RAISE YOUR F

"Everything is made of frequencies. What if you could become conscious of the messengers and numerical frequencies ready to provide deep insights, guidance, and advisement? Melissa's book is the most astute and practical guidebook I have ever read and employed for receiving these spiritual messages—from over a thousand numbers and three thousand guardians and guides. This is an invaluable roadway to joy and more wondrous than any other."

—Cyndi Dale, author of 30-plus books about energy healing

"This book is impressive! Melissa has gone above and beyond in providing the answers and all the pieces of the puzzle of living. In *Raise Your Frequency Through Number Messages*, the power of matching vibrations shines a light on your path by using numbers, animals, nature, gemstones, and the Universe to guide you. There are many messages for you in this book. This book is a must-have!"

—Margaret Ann Lembo, author of
Animal Totems and the Gemstone Kingdom

"Melissa Alvarez goes beyond the typical numerology descriptors to bring you a whole new way to access your guidance through numbers, Intuition & the universe! One of my favorite methods she uses is to tune in for yourself and intuit how your messages apply to your life! A must keep for your shelf!"

—Melanie Barnum, author of *The Book of Psychic Symbols*

"Melissa Alvarez always imparts an abundance of information to her readers. This book eloquently showcases her expertise in energy frequencies and is filled with her unique insights into hidden messages behind each number. Her interpretations of number frequencies are packed with three powerful messengers. Readers will find her book offers a valuable in-depth understanding that leads to greater self-realization."
—Sally Painter, author and paranormal content writer

"I absolutely LOVE this much-needed book! Melissa has successfully woven the magical messages of numbers with animals, nature, and the universe to reveal a deeper look into how we are constantly being guided in our cosmic dance.
She has created a reference book and a guidebook, teaching us how to use our intuition with each meaning she has so wonderfully brought together. This is definitely a book you will want handy at all times!"
—Betsey Grady, Psychic Medium, Akashic Records Consultant

"Big and bold, wise and wonderful... What can I say but: *Wow, this ain't your mama's number book!*

With well over a thousand entries plus an extensive index, *Raise Your Frequency Through Number Messages*, by Melissa Alvarez, is a brilliant tour de force, an encyclopedic resource as expansive in its scope as it is insightful in its content. And I do mean insightful. I've been working with it for several days now and am finding its number messages to be remarkably accurate overall. Also accessible. This is the sort of book that feels as though it's speaking directly to you, comprehensive and conversational both. Whatever I ask it, I get an astute answer. Besides which, I have to add, it is really fun to use—almost addictive, in fact. Be warned, once you start perusing the pages, you may find it difficult to stop. I know I do. In all honesty, just the act of reading this book raises my frequency. It radiates positive energy.

At its core, the book covers the numbers from zero to 1111, and for each and every one, Ms. Alvarez has intuited not only its special message, but also three related synchronicities (additional messengers, if you will, drawn from the realms of animal guides, Nature, and Universal energies), making this a truly unique reference. I know of no other quite like it, and I am so impressed by how well the author knit everything together. The synchronicities dovetail beautifully with the number messages.

For the record, I've read almost all of Melissa Alvarez's books, and they never disappoint, but I think this one is my favorite so far. *Raise Your Frequency Through Number Messages* is destined to be a classic. I highly recommend this marvelous book!"

—Mimi Riser, author of *The Kitchen Witch Collection*

RAISE YOUR FREQUENCY
Though
NUMBER MESSAGES

Awaken to the Meaning of Number Sequences and Synchronicities from Animals, Nature, and the Universe

Messages for the Numbers 0 to 1111
from 3336 Messengers
Search by Number or Messenger

MELISSA ALVAREZ

Adrema Press

Raise Your Frequency Though Number Messages: Awaken to the Meaning of Number Sequences and Synchronicities from Animals, Nature, and the Universe© 2023 by Melissa Alvarez. All rights reserved. No part of this book may be used or reproduced in any manner whatsoever, including Internet usage, except in the case of brief quotations embodied in critical articles and reviews.

Published by Adrema Press April 19, 2023

ISBN: 978-1-59611-155-4

Cover Design by Melissa Alvarez at BookCovers.us
Interior Design by Melissa Alvarez

Animal Frequency® is a registered trademark of Melissa Alvarez

OTHER BOOKS BY MELISSA ALVAREZ

365 Ways to Raise Your Frequency
365 Days to Raise Your Frequency Journal
Llewellyn's Little Book of Spirit Animals
Earth Frequency
Earth Frequency Journal
Your Psychic Self
My Psychic Journal
Animal Frequency®
Animal Frequency® Journal
Animal Frequency® Oracle Cards
The Spirituality of Coziness
The Spirituality of Coziness Journal
Believe and Receive
Believe and Receive Journal
Believe and Receive Mini Meditation Cards
Simply Give Thanks
Simply Give Thanks Gratitude Journal
Chakra Divination® Card & Charts Activity Book
Chakra Divination® Ultimate Balance Journal
The Essential Guide to Chakra Divination®
Chakra Divination® Card Deck
The Phoenix's Guide to Self-Renewal
Your Color Power
Analyze Your Handwriting
Ghosts, A Spirit Guide and A Past Life
Paranormal Investigative Groups Around the World

WRITING AS ARIANA DUPRE

Night Visions
Talgorian Prophecy
Talgorian Dragon
Briar Mountain
Paradise Designs
Paranormal Adventures

And many more...
Please visit http://MelissaA.com for the complete booklist.

ABOUT THE AUTHOR

Melissa Alvarez is a bestselling author, editor, and book cover designer who has written over thirty-two books, novels, short stories, and mind/body/spirit nonfiction titles as well as nearly 500 articles on self-help, spirituality, and wellness. As a professional intuitive coach, energy worker, spiritual advisor, medium, and animal communicator with over 35 years of experience, Melissa has helped thousands of people bring clarity, joy, and balance into their lives. Melissa teaches others how to connect with their own intuitive nature and how to work with frequency for spiritual growth. She has appeared on numerous radio shows as both a guest and host. Melissa is the author of *365 Ways to Raise Your Frequency*, *Your Psychic Self*, *Animal Frequency*, *Earth Frequency*, *Llewellyn's Little Book of Spirit Animals*, *The Spirituality of Coziness*, *Simply Give Thanks* and many other titles. Her books with Llewellyn have been translated into multiple languages worldwide including Romanian, Russian, Chinese, French, Czech and Spanish. Please visit her website for a full list of her current titles.

Find Melissa Online at:
https://MelissaA.com
https://www.facebook.com/melissaalvarezauthor (main profile)
https://www.facebook.com/IamMelissaAlvarez (author page)

Other websites:
https://BookCovers.us
https://ThornRidge.com Online retail store
http://TopHatFriesians.com Barock Pinto & Friesian horses

DEDICATIONS

This book is for you, the reader. For your dedication to reading my books and for spreading the word through social media. For actively working on your psychic selves and growing on your spiritual paths. You are the reason I keep writing. Thank you for being you!

This book is also for my husband, Jorge. I'm releasing this book on what would have been your 63rd birthday. You were such a gift, the love of my life. It's been a year since you left us and I don't think I'll ever adjust to your absence, even though you're here with me in spirit every day. Happy Birthday! I love you!

CONTENTS

Introduction   1

Numbers, Messages, and Messengers (Zero to 1111)   *15*

Conclusion   571

Bibliography   572

Website Resources   574

Messenger List and Index   575
    Animal Messengers   575
    Nature Messengers   584
    Universe / Energy Messengers   592

INTRODUCTION

It's amazing to me how interconnected the Universe is in all ways. From the expanse of the universe, both physically and spiritually, to the interconnectedness of the people, animals, and all of nature on planet Earth. When you really think about it, we are just little pieces of the whole, but we can make a profound impact on our own spiritual growth if we listen to the Divine messages sent to us while we're living on the earthly plane of existence.

In my books *Animal Frequency*, and *Llewellyn's Little Book of Spirit Animals*, I discuss how energy animals, also known as your animal guides, power animals, and spirit animals, will appear to you repeatedly when they have an important message to share with you. In *Earth Frequency,* I discussed how you can connect to the energy of sacred sites, vortexes, Earth Chakras, and other transformational places around the world. In *365 Ways to Raise Your Frequency*, I gave you a year's worth of exercises and things to do to increase your frequency to higher levels. The purpose of *Raise Your Frequency through Number Messages* is to address the appearance of repetitive numbers and to help you raise your frequency to higher levels as you awaken to the meaning of number sequences and synchronicities through messages from animals, nature, and the Universe. To achieve this goal, I'm incorporating messengers from the animal kingdom, nature, and Universal energy (Universe/Energy). The messages from these messengers and the number itself can guide you when you see repetitive numbers. Typically, seeing repetitive numbers is often thought to only be related to messages from your guardian angels. I too, find this is true, and angels can indeed send you messages through the numbers. But I also believe energy animals, elements of nature, and the energy and frequency of the Universe also act as guardians and guides, and therefore it is important to be aware of their messages when you see repetitive numbers. If you're seeing a repetitive number or any of the messengers (animal, nature, or Universe/Energy) at the same time, then it's important to look up both the number you're seeing and if you're seeing a messenger repeatedly, to use the index in the back of this book to find the messenger and look up the meaning of the number associated with that messenger as well.

There are plenty of books on the market regarding angel numbers and numerology, so you can also cross-reference the number you're seeing with one of those books too. In numerology, the numbers 0 to 9 have specific meanings, so books on numerology would also be a good cross-reference to examine because I am not associating the standard 0-9 meanings of numbers from numerology to the numbers and number messages in this book.

Energy animals, nature elements, the Universe and energy will show you signs until they get your attention. They will appear on television, in person, in print, and well, it wills seem like you're seeing their image just about everywhere until you stop, pay attention, and actively seek out the message they're trying to deliver. When repetitive numbers are used to get your attention you'll see the number sequence in the same manner, in print or radio advertising, on your clock, within phone numbers, on car tags, in songs, on the side of a business vehicle, on road signs, and just about everywhere until you realize that something bigger is going on and there is a message for you and it is associated with that number. You may even dream about the number and the messenger at the same time. I know I have.

HOW TO USE THIS BOOK

I did not include number messages in my previous books because I felt that this topic deserved its own book. In *Raise Your Frequency Through Number Messages*, there are a total of 3336 different messengers for 1111 numbers plus zero. Each number has an animal, nature, and Universe/Energy messenger so, as I have done with previous books, I again called on the energy animals, elements of nature, and Universal energy to guide me intuitively as I wrote the messages associated with the numbers. I just transcribed what I heard, felt, or saw during the sessions I held while writing the book. When you read the message, you'll intuitively know, based on your own personal situation, which part of the message came from which messenger and how to apply it to your life. You might have to think deeply and consider different possibilities, but that's when the most forward movement is made and when solutions come to you.

This book is chocked full of important messages that can be as large as the Universe when applied to your current situation. It's handy because you never know when an eagle will soar past you, or you repeatedly see 333, 444, 1111, 697 or 231 everywhere you look, or you notice waterfalls at every turn. The messages you receive from these messengers often give you something to think about in regards to your current situation, that will bring about a change in perspective, opportunities to grow on both a personal and spiritual level, to learn lessons important to overall growth, or to balance karma, and to guide you through life with insights, calming words, or messages that wake you up to your true spiritual nature.

It's important to also trust your own intuition when interpreting the meaning of the message delivered by the messenger. Sometimes, if I'm not clear about what the message means, I'll say, *show me a sign to clarify please*. Then, I might see another number or another messenger, and, when I look up that number or messenger, the meaning becomes very clear. The hardest thing about asking for a sign is that you can't second guess what the sign is. Typically, it is the very next thing you see, or it might be something someone says on the television that jumps out at you as if it applies directly to you. Go with your *first* impression. When you second guess yourself and the message, you might just miss it, which will only cause confusion. When you ask for clarity, it usually comes very quickly.

IDENTIFYING NUMBER POSSIBILITIES

The numbers in this book start at 0 and go up to 1111 for a total of 1112 numbers. So how would you interpret a number that is outside of this range? Let's look at the number 158777 as an example. First, we're going to break it down into two or three equal parts. In this example, you'll look up the numbers 158 and 777 for their meanings. To get a deeper meaning with big numbers like this you can break it down ever further to 15, 87, and 77. Then you examine the meanings of all five number sequences and see how they apply to your situation. For three-digit and four-digit numbers you can look up the first two or three digits and then use the third or fourth digit for clarity or for a deeper meaning.

Because I love playing with numbers, another thing that I will do is break larger numbers into smaller ones or add the numbers up to obtain even more assistance from the Universe. So, for 158777 I would add it all up as single digits so 1+5+8+7+7+7=35. Then I'd look up 35 and then add 3+5=8 so I'd look up 8 too. You could also add it up as double digits so it would be 15+ 87+77=179. I'd look up 179 as individual numbers 1, 7, 9, then take the first half to get 17 and the second half to get 79 and look both of those up too. Then I'd add the 1, 7, and 9 to get 17 and I'd look up 17. Add the 1 and 7 of 17 and I'm back to 8, which I'd just looked up. In the above scenario the total possible numbers are: 1, 5, 8, 7, 158, 777, 35, 15, 87, 77, 179, 9, 17, 79, which gives me 14 different number messages to read. There is some repetition breaking the number down this way (8 and 17 repeats in this example), so I'd pay extra attention to repeating numbers. I'd then consider how the messages from all these numbers can be applied to my life or situation. If I still feel confused and don't understand the message, I shut the book, ask my guides to show me the one number message that best applies to my situation for clarity and then open the book to a random page. The first text you look at is the answer. Don't second guess it or choose another number message on the page. Read the one you saw *first* because that's your clarifying answer.

THE MESSENGERS

Let's take a minute and go over the messengers in this book. They are the number itself, the animal messengers, nature messengers and the Universal/Energy messengers for a total of four messengers per message. While seeing the repeating number may be the only reason you started investigating what that number meant, the other three messengers add to the message and can give you clarification and a deeper understanding of the information the Universe is trying to send to you.

It is important to remember that while the number itself is the primary messenger, the message is also coming from the corresponding messengers. For example, if, in addition to seeing a repeating number, you also keep seeing a particular animal, a specific kind of tree, or are feeling a certain way when you see the number, you can use the index in this book to look up the animal, tree, or feeling to find the corresponding number associated with it and read that number's message too. The number was the catalyst for your research and the rest gives you a plethora of information that will help you on your path. There are unlimited possibilities in this book to discover information and messages that will help you on your journey throughout your lifetime.

If you're not familiar with a particular messenger, please look it up when you have time to gain further insight into how it could be applicable to your life. I've included the main species or a brief description in parentheses to give clarity until you can do more research on your own.

The Animal Messengers: In the animal messenger section, I included species and sub-species of all different types of living creatures. As you consider the animal messenger, think about its characteristics, behaviors, where it lives, what it sounds like, its color or if it has any particular habits. What are its strengths, weaknesses, or preferences? Can its natural instincts or actions be beneficial to your situation if you were to behave in the same way? Animal messages can bring powerful messages and they typically don't give up until you get the message. Spend time thinking about the animal and seeing how you feel about it as you read the messages. While researching, you may discover new information about the animal that you never knew before you started. That information may be exactly what you need to know right now to help you with your current situation. Messages aren't always what you read on the page, but they are also how they make you feel and light bulb moments in your mind as you read them and make a connection.

The Nature Messengers: In the nature section you'll find species and sub-species of plants, flowers, marine plants, trees, fruits, vegetables, and beans, as well as rocks, minerals, fossils, gemstones, and weather situations. Now you might ask how a vegetable or bean, or any of these other things in nature, could possibly give a message. They can, you just have to look for the meaning. Here's an example: cucumbers are known to be soothing for the eyes, so its message may be to take time to do something for yourself to help you relax. Navy beans are known to cause excessive flatulence in many people, which could be interpreted as making sure you're not *full of hot air* or *boasting* about something in your life. For weather, I have included all kinds of weather and natural events so it's important to look at both the positives and negatives they bring instead of solely focusing on one or the other. A thunderstorm has lightning that can be dangerous, but it also brings rain that the Earth needs. So, its message may be to avoid highly charged situations and hydrate more. A tornado is destructive, but it could be a message to pay more attention to your actions or feelings so you're not spinning out of control and to focus on your inner strength to move forward on your path of spiritual growth.

The Universe/Energy Messengers: The Universe/Energy section contains messengers that are intangible or less tangible than those in the animal and nature categories. You'll find messengers related to energy such as natural phenomenon, weather phenomenon (that fit better in this Universe/Energy category than the nature category) and events. This category also contains actions you can take, emotions, feelings, sensations, sounds, colors, scents, and other messengers that are positive, inspirational, or that can help you raise your frequency if you do them, use them or acknowledge them. All of these have energy, and as spiritual beings made of energy, we can connect our energy with the messenger and message to gain spiritual insight and growth. By doing the actions or sitting quietly and experiencing the sounds, scents, and colors or examining your feelings, you will often find that you will realize something about your situation through this messenger that you may not have received if you hadn't actively participated in what the messenger represented. Sometimes just reading a message doesn't deliver the entirety of it and the best way to get all the information you're supposed to receive is to take action in regard to the messengers.

Will you find any duplications within the messengers? It's possible. I did my best to connect with 3336 different messengers for you within the three categories, but I can't guarantee that I didn't duplicate something along the way. There may also be similarities in the messengers but while they may be similar, they are also different. It's important to consider the differences. For example, I included the general term *bear* plus a lot of different sub-species of bears as messengers. A black bear, a grizzly bear, and a polar bear can all offer distinct types of messages, even though they're all bears. And the term bear by itself makes you think of all bears. It's the same thing for plants, gemstones, rocks, flowers, and all of the other things in nature and the Universe. You may see a fruit or flower under the nature section and then see the scent of that same fruit or flower under the Universe/Energy section. Why? Because eating the fruit or planting the flower in your garden for a specific purpose and smelling the scent of that fruit or flower can evoke completely different energies and messages.

To give you 3336 messengers I had to include both species and sub-species. In the messenger section of each number beside the sub-species or sub-categories that aren't well known, I have included, in parentheses, the common or generic names of the main species or category and/or a brief description. This will help you get a better idea of what the messenger is if you don't have time to look it up when you read it. For example, a weevil is an insect, so I put (insect) beside the name, a quagga is a sub-species of zebra, so it says (equine) beside it. I did this for all three categories of messengers to offer clarity of what the messenger is if the word isn't a common word or if it doesn't say what it is in the name. For example, crabgrass has grass in the name so you'll know it's a type of grass, a snapping turtle is a type of turtle, a supernumerary rainbow is a type of rainbow so those entries will not have anything in parenthesis because what it is, is already part of the name. By listing the messengers in this way, each is relevant to the message, and you can choose which term you like best as you interpret the material. In the index the messengers are also divided by category for easy reference. I would have loved to give you tons of information about each messenger like I did in *Animal Frequency* and *Earth Frequency*, however, with the number of messengers in *Raise Your Frequency through Number Messengers*, it simply wasn't possible. Please look up details about each animal, nature, or Universal/Energy messenger to discover even more details about each one. Details about the messenger will often provide information that is applicable to your situation in addition to the message itself.

The generic version of the messenger is equally as important and relevant as the unique variation that is referenced. You can choose which one feels right for you in your situation. For example, if I have the messenger as triggerfish (fish) but you instantly imagine a catfish when reading the message, then you should go with the catfish as the messenger because it is calling out to you in that specific moment. In this case, the generic category of fish spoke to you more than the sub-species of triggerfish. When it comes to receiving messages, you must always go with your gut instincts and intuitive impressions and use whatever book you're reading as a guide on your journey.

Once you read the message, what do you do with it? The first thing is to really think about how the message applies to your life. Since seeing random numbers doesn't often tell you exactly what area of your life it applies too, you'll have to think about it and decide for yourself. For example, if I was frustrated at work but couldn't put my finger on exactly what was causing my frustration, then I started seeing a specific number and looked it up and the message says to take a step back and be aware of those around you, I would immediately do exactly that. Because by being aware of the people around me, I can probably find the cause of my frustration, or I could avoid being pulled into a situation that I might not want to be in at work. Let's also say that my messengers were a canary, peanuts, and walking. I would think that the canary means I need to add some bright colors and music to my daily routine to help avoid bringing my work frustration home. The peanuts might mean that I should add more protein to my diet, and the walking would mean that I could get rid of some of the frustration through exercise by taking a walk outside. In addition to looking up the number in the book you can also engage with the messengers. You might decide to meditate with one specific messenger or, if it's an edible plant, you might want to eat it. Or maybe the messenger is in a country different from yours and you're unable to access it. Then you'd need to think about its benefits and see if there is another way to gain those same benefits in your life. If the messenger is a feeling, sensation, or other emotion, then you'd need to consider things you like to do that cause you to feel that same emotion and then do them.

It's important to look at aspects of each messenger as well as the messenger itself to make it work for you to bring more positivity and joy into your life.

GUIDED MEDITATION

Doing a guided meditation regarding the message is always helpful because you may gain further insight into the message while doing so. Here's one way to go about it. Once you find the number and the messengers in this book, find a place to sit quietly so you can consider each one. Close your eyes and think of the number, see it in your mind's eye. Does it stay the same or does it change into additional numbers? If it stays the same, then that is the main message. If you see it changing into other numbers, consider those messages as well. Take all the time you need to feel the importance of the number. Ask it if there is any other message it would like to deliver to you at this time. Wait for the answer. Now think about the animal messenger. What does it look like, does its color have significant meaning? Does it have hooves or claws? How is that important to your situation, should you run, or sink your claws in? Look at the nature messenger. Is it a lake, a plant or something you might eat? Now look at the energy, does this messenger connect with the other two and the number? Is there something you should do to complete the connection in your life with all their information? Think about each of the messengers both individually and in connection with the other messengers as you read the message. Now, see yourself applying the information in the message to your life. Does it offer a resolution? Can you see a benefit in the message? Plan a course of action based on the information you've received from the messengers and the message itself. Feel it, embrace it, and own the result. Now slowly open your eyes. Take your plan that you've just made and put it into action in your life.

Getting messages through numbers, animals, nature, the Universe, and energy is helpful in all walks of life. Seeing repeating numbers or other messengers is always a random event that happens when you're not expecting it, but, if you're aware, and pay attention to the signs around you, then you'll be guided through meaningful messages received in a wonderful variety of ways.

The Number, Message, and Messengers

0

Surround yourself with peaceful calmness to experience purity of your inner light, balance of the spirit, and hope in all things. Positive solutions and new beginnings are yours. Acceptance of yourself is important. You cannot change what is happening so look for the gift within the experience. As things change, look through the windows around you to gain clarity of action and discover new possibilities.

Messengers:

Animal: *Dove (bird)*
Nature: *Moss*
Universe/Energy: *Contentment*

1

Expand your vision to chart your course. Hold to your dream, focus on your path, and don't hold back. Command authority. Offer inspiration and protection and rise above negativity. Open to your inner self and spiritual consciousness to bring about stability and a clear path to achieving your goals. Look for messages within the clouds above you for confirmation of your path and questions.

Messengers:

Animal: *Eagle*
Nature: *Cumulus Clouds*
Universe/Energy: *Astuteness*

2

You will enjoy the sweetness of success. Creativity is important in attaining your goals. Managing others in a busy environment leads to a joyful sense of accomplishment. When success is achieved, enjoy the fruits of your labor before jumping into the next project. Make a conscious effort through the practice of creative visualization to purposefully find negativity to which you are currently connected. See yourself disconnect it from your spirit and release it from your life.

Messengers:

Animal: *Bee*
Nature: *Broomstraw*
Universe/Energy: *Candor*

3

Don't take yourself too seriously. Laughter, including laughing at yourself, is of utmost importance right now. It reduces stress, elevates your frequency, and lets you see humor in difficult situations. Think out of the box, not in absolutes, so you can visualize a clear path in front of you. Find the fun in life and enjoy it to the fullest.

Messengers:

Animal: *Coyote*
Nature: *Seashells*
Universe/Energy: *Time*

4

Pay attention to any protective spiritual armor you may have placed around yourself. Is it still necessary or can you let it go now? Open to others so you can shine. Trust doesn't come easy to you but when you give it, you give it all. Know when to retreat and when to brave the unknown and forge ahead. Make sure to follow through on plans, protect your ideas, and use your incredible talent to bring your ideas to the world.

Messengers:

Animal: *Clam*
Nature: *Rock Formation*
Universe/Energy: *Smiles*

5

Take stock of your surroundings and the true intentions of others. Move forward slowly, digging for what's underneath. This is a time for cautiousness and adaptability as you prepare for positive changes. Growth starts from the smallest beginnings and the results can be extremely large. Consider the Redwood and plant seeds that will help you attain all the growth you desire.

Messengers:

Animal: *Aardvark*
Nature: *Flaxseed*
Universe/Energy: *Truth*

6

There is a time for all things and all things change over time. Look carefully within to see if the time has come to make any changes in your life. Are you ready to soar? To accept that you have the abilities and the desire to reach great heights? Reaching the goals you've set results in a renewed sense of freedom, of accomplishment, and pride in yourself. Take a deep breath and own what you have been able to achieve. You've worked hard for it.

Messengers:

Animal: *Bald Eagle (bird)*
Nature: *Oxygen*
Universe/Energy: *Self-care*

7

It may seem that the world is heavy around you with negativity coming at you at every turn. But you are lightness of being, purity, and high levels of positive energy. You are connected to the Universe at every level. This is a time of transformation and enlightenment, a time to look within yourself and recognize your true vibration, and then raise it even higher. When you set your mind to something you don't give up, but instead push forward to your goals.

Messengers:

Animal: *Dragonfly*
Nature: *Wind Speed*
Universe/Energy: *Diligence*

8

Do your due diligence. You're approaching a time of challenging work where the significant effort you'll put in will produce rewarding results. Make sure you're doing everything correctly from the ground up to avoid problems later. Listen to your hunches and if something doesn't feel right, don't do it until you investigate further.

Messengers:

Animal: *Honeybee*
Nature: *Dew*
Universe/Energy: *Lightheartedness*

9

Do you have an inflated opinion of yourself or your accomplishments? It's a good thing to be proud of what you've done but it's another thing to constantly brag about yourself and what you've done. Recognize your accomplishments in your heart and mind. If other people notice, then accept their praise with gratitude. If no one notices that's fine too because you know.

Messengers:

Animal: *Puffin (bird)*
Nature: *Kumquat*
Universe/Energy: *Acceptance*

10

You're never too old to find joy in silliness or to be overwhelmed with a sense of wonder. Give in to your impulses. Be mischievous. Look at the world through the eyes of a child to see the awesome wonders around you.

Messengers:

Animal: *Pygmy Goat*
Nature: *Acacia Tree*
Universe/Energy: *Eucalyptus (scent)*

11

Sometimes searching for a reason, explanation, or cause will not give the results you seek, that is when you must change your thinking and look inward. Let yourself rise and fall to excel in your daily life. Be fluid and fluctuate but never give up.

Messengers:

Animal: *Inchworm*
Nature: *Gravity*
Universe/Energy: *Persistence*

12

Grin for no reason. Smiling brings joy to you even if you're in a bad mood. Turn situations around with a smile. Step outside, take a deep breath of fresh air. Put a little skip into your walk. Movement, facial expressions, and being in the moment adds joy to your life and will influence those around you in a positive way.

Messengers:

Animal: *Ibis (bird)*
Nature: *Seawater*
Universe/Energy: *Eloquence*

13

A path may be rocky and hard but use the rocks as steppingstones to attain your goals. A happy attitude can brighten your day and lift the spirits of those around you. Give them often. Truth will always rise to the surface, be honest in all that you do. You are in balance and bring a sense of equilibrium to those around you.

Messengers:

Animal: *Pelican*
Nature: *Silver*
Universe/Energy: *Harmony*

14

Your mind is like the ocean. Thoughts flow in waves and ebb like the tides. Pay attention to your thought processes to work through situations, examine what you're doing, and to make plans. Will you move forward or take a step back?

Messengers:

Animal: *Maned Wolf*
Nature: *Glacier*
Universe/Energy: *Alertness*

15

Make your true feelings known when asked to do something. If you really don't want to do it, don't hide but instead step up and express your reasons for saying no with conviction and sincerity. When you speak from the heart and really mean what you say, others will see the truth and respect your decision. Doing things that you don't want to do will affect you negatively.

Messengers:

Animal: *Quail*
Nature: *Black Cumin (spice)*
Universe/Energy: *Refreshed*

16

A "word to the wise" may be given to you from someone in a random place like the grocery store or gas station. Pay attention because this is a message from the other side and the individual is just the delivery person. The message may seem shrouded and vague, but you'll know exactly what it means. Listen closely.

Messengers:

Animal: *Snowy Owl*
Nature: *Mist*
Universe/Energy: *Accuracy*

17

When you understand the world you live in, the easier it makes life. Venture into the unknown to discover more. Look for similarities and contrasts regarding the things you already know and expand your horizons by obtaining new knowledge. Travel the world, even if it is through your imagination or by reading about other locations and seeing pictures of them in books while sitting in the chair in your living room or through websites via your phone or computer.

Messengers:

Animal: *Sea Turtle*
Nature: *Zinnia (plant/flower)*
Universe/Energy: *Buzzing of Bees (sound)*

18

Do not deceive yourself. Instead, look at the truth of your soul and situation to make the most of it. Surprises abound when you delve within. Don't mask what you're learning about yourself with doubts but instead embrace and accept who you are. It's time to celebrate the uniqueness of you.

Messengers:
Animal: *Wild Turkey*
Nature: *Green Onion*
Universe/Energy: *Pop of a Cork (Sound)*

19

When you have more than you need, share. You never know when someone is hiding the fact that they are doing without, that they're digging deep just to survive. Celebrate the fruits of your labor by offering what you don't need to another. Helping in this way will make your heart swell with joy.

Messengers:
Animal: *Vole (rodent)*
Nature: *Apple*
Universe/Energy: *Abundance*

20

If money is tight, find unique ways to make it stretch. When you have extra, pay things off and save. To avoid feeling frenzied and overstressed when it comes to money, make a budget, and do your best to stick to it. After you've eliminated some debt or saved a nest egg, the result will be less stress, more money, and peace of mind.

Messengers:
Animal: *Whale Shark*
Nature: *Basalt Dacite (rock)*
Universe/Energy: *Sing (action)*

21

You are being sent messages that you've ignored because you've been too focused on the amount of work you need to do. There is also fear of accepting the intuitive part of yourself because you're unsure about psychic and paranormal experiences. You can choose what information you'd like to receive by telling the Universe and your guides what you're ready for and what you'd like to avoid.

Messengers:
Animal: *Zebu (cattle)*
Nature: *Bald Cypress Tree*
Universe/Energy: *Divine Guidance*

22

Learn to laugh at yourself. You are a unique gem with many facets. Find your joy in each part of your being. While seriousness is sometimes needed, laughter brings joy and a lightness of being and an easy acceptance of yourself.

Messengers:

Animal: *Wolf Spider*
Nature: *Blue Diamond (gemstone)*
Universe/Energy: *Attunement*

23

You can't believe everything you hear. Now is the time to do your own research, to light up your own life from the information you discover that resonates with your soul. Don't hide in the sand waiting for others to make decisions for you.

Messengers:

Animal: *Sand Boa (snake)*
Nature: *Thunder*
Universe/Energy: *Electricity*

24

Blessings come in many forms. Sometimes you must work through difficulties to receive the blessing. It can involve demanding work, be frustrating, and feel as if you're fighting against the wind. Hold on and keep knocking out the work because the delights of success are right around the corner.

Messengers:

Animal: *Yellow-bellied Sapsucker (bird)*
Nature: *Updraft (weather)*
Universe/Energy: *Serenity*

25

You are on the hunt for change and to experience more beautiful things in your life. To start, clear out things you don't need. When your life is cluttered and full there is no space for the exciting new possibilities coming your way.

Messengers:

Animal: *Bengal Tiger*
Nature: *Jewels*
Universe/Energy: *Aurora Borealis (Northern Lights)*

26

You're holding onto stress. To let it go, take a big breath and release it. Do it again, this time shake out your body on the exhale. Keep doing this until you feel the stress leaving and your body starts to relax. Your foundation is strong so you can take a solid stance and grow by leaps and bounds.

Messengers:

Animal: *Snowshoe Hare*
Nature: *Lettuce*
Universe/Energy: *Sighing (Sound)*

27

Let love and compassion break you out of the fears holding you back from expressing your feelings to others. There is no right or wrong way to feel; it's only how you as an individual feels that is truth for you. Avoid aggression. Pay attention to your eyesight. If you need glasses don't put it off.

Messengers:

Animal: *Tapir (mammal)*
Nature: *Velvetleaf (plant)*
Universe/Energy: *Focused (feeling)*

28

You may find yourself in a tough, harsh situation but you know how to survive when things get rough. This experience will bring about healing and balance in your life. Spend some time with animals to bring even greater balance. Add more of the color green to your living space.

Messengers:

Animal: *Polar Bear*
Nature: *Serpentine Stone (gemstone)*
Universe/Energy: *Observe nature (action)*

29

Purity, innocence, and goodness surround you. This will help you know who you are as you see just how much you're capable of doing in your life. Look for moments where you can guide as a teacher or where others will guide you. Your work will benefit a great cause even if it's on a small scale.

Messengers:

Animal: *Stoat (mammal weasel)*
Nature: *Echinacea (herb)*
Universe/Energy: *Embrace A Moment (action)*

30

Take care in all you do right now. Pay extra attention as you work so you avoid injury. Now is the time to be extremely focused instead of playing around or goofing off. Make sure you're drinking plenty of water especially if you're working outside.

Messengers:

Animal: *Thorny Devil (reptile)*
Nature: *Badlands (terrain)*
Universe/Energy: *Electric Saw (Sound)*

31

Moving fast, standing tall, and drawing the attention of others is happening to you all at once. Take it in stride. Use your weaknesses to inspire growth in whatever you do. You have chosen to experience life instead of sitting back and watching it pass by.

Messengers:

Animal: *Skink (Reptile)*
Nature: *Pinyon (tree)*
Universe/Energy: *Attraction*

32

Learn to say no, to not overburden yourself because someone else is expecting more than you can give or they are taking advantage of your kindness. You have the faithful nature to understand that when your life feels the most derailed is when it will soon be back on track. Do not be afraid of what you don't understand, but instead take some alone time to figure it out.

Messengers:

Animal: *Unicorn Crestfish*
Nature: *Solstice*
Universe/Energy: *Heart Chakra*

33

You are in a phase of magical transformation and will have unique abilities come to the surface. Abilities you never imagined you could do. You will become the guardian of something very sacred and divine. Great spiritual and intuitive growth is upon you.

Messengers:

Animal: *Water Dragon (reptile)*
Nature: *Ice Crystals*
Universe/Energy: *Blush (color)*

34

Look for multiple meanings in everything. There is a lot of information coming at you from many directions right now. You're changing, having unbelievable experiences which are proving to you that things you can't see do exist in reality and not just in someone's mind. Embrace your new normal.

Messengers:

Animal: *Kite (bird)*
Nature: *Water Lily (plant)*
Universe/Energy: *U Burst (weather)*

35

Analytical skill and intuitive insight are needed for self-preservation at this moment. You're a stable person, dependable and kind but also fiercely protective. This is a time of self-examination and spiritual growth. Are you taking on too much? Are you allowing someone to take advantage of you because you can't say no? Evaluate the situations of your life and then take action.

Messengers:

Animal: *Donkey*
Nature: *Tempest (plant)*
Universe/Energy: *Thrill*

36

To feel grounded, talk a walk in nature at sunrise. Listen to the sounds of nature, and to the silence. Feel the temperature of the air. Is there a mist? Fog? Can you lose yourself in your surroundings? Experience the peace and freedom you have attained in your life.

Messengers:

Animal: *Mourning Dove*
Nature: *Fog*
Universe/Energy: *Silence (Sound)*

37

Do something different to shake things up and get yourself out of stagnant patterns. You're a rarity in that you can change the moments of your life immediately. You have the ability to see the different futures ahead of you based on the paths you choose to walk.

Messengers:

Animal: *Quagga (equine)*
Nature: *Honeycomb*
Universe/Energy: *Crown Chakra*

38

You are the guardian of secrets. You possess ancient knowledge, infinite wisdom, and truth of being. Mysteries of the Universe make sense to you at a soul level. Now is the time to hold all secrets close. You draw others to you because of your inner light.

Messengers:

Animal: *Lynx (feline)*
Nature: *Fancy Sapphire (gemstone)*
Universe/Energy: *Deep cerise (color)*

39

Secrets are being kept. Look for the little signs, the stolen glances, the nuances that reveal what is going on beneath calm waters. There is a giant discovery waiting to be revealed. It will be hard to wait, your mind will work overtime trying to figure it out, but when the announcement is made, joy will abound.

Messengers:

Animal: *Beluga Whale*
Nature: *Java-Plum (fruit)*
Universe/Energy: *Squeak of the Floor when Stepped On (Sound)*

40

One part of life which is an inevitability is that everything will change. Adjustments are always being made, people alter their decisions, and plans are rearranged. The only constant is change because that is how you grow in this life, how you learn and excel. Expect and flow with it.

Messengers:

Animal: *Mackerel (fish)*
Nature: *Snowflakes*
Universe/Energy: *Hybrid Eclipse*

41

If you had the chance to do one thing over, what would it be? Look at past events and try to correct any wrongs or make changes that will push you into a different result. If the past can't be changed, fully accept it in your heart and mind so you can move forward from it.

Messengers:

Animal: *Urial (wild sheep)*
Nature: *Augite (mineral)*
Universe/Energy: *Thrilled (emotion)*

42

A strong sense of loyalty, protection, and service is how you feel about the people around you. It is an important part of how you see yourself. Make sure you are strong and pure in your intentions. See the good over the bad, the hope over the despair, and elevate your energy to match the good things happening to you and those you love.

Messengers:

Animal: *Dog*
Nature: *Bonsai Tree*
Universe/Energy: *Awe*

43

Plant seeds wisely because you'll reap what you sow in abundance. Positivity erupts in your life, displacing negativity and bringing gifts of blessings and joy. You are physically connected to your soul self and the divine at this time.

Messengers:

Animal: *Weevil (insect)*
Nature: *Geyser*
Universe/Energy: *Emotional Bonds*

44

Tread carefully for the road is slippery. Take careful, measured steps as you move forward toward your goals. Stay with the herd, appreciate the differences between each person in your life. Feel blessed by their uniqueness. This will open your eyes so you see their truths at a soul level.

Messengers:

Animal: *Zonkey (equine)*
Nature: *Sleet*
Universe/Energy: *Realization*

45

Get excited about something and let your excitement build until your momentum is at an all-time high. The more you care, the better the results. There will be times when you'll need to pause and just float for a moment but then you'll take off again and fly. Look for predictive signs along the way.

Messengers:

Animal: *Wood Duck*
Nature: *Turnip*
Universe/Energy: *Protective (feeling)*

46

Life will give you what you don't want to deal with until you accept it and learn the lesson. Once you do, you'll stop repeating it so you can move forward. It's time to face the things that are difficult for you instead of denying or ignoring them.

Messengers:

Animal: *Yellow Tang (fish)*
Nature: *Vanilla*
Universe/Energy: *Time Passing (sensation)*

47

You are stronger than other people give you credit for. You know that deep down, but you sometimes let other people's opinion of you matter too much. You can achieve great things so set your mind on what you want and go for it. Absorb knowledge of all kinds.

Messengers:

Animal: *Scarab Beetle (insect)*
Nature: *Turquoise Stone (gemstone)*
Universe/Energy: *Awareness of Self*

48

Sit, wait, watch, and then make your move. Patience is important now as you wait for everything to fall into place, to come together at the right moment. Negativity is being neutralized. Fear, stress, and depressing thoughts are dissolved. Calmness, surety, and a courageous outlook are taking their place.

Messengers:

Animal: *New Caledonian Owlet-Nightjar (bird)*
Nature: *Smoky Quartz (crystal)*
Universe/Energy: *Meaningful occurrences*

49

You see it happening. You know it's your intuition but still you doubt. Now is the time to believe in what your visions are telling you. They may be acting as an early warning system, so you'll know if you need to retreat from a situation or prepare to strike out. Listen and act if or when it is needed.

Messengers:

Animal: *Pit Viper (snake)*
Nature: *Quackgrass (plant)*
Universe/Energy: *Visions*

50

You might feel like a little fish in a big pond right now as you're going through a time of change. Hang on because the situation will be disrupted and blown around. You'll find yourself in a position of greater authority. It will come as a surprise and fill you with a sense of awe that you have been recognized in such a fantastic way.

Messengers:

Animal: *Anchovy (fish)*
Nature: *Termite Mounds*
Universe/Energy: *Respected (feeling)*

51

Keeping to yourself is fine, just don't become a hermit who is rarely seen by others. Don't trick yourself or be misguided by believing in something that is not your own personal truth. Every moment in life is precious and can be filled with excitement and wonder, if you'll only let it be that for you.

Messengers:

Animal: *Oarfish*
Nature: *Fool's Gold (pyrite mineral)*
Universe/Energy: *Living in the Moment*

52

Change is a normal part of life and you're embarking on a journey of many changes. Look for opportunities after endings; joy after sadness; and connect to the energy of the earth. Releasing emotions helps with healing. Don't hold everything inside.

Messengers:

Animal: *Komodo Dragon (reptile)*
Nature: *Zoisite (mineral)*
Universe/Energy: *Time standing still (feeling)*

53

There will always be some difficulties to face. Instead of fearing what is lurking around beneath the waters, learn to understand yourself and how you react to situations. Be grounded by going barefoot and having a direct connection to the Earth.

Messengers:

Animal: *Nurse Shark*
Nature: *Terra (land)*
Universe/Energy: *Perception (feeling)*

54

What goes around comes around. Look at your current behavior. Are you screaming, acting up, or doing things you know are out of character for you and you shouldn't be doing them? Stop. Find a place of balance and just let yourself settle for a bit. Now start over with good behaviors, a happy attitude, and a joyful presence. Reboot yourself.

Messengers:

Animal: *Screech Owl*
Nature: *Yew (tree)*
Universe/Energy: *Drumbeat (sound)*

55

Look for your hidden gifts through meditation, inner visions, or dreams. Enjoy time outside in the sun to promote rejuvenation during challenging times. Shed what surrounds you that is holding you back in order to grow more. Bask in the sun and spend time around water to bring your desires to fruition.

Messengers:

Animal: *Lizard*
Nature: *Larimar (gemstone)*
Universe/Energy: *Manifesting*

56

You're in tune with the energy in your body so use that attunement to send healing energy within yourself. You're able to find balance when it's evasive. You're flexible in mind and spirit and have above average intelligence. You intuition is an important part of your being and you embrace it.

Messengers:

Animal: *Coati (mammal)*
Nature: *Dill (herb)*
Universe/Energy: *Touch healing (sensation)*

57

Spiritual changes are happening inside of you. It's time to celebrate all the good things in your life. You're standing on solid ground and can move forward on whatever path you want to take. Work with your hands doing something creative. The future is in your hands, all you have to do is let your intuitive abilities guide you.

Messengers:

Animal: *Macaw (bird)*
Nature: *Chert Bituminous Coal (rock)*
Universe/Energy: *Floral (scent)*

58

Be yourself instead of struggling to be someone you're not. Let yourself dance in the rain or climb to great heights. Enjoy the luck and protection that is yours at this time. Your own happiness is completely up to you and is based on the decisions you make for your life.

Messengers:

Animal: *Roadrunner (bird)*
Nature: *Lady Fern (plant)*
Universe/Energy: *Freezing (natural phenomenon)*

59

Let your vision soar to great heights so you can see with clarity and perception. Look at situations from an elevated point of view, as if you're seeing them from above. You are dependable, reliable, and are a blessing to those around you.

Messengers:

Animal: *Peregrine Falcon*
Nature: *Siberian Iris (flower)*
Universe/Energy: *Mango (scent)*

60

You see things others cannot. You know what is really happening even when others are trying to hide it. You can be overcome with emotions quickly and sometimes find it hard to pull yourself out of the feelings.

Messengers:

Animal: *Snow Leopard (feline)*
Nature: *Winterberry Holly (plant)*
Universe/Energy: *Sit by a fire (action)*

61

State the facts and only the facts. Keep your beliefs and judgements out of the situation you are currently in. There are times when you can attack and other times when you need to just keep moving and watch what happens. This is a time to wait and watch.

Messengers:

Animal: *Tiger Shark*
Nature: *Water*
Universe/Energy: *Tingling (sensation)*

62

Just like the buttercups blooming from beneath a spring snow, you are in a time of uplifting growth. You have the support of those around you to help you along the way. Take time to enjoy the sweetness of life as you grow into the person you were meant to become.

Messengers:

Animal: *Gar (fish)*
Nature: *Thaw (weather)*
Universe/Energy: *Frosting (Scent)*

63

Enjoy doing a meaningless task and don't feel guilty about it. You tend to work tirelessly but everyone needs some time to do nothing. Sleep late, watch cartoons, read a magazine. Do something that will pass the time (that isn't work) or do nothing at all.

Messengers:

Animal: *Wallaby (mammal)*
Nature: *Variscite (mineral)*
Universe/Energy: *Consolation (feeling)*

64

Life is about balance. To fully enjoy the fruits of life, you also need to completely feel and understand the parts that cause you to feel unhappy. Being sensitive to your own needs will help you to stay balanced, will help you to ground yourself, and allow happiness to come to you.

Messengers:

Animal: *Vampire Bat*
Nature: *Sensitive Plant*
Universe/Energy: *Sketching (action)*

65

You work and work and never cut yourself any slack. Don't be too hard on yourself. Life is more than working yourself into the ground, especially when the joy has gone out of the work. You are surrounded by the power of love. Make sure you love yourself as much as you love others.

Messengers:

Animal: *Whitetail Deer*
Nature: *Lime Tree*
Universe/Energy: *Swinging on a swing (action)*

66

Don't get discouraged by your current circumstances. When you chose to live this life, you also chose lessons that would enable you to grow on a spiritual level. Every circumstance you find yourself in is an opportunity to gain experience in some way.

Messengers:

Animal: *Perch (fish)*
Nature: *Zucchini Squash*
Universe/Energy: *Observe Patterns*

67

Imagine that you can attract as much money as you need, or want, in life. Work to manifest the funds you desire by taking time out of each day to meditate and visualize the money coming to you. Remember it is rare for something to just be handed to you without you doing anything to earn it.

Messengers:

Animal: *Willet (bird)*
Nature: *Collard Greens*
Universe/Energy: *Writing (action)*

68

You see good omens at every turn. You're either in or are entering a phase where everything you touch is successful. You have managed to release fear and are balanced and grounded. Now is the time to act and make decisions. Counter any negativity with a smile and with grace.

Messengers:

Animal: *Gannet (bird)*
Nature: *Tiger's-Eye (gemstone)*
Universe/Energy: *Yodeling (action)*

69

Do you cling to things? Are you afraid to let go? Take a moment to examine what makes you feel secure. Are you able to stand on your own or do you feel as if you need someone else to support you? Now is the time to become independent.

Messengers:

Animal: *Sooty Tern (bird)*
Nature: *Valley*
Universe/Energy: *Zest*

70

It's time to dig deeply into your spiritual consciousness to learn where your path will lead. Watch out for boundaries with others. You may be stepping over some lines that make another person uncomfortable or they may be doing the same thing to you.

Messengers:

Animal: *Woodchuck*
Nature: *Storm Surge*
Universe/Energy: *Fire in a fireplace (scent)*

71

Look to the night sky, believe in what you can't see, sing a song that has no words. The mountains are high, and the valley is low, but it is what lives in the mystical places in between that draw you. There is magic in the air.

Messengers:

Animal: *Fairyfly (insect)*
Nature: *Volcanic Rock*
Universe/Energy: *Broaden Your Horizons*

72

Resourcefulness guides you. Be loyal to family and yourself. Home is your safe place, your shelter from the storms of life. Seek out new projects. They will be prosperous and rewarding. Dream bigger than you dare and take on tasks that seem monumental. Start small and build big while paying attention to details.

Messengers:

Animal: *Beaver*
Nature: *Lemon Tree*
Universe/Energy: *Attention to Details (action)*

73

Answer the call of the sea. When the water calls you, you must go. With your toes in the sand, the water flowing over your ankles, answers will be made known, and your soul will heal. If you can't visit in person, travel there in your mind's eye, and imagine how it feels to be at the beach with the wind, water, and sand.

Messengers:

Animal: *Porpoise*
Nature: *Ammolite (gemstone)*
Universe/Energy: *Wonderment (feeling)*

74

Before bed, figure out your problems and plan for the next day. That way, you'll have a good night's rest and wake up with a smile in your heart. When problems aren't resolved they can cause you to lose sleep and toss and turn, resulting in your feeling groggy and tired the following day.

Messengers:

Animal: *Neon Tetra (fish)*
Nature: *Yellow Diamond (gemstone)*
Universe/Energy: *Strength*

75

There is negativity at work in your life that is holding you back. Seek it out and find a way to release it. Good things can come from the worse scenarios in life. Clearing out the bad is a form of rebirth. Now is a suitable time to start a new program or to take a class.

Messengers:

Animal: *Maggot*
Nature: *Whirlwind*
Universe/Energy: *Reading (action)*

76

Determination is at the forefront now. You're a strong, wise person who prides yourself on doing an excellent job in everything you do. The tasks before you are difficult ones, but you will be able to prevail. Success doesn't always come easy for you, but it always comes because you don't give up.

Messengers:

Animal: *Sockeye Salmon (fish)*
Nature: *Vernal Witch-hazel*
Universe/Energy: *Tan (Color)*

77

You are embarking on an adventure of spiritual growth and transformation. Your dreams become prophetic, you know things before they happen, and you're developing new intuitive abilities. It may seem as if you're an emotional wreck but that's because your frequency is rising, and it can be a bit unsettling as it does so.

Messengers:

Animal: *Angelfish*
Nature: *Wolfsbane (plant)*
Universe/Energy: *Dark Sienna (color)*

78

Always think for yourself, follow your heart and dreams. There are times when you will seek the advice of others but that doesn't necessarily mean you'll follow their advice. Listen to different perspectives and then make up your own mind based on what you learn.

Messengers:

Animal: *Palila (bird)*
Nature: *Zinc*
Universe/Energy: *Cream Soda (Scent)*

79

Watch for someone who is trying to trick you though shock and awe. The words are hiding something that is meant to entice you to do something you really don't want to do. Be slick and move quickly, rippling the waters of their plan to keep yourself from being caught.

Messengers:

Animal: *River Otter*
Nature: *Venus Fly Trap*
Universe/Energy: *Joyful Surprise (emotion)*

80

You're a great communicator but beware of talking too much or bringing too much attention to yourself. Listen closely and use the information you learn to your advantage. Be clear and concise in your speech so there isn't any chance of misunderstandings.

Messengers:

Animal: *Gray Catbird*
Nature: *Waxed Beans*
Universe/Energy: *Vacuuming (Sound)*

81

Home is the place where you feel most comfortable, at ease, and peaceful within yourself. You may live in a big house, a little house, a camper, or a cabin in the woods, or maybe you share a space with friends or a roommate. It doesn't matter where you live as long as you make your space feel like a warm and cozy home.

Messengers:

Animal: *Softshell Turtle*
Nature: *Pineapple*
Universe/Energy: *Jasmine (scent)*

82

Immerse yourself in stillness. Don't move, don't think, just be. Breathe deeply and slowly. Pay attention to each breath you take. Feel the air moving through your body sustaining your life. Be one with nothing, yet with everything at the same time. The Universe guides you. Follow its lead.

Messengers:

Animal: *Marten (mammal/weasel)*
Nature: *Eggplant*
Universe/Energy: *Festive (feeling)*

83

Take some time to cook today simply for the joy of cooking. There are messages all around you and the kitchen is the gathering place. As you create a delicious soup, meal, or dessert, feel the calmness and joy that creating food gives you.

Messengers:

Animal: *Sambar (mammal/deer)*
Nature: *Chervil (herb)*
Universe/Energy: *Fudge (Scent)*

84

Sometimes you must take a step back to see the truth of the matter. When you're unsure of which way to go, looking from a distance gives clarity and vision. Remember that you don't have to catch every ball thrown your way.

Messengers:

Animal: *Loach (fish)*
Nature: *Black Ash Tree*
Universe/Energy: *Courageous (feeling)*

85

You have few enemies but those who are can be venomous towards you. Now is the time to put up a protective wall around your spiritual self and empower it with the energy of quartz. This will help to keep the negativity at bay. Pay extra attention to those you love and who love you.

Messengers:

Animal: *Sea Wasp (jellyfish)*
Nature: *Quartz*
Universe/Energy: *Exercise (action)*

86

You're on a path of personal growth and increased self-esteem. Do not hesitate or be afraid. See things as they really are and not how you want them to be. Mysteries will be revealed to you. Decide what you will do with the information before acting on it.

Messengers:

Animal: *Boar*
Nature: *Jasmine Flower*
Universe/Energy: *Positive Thinking*

87

Do not hold on to regrets. Look at them from a place of quiet calmness and try to understand why the situation happened the way it did. Release them if possible. Your looks are unique, and you also have exceptional abilities that often surprise those around you.

Messengers:

Animal: *Red-lipped Batfish*
Nature: *Cherry Tomato*
Universe/Energy: *Orchids (scent)*

88

Do not fear your own power. You shine and sparkle with brightness and color. Others want to emulate you because watching you makes them happy. Take care to stretch your muscles and use deep breathing techniques to ground and center yourself.

Messengers:

Animal: *Puma (feline)*
Nature: *Colored Diamond (gemstone)*
Universe/Energy: *Freshly cut grass (scent)*

89

There are unknown invisible attachments that are bringing your energy level down. Using creative visualization, look over your entire body to find them and disconnect them from your energy. Watch as they bounce back to where they came from. Something or someone will be hidden from view for a brief time but will then come back around to you when you least expect it.

Messengers:

Animal: *Jackrabbit*
Nature: *Solar Eclipse*
Universe/Energy: *Slow down (action)*

90

Sensitivity is needed at this moment. You'll be consulted about a delicate matter that will require gentleness and grace. Hidden deep within are glorious creations that inspire and touch your heart. Sit and enjoy what you have discovered for a while. Healing is upon you.

Messengers:

Animal: *Axis Deer*
Nature: *Geodes*
Universe/Energy: *Meditation*

91

Above and beyond, looking down from eternity, wrapped in the energy of the Universe is where you'll find your true reason for being. Scraping off the old, embracing the new is important now. You are no longer a fish out of water but have delved deep within the depths of your own ocean.

Messengers:

Animal: *Herring (fish)*
Nature: *Pumice Rhyolite (rock)*
Universe/Energy: *Out-of-Body Experience*

92

Sometimes it's hard for you to see what's right in front of you. Make a special effort to uncover information. This is a time of connecting with likeminded people who are embracing new ideas and connecting with the spiritual realm and the Divine.

Messengers:

Animal: *Guinea Pig*
Nature: *Watermelon*
Universe/Energy: *Make a choice (action)*

93

There is clarity in the air. You may feel comfortable in the coldness of winter and at home with the warmth of summer. Scents fill the night drawing wildlife to you. This is a time of commitment to yourself. Of transformation within and change without. You are ready.

Messengers:

Animal: *King Eider (sea duck)*
Nature: *Nottingham Catchfly (plant)*
Universe/Energy: *Bells (Sound)*

94

Now is the time to seek guidance from your spirit guides and those on the other side. You are in the middle of a tremendous amount of spiritual growth and are directly connected with the Divine. Listen to the messages you receive.

Messengers:

Animal: *Moray Eel*
Nature: *Forest*
Universe/Energy: *Clairaudience*

95

When the storm is raging all around you, be patient and wait for the calmness to settle in. You will feel an easy peacefulness in the quiet. The sting of someone's words is surprising and unexpected and will hurt your feelings. Little jabs have a big punch. Feel it and let it go.

Messengers:

Animal: *Blue Dragon (sea slug)*
Nature: *Eye of the Storm*
Universe/Energy: *Reconnect with someone (action)*

96

Manual labor is at the forefront right now. Make sure you're getting plenty of water and are eating plenty of well-balanced meals as you do the work to keep your strength up. Stick to your plans and you'll attain success. Don't play around, instead make advance plans to stay on track.

Messengers:

Animal: *Leopard Seal*
Nature: *Diatomite Dolomite (rock)*
Universe/Energy: *Barometric Pressure*

97

You work between worlds. Your intuition is strong, and you have the abilities of a medium and can travel between worlds. You're often contacted to pass messages from the other side to those in the physical realm, which you do with honor and ease.

Messengers:

Animal: *Squirrel Monkey*
Nature: *Spider Webs*
Universe/Energy: *Play (action)*

98

You may be in direct connection to the other side through paranormal experiences. Protect yourself through positive energy and healing light. If it is too much for you to understand, ask your guides to take it from you. A message is trying to be delivered. Listen and pay attention to your experiences. Once the message is received, the encounters will stop.

Messengers:

Animal: *Kit Fox*
Nature: *Lacy Blue Self-Heal Plant*
Universe/Energy: *Phantom Phone Call/Text*

99

To find clarity, you must get dirty. Get outside. Feel the rain on your skin, the dirt in your hands, the wind in your face. This will allow you to connect to your higher self, to elevate your personal vibration, and find ways to grow on your spiritual path.

Messengers:

Animal: *Chinchilla*
Nature: *Ladyfinger Cactus*
Universe/Energy: *Gold (color)*

100

Physical exercise often leads to the most enlightening experiences. When you're doing mundane labor-intensive tasks, your mind often wanders into a quiet place. This is when it is easy for messages to be delivered to you from the Universal consciousness. All while getting a great workout.

Messengers:

Animal: *Antechinus (marsupial)*
Nature: *Seagrass*
Universe/Energy: *Rolling Ocean Waves (Sound)*

101

Are you bringing on pain by being too critical of yourself? Make sure you're not putting yourself in situations where you know you'll be hurt emotionally. You are pure and evergreen. Appreciate yourself and ask for more of what you *really* want out of life.

Messengers:

Animal: *Sole (fish/ray)*
Nature: *Cypress (tree)*
Universe/Energy: *Confident (feeling)*

102

Relax. Let go of stress. Get more sleep. Pay attention to what your body is saying to you. Eat more vegetables, drink more water, get more rest or exercise. You're in the process of attuning to higher frequencies.

Messengers:

Animal: *Koala (bear)*
Nature: *Tertiary Rainbow*
Universe/Energy: *Positive Self-Talk*

103

Your home is a sanctuary. A place where you let all the stresses of the day fall away. Outside of your home you tend to have quick movements and are constantly on the go all day with your work. Once home though, that changes and you're able to slow down. Maybe a bubble bath is in order tonight before bed for complete relaxation.

Messengers:

Animal: *Pika (mammal)*
Nature: *Starflower (herb)*
Universe/Energy: *Burn your favorite Candle (action)*

104

You're curious and think deeply about things. Puzzles intrigue you. Put one together now and pay attention to the high frequency thoughts that come to you. You're one of those people who think a thousand different thoughts a day instead of thinking one thought a thousand separate times. Use a journal to keep up with your plethora of ideas.

Messengers:

Animal: *Arctic Fox*
Nature: *Colt's Foot (plant)*
Universe/Energy: *Feel the wind on your face (sensation)*

105

Experience is the best teacher. There are plenty of things you can read about in books but until you actually experience the situation in real time in the real world, it's not your personal reality. Once you have the experience firsthand, then you will learn the lessons that go along with it.

Messengers:

Animal: *Pink Salmon (fish)*
Nature: *Golden Currant (plant)*
Universe/Energy: *Journeying*

106

You can help others who are going through things you have already dealt with in your life. It feels as if you're stepping out of your comfort zone to help, and you are. The courage it takes to reach out to someone who hasn't asked for help, is part of your core being, and will lead to great spiritual growth for the both of you.

Messengers:

Animal: *Sora (bird)*
Nature: *Uraninite (mineral/ore)*
Universe/Energy: *Leather (Scent)*

107

Do not let what could destroy you win. Instead let it propel you to great heights, so you soar though the atmosphere of happiness and love. You have many blessings to celebrate, and you work hard to get through the challenging times with courage and strength.

Messengers:

Animal: *Golden Eagle*
Nature: *Atmosphere*
Universe/Energy: *Sing a song in your mind (action)*

108

It's time for a decision. It may be something sharp and prickly on one hand and something else smooth and sleek on the other. When deciding, do not choose the easiest path unless it is the right one. Sometimes a road that is harder to walk brings about greater and more rewarding results.

Messengers:

Animal: *Bichir (fish)*
Nature: *Chestnut*
Universe/Energy: *Fork in the Road*

109

You do not see yourself in the same way that other people see you. You may not give yourself the credit you deserve, or you may not see your true beauty both inside and out. You may downplay your abilities or achievements. Appreciate yourself every single day. You are worthy!

Messengers:

Animal: *Hoopoe (bird)*
Nature: *Sediment*
Universe/Energy: *Gardenia (Scent)*

110

The weight on your shoulders is getting too heavy. It's time to put some of it down, let others handle some of the responsibility. You don't have to do everything yourself. It's okay to give up some control. After you adjust, you'll feel freer and wonder why you didn't do this sooner.

Messengers:

Animal: *Llama*
Nature: *Cold Front*
Universe/Energy: *Hammering (Sound)*

111

You do your best work in the dark. You move with quiet stealth and sneak up on the unexpecting when needed. You're very aware of the world around you and your feelings. These are good traits to have in a competitive business. You're successful in what you do. There is wisdom and benefits to looking at the shadow parts of your work. Look for and don't doubt the messages in the shapes of the clouds.

Messengers:

Animal: *Barn Owl*
Nature: *Meteors*
Universe/Energy: *Watch the Clouds (action)*

112

You'll find yourself jumping from one thing to another without completing the task. Slow it down some and finish what you start. When you have too many irons in the fire it can erupt on you and turn to ash. This is a time of happiness and joy. Relish in it.

Messengers:

Animal: *Ringtail Lemur*
Nature: *Volcanic Ash*
Universe/Energy: *Ecstatic*

113

It's time to rely on all your six senses to help you through a situation. Don't discount anything. Instead pay closer attention to what is going on around you. You may feel like you're all alone in these waters, but you're not.

Messengers:

Animal: *Black Racer (snake)*
Nature: *Chickpea*
Universe/Energy: *Go rafting (action)*

114

Sleeping all day and staying up all night? Or your dreams are so intense that you feel like you haven't slept at all. To reset your clock, stay up longer than you thought possible and then try to sleep at your normal evening time.

Messengers:

Animal: *Sugar Glider (marsupial)*
Nature: *Water Chestnut (plant)*
Universe/Energy: *Enthusiasm*

115

There are times when you cross over turbulent waters and are shielded in safety from above. There are other times when the waters run so deep that you find yourself swimming at great depths just to survive. If you need comfort, but there's no one to give it, comfort yourself.

Messengers:

Animal: *Wahoo (fish)*
Nature: *Swaddled Babies Orchid*
Universe/Energy: *Absorption (phenomenon)*

116

Sometimes the chase can be more exciting than the end result. Your energy levels are high and flowing in abundance. Focus your attention and enjoy going after what you want. This is a time to pay attention to your money and save.

Messengers:

Animal: *Clouded Leopard (feline)*
Nature: *Vanadinite (mineral)*
Universe/Energy: *Mandalas*

117

You know you are different on the inside than how others perceive you on the outside. Intuitive abilities, paranormal events, and just knowing things without knowing how you know them, are all an intrinsic part of your spiritual self. You can do more with your abilities than you'll ever let other people know. Not because you're ashamed, but because keeping it secret is its power.

Messengers:

Animal: *Oilbird*
Nature: *Dryhead Agate (gemstone)*
Universe/Energy: *Telekinesis*

118

How influential do you want to be? A famous social media influencer? You can create the most change and awareness when others don't realize that's what you're doing. Take a stealthier approach because you can be much more influential when others aren't aware of your influence in their lives.

Messengers:

Animal: *Heron*
Nature: *El Niño*
Universe/Energy: *Fulfillment*

119

Anything you want can be achieved through creating and seeing it in your mind's eye. Practice manifesting it daily. It's time for you to stand strong but to always sway in the winds of change. Do not demean your value when it comes to work. Charge more for services than less because you are worth the higher fee.

Messengers:

Animal: *Turbot Fish*
Nature: *Pine Tree*
Universe/Energy: *Creative Visualization*

120

Now is the time to learn more about your spiritual self and your life purpose. You may feel as if you've been wandering, without any specific direction. Reconnect with your past and personal heritage to get started. Spiritually, you connect to the Divine to discover the best way to learn the lessons you planned prior to birth.

Messengers:

Animal: *Yak*
Nature: *Blizzard*
Universe/Energy: *Crowd Chatter (Sound)*

121

Victory is near. You've worked hard, taken a unique approach, and worked in a colorful and meaningful way. While you wait for the result to be announced, take some time off, visit the waves and sand of the beach or go to the fair and have fair food. Maybe just take a few days off and do nothing. You deserve it.

Messengers:

Animal: *Secretary Bird*
Nature: *Beach*
Universe/Energy: *Caramel Apples (Scent)*

122

When you offer advice, speak from the heart and with truth. Your words should be useful and helpful, not filled with criticism or disapproval. It is not your place to judge someone else, but you can lift them up when they're down.

Messengers:

Animal: *Spanish Mackerel (fish)*
Nature: *Quartzite Muscovite Schist (rock)*
Universe/Energy: *Purposeful realization*

123

Don't take anyone or anything for granted. You have a deliberate focus that helps you get to the heart of the matter quickly. Listen to the whispers around you, whether spoken on the physical plane or the spiritual plane. Words have power.

Messengers:

Animal: *Seahorse (fish)*
Nature: *Titanium*
Universe/Energy: *Make a request (action)*

124

In life, there are people who will not live up to your expectations. People who will let you down time and time again. You are loyal to a fault and will always be there for others when they need you. Surround yourself with people who will always be there for you too and let those who are only using you drift away.

Messengers:

Animal: *Red Mullet (fish)*
Nature: *Lepidolite (gemstone)*
Universe/Energy: *Loyal*

125

You have the gift of being able to interpret what you see not only with your mind but on a deeply intuitive level as well. People don't have to talk for you to know things from just looking at them. This ability can cause others to be wary around you because they fear you will know more about them than they want you to know.

Messengers:

Animal: *Andean Condor (bird)*
Nature: *Columnar Basalt (rock)*
Universe/Energy: *Declutter Your Space (action)*

126

Allow yourself to wait. Just hang out and do nothing. Put your phone away, turn off the television, and just be. As you wait, you'll find your mind drifting back and forth, reaching into places that you wouldn't have gone if you'd been on the phone, reading a magazine, or doing an activity.

Messengers:

Animal: *Possum*
Nature: *Dacite Diabase (rock)*
Universe/Energy: *Inchworm Green (color)*

127

Are you hiding behind a false glossy veneer that covers the real you? Are you craving more than you have and don't know what to do to get it? Now is the time to plan. Be guarded but not cold. Be guided but not weak.

Messengers:

Animal: *Arctic Char (fish)*
Nature: *Fatsia (plant)*
Universe/Energy: *Pay Attention to Your Surroundings (action)*

128

It's easy to take the little things in life for granted. Make sure your words have meaning and you're not just repeating what you've heard others say. This can cause people to avoid you because you don't have your own opinions. The little things matter and can grow into something tall and strong.

Messengers:

Animal: *Magpie (bird)*
Nature: *Pine Nut (seed)*
Universe/Energy: *Babble of a Brook (sound)*

129

Don't be surprised to discover what you thought was truth is wrong. You will be able to see another person's true colors and it may make you feel guilty for misjudging the person. Now is the time to make amends. Sharing a meal is always a wonderful way to overcome differences.

Messengers:

Animal: *Amazon Dolphin*
Nature: *Labradorite (gemstone)*
Universe/Energy: *Pastries (Scent)*

130

Are you having a tough time contacting someone important in your life? Go the extra mile to reach them even if it means driving to their house to say hello. This is not the time to sit back and relax but to squeeze someone in a big hug.

Messengers:

Animal: *Anaconda (snake)*
Nature: *Ghost Orchid (plant)*
Universe/Energy: *Rest (action)*

131

If you're feeling small and helpless due to your current situation, then you're headed in the wrong direction and need to make a U turn. This is a warning from your spiritual self that you're on the wrong path and need to make a change.

Messengers:

Animal: *Newt (amphibian)*
Nature: *Forget-Me-Not (plant)*
Universe/Energy: *Go for a drive (action)*

132

Be careful not to get caught up in a web of lies. You're starting a new project but there is some dishonesty involved at the beginning. Be very aware and sort through what people say until you get to the truth. This will enable you to be more successful by weeding out those people in the beginning.

Messengers:

Animal: *Spider*
Nature: *Mango*
Universe/Energy: *Aspire*

133

It's time to take inventory of your inner self. Consider all of your positive and negative attributes. This enables you to find characteristics that you like and dislike about yourself, then you can begin to make positive changes and let go of any negative attributes. Do not think this will be easy. Making character changes is difficult at times but it can be done.

Messengers:

Animal: *Barred Forest Falcon*
Nature: *Slate (rock)*
Universe/Energy: *Blessings*

134

Get some exercise in a fun, outdoorsy way today. Take a stroll in the forest and look for the spirits that live within or simply go for a walk in your neighborhood. Just get yourself outside so you can be in the world instead of staying inside your home. There doesn't have to be a purpose other than your own enjoyment.

Messengers:

Animal: *Zebrafish*
Nature: *Japanese Maple (tree)*
Universe/Energy: *Hilarity (feeling)*

135

Do you take care of your inner child? Consider how you take care of that little person inside of you. Are you holding onto things from your past that you no longer want in your life? You are the parent to your inner child. Love and embrace that spirit so you solve any unresolved feelings from your past.

Messengers:

Animal: *Goliath Birdeater (spider)*
Nature: *Earth's Crust*
Universe/Energy: *Horse Running (Sound)*

136

If it feels like the people around you are acting cold toward you, then look for the source. Someone is messing with you in a very indirect way and is playing a game you don't even know you're participating in. Be very aware right now and hunt down the culprit so you can put an end to it.

Messengers:

Animal: *Auk (bird)*
Nature: *Chickweed*
Universe/Energy: *Play a Game (action)*

137

Get in touch with your emotions by letting them out. Write in a journal, compose a song or poem. Simply take the time to quietly sit and think about your feelings. Accept yourself, others, and situations in which you are involved. Most of all have faith that you are doing your best and trust that things are going to work out as they are supposed to.

Messengers:

Animal: *Manatee*
Nature: *Roll Cloud/Morning Glory Cloud*
Universe/Energy: *Delight (feeling)*

138

You have a knack for being at the right place at the right time and will be successful in your ventures through your creativity and talent. You don't need to keep others around that may hold you back or cause problems. Venture out on your own and find new opportunities.

Messengers:

Animal: *Pencil Urchin (sea urchin)*
Nature: *Apricot*
Universe/Energy: *Commitment*

139

Practice makes perfect. You have the unique ability to get yourself out of any situation that you don't want to be in. You're slippery and deep and have the gift of gab. You can talk your way out of just about anything. Take some time to spice up the romantic areas of your life.

Messengers:

Animal: *Click Beetle*
Nature: *Mudslide*
Universe/Energy: *Gingerbread (Scent)*

140

Now is the time to be playful and to not take yourself seriously at all. It's time for fun, for enjoying the company of others, and being silly. It's been a long time since you let loose and had a fun time without worrying about your responsibilities. Go for it!

Messengers:

Animal: *Macaque (primate)*
Nature: *Barite (mineral)*
Universe/Energy: *Amusement*

141

Completing projects and tying up loose ends is important now. As you do, you'll discover new connections coming into your life that will lead to new prospective jobs. If you've ever wanted to start a business and be your own boss, you can now spin your own web of wonders.

Messengers:

Animal: *Garden Spider*
Nature: *Ametrine (gemstone)*
Universe/Energy: *Conformity*

142

On tiny feet lives a heart of gold. Be aware of a giving, loving, and independent spirit that would rather spend time with you than with the herd. When one door closes, another will open. Opportunities seem to come from all sorts of places right now and you're not sure which one to go for. Take your time and decide. You'll pick the right ones.

Messengers:

Animal: *Falabella (equine)*
Nature: *Chinquapin Oak Tree*
Universe/Energy: *Door Opening and Closing (Sound)*

143

143 means I love you. Messages of love from the other side are abundant. Pay attention to what is around you, look for hidden messages in the clouds, or for shadow animals. The animal kingdom is reaching out to you, pay attention to the signs and messages. They are sending you messages of hope, love, and strength during challenging times. Love will see you through.

Messengers:

Animal: *Friesian (equine)*
Nature: *Lemon Balm (herb)*
Universe/Energy: *Expression*

144

Not everything has a sting or bite to it. When you're looking for the negative, you'll often find it. Instead, look for goodness, truth, and light in every situation. You have a clear understanding and a keen knowledge of people and situations that is unexplainable. This is your intuitive gift.

Messengers:

Animal: *Mud Dauber (insect)*
Nature: *Gem Silica (mineral)*
Universe/Energy: *Claircognizance*

145

Protect your inner self as you delve into your soul's purpose. Walk your own path instead of following others. Avoid telling too much at this time, even to those closest to you. Water is important for spiritual cleansing, releasing frustrations, and protecting yourself from negativity. Change your perspective from time to time to gain clearer vision.

Messengers:

Animal: *Armadillo*
Nature: *Novaculite Phyllite (rock)*
Universe/Energy: *Lucid Dreaming*

146

The time of great expectations has come to an end. Now you will experience the parting of ways, whether it is in your personal life or in business. There's a storm brewing and you're getting out just in the nick of time.

Messengers:

Animal: *Screamer (bird)*
Nature: *Tropical Storm*
Universe/Energy: *Satisfied (feeling)*

147

That which you can't see can burn the brightest. Mind your manners and act with simple grace. There will be a homecoming of sorts and you'll be amid the excitement. You've wandered far but home has always been where your heart is the happiest. Travel back to become complete.

Messengers:

Animal: *House Wren*
Nature: *Ultraviolet Light*
Universe/Energy: *Open the door for a stranger (action)*

148

Look for answers to what you don't understand by considering all possibilities with an open mind. Family, traditions, and getting back to your roots are important now. Make plans so you don't veer off your path. There's more being said by others than what you hear so listen closely.

Messengers:

Animal: *Lemur (primate)*
Nature: *Poppy (plant)*
Universe/Energy: *Water Sky (natural phenomenon)*

149

Remember to project into the world what you would like to receive back in your life. From the smallest thought to the biggest dream, and everything in between, you will receive what you radiate. Listen closely to the messages being sent your way as time will not wait but will steadily move on. If you're ready, you will capture the vibrancy of life.

Messengers:

Animal: *Sea Anemones*
Nature: Thermal Pools
Universe/Energy: *Cuckoo Clock (Sound)*

150

Preparing for the future is a smart strategy. If you can, stockpile now so you have what you need in the short term. Make future financial plans and investments for the long term. If you do your preparations now, you'll have more security later in life. It's never too late to start saving and planning for the future.

Messengers:

Animal: *Squirrel*
Nature: *Zebra Haworthia (plant)*
Universe/Energy: *Strong Feeling of Belonging*

151

Be on the lookout for deceit, unfaithfulness, and a venomous attack. The energy surrounding you is chaotic and out of sync with your own inner stability. You will need to draw on your inner strength and listen to your own intuition for guidance.

Messengers:

Animal: *Mamba (snake)*
Nature: *Peanut*
Universe/Energy: *Eternal Flame*

152

Brainstorming is at the top of the agenda. There's a new project you'll be involved with starting from the ground up. There will be lots of planning and tension will be high. Some people will lose their temper and snap at others on the team. Just make sure that person isn't you.

Messengers:

Animal: *Alligator Snapping Turtle*
Nature: *Chicory (vegetable)*
Universe/Energy: *Explore Ideas*

153

Balance, peacefulness, and reconnecting to your higher self is of importance now. Filter out the good from the bad even if it means retreating within yourself for a bit. You're sensitive to the energy of others, both intuitively and emotionally, especially when the intention behind that energy is unclear. Take the time you need to sort it out for yourself.

Messengers:

Animal: *Oyster*
Nature: *Heliconia Flower*
Universe/Energy: *Use Reason*

154

Storms may rage around you but you're in a happy place where no one can alter your emotions. Let the others rant and act out. Keep to your own plan, enjoy the life you're living, and be supportive if possible. What is affecting those around you isn't affecting you. Don't be drawn into the drama of others.

Messengers:

Animal: *Moorhen (bird)*
Nature: *Nor'easter*
Universe/Energy: *Tapping (sound)*

155

There are some personal things that you just shouldn't tell others. When you ask someone to keep your secrets you're putting them in an uncomfortable position, and while they might be supportive, you may worry that they will tell someone else. Consider whether you might feel this way and if you think you will, then you shouldn't be sharing your secrets. Keep them to yourself.

Messengers:

Animal: *Amur Leopard*
Nature: *Sandhill*
Universe/Energy: *Kettle whistling (sound)*

156

Look at the patterns around you. Do you sense anything about them? Patterns can be a connection to the Divine. They can help, through their intricate weavings, to uncover deeper meanings and new information. You may feel hot and bothered by this information, but it is necessary for your spiritual growth.

Messengers:

Animal: *Tiger Snake*
Nature: *Humid Climate*
Universe/Energy: *Elation (emotion)*

157

To find balance, you must detach yourself emotionally from events in the past. This is a difficult lesson to learn but you will achieve it when you bring balance to both your aura and your chakras. Work on those areas first so that you can look at your past with a calm understanding instead of emotional upset.

Messengers:

Animal: *Black Dolphin*
Nature: *Golden Barrel Cactus*
Universe/Energy: *Aura Balancing*

158

Plans have stalled and you're not sure what to do to get them moving again. It's time to reevaluate what you've set out to achieve. What changes can you make to get things moving again? Or has the outcome been affected and you need to start over with a different plan?

Messengers:

Animal: *Marsh Rabbit*
Nature: *Pin Oak (tree)*
Universe/Energy: *Accomplishment (emotion)*

159

You may find yourself getting sudden flashes of inspiration. Consider the frequencies around you. Is it music to your ears? Does it make you want to leap around and enjoy yourself through dance? Act on what inspires you so you will grow to higher energetic levels.

Messengers:

Animal: *Springbok (antelope)*
Nature: *Wintergreen Tree*
Universe/Energy: *Sizzle (sound)*

160

Emotions such as fear and self-doubt can keep you sitting on a fence, unable to decide one way or the other. You're not contained by the way you think and can break free of negative emotions at any time you choose.

Messengers:

Animal: *Willow Ptarmigan (bird)*
Nature: *Gabbro Granite (rock)*
Universe/Energy: *Climb over a Fence (action)*

161

Someone may want to fight your battles for you to be your protector. To grow both as a person and in spirit, you need to take up the fight for yourself. While the other person means well, until you can stand up for yourself, you will not have the confidence to be your true spiritual self.

Messengers:

Animal: *Dog Salmon (fish)*
Nature: *Rodgersia (plant)*
Universe/Energy: *Running Water (Sound)*

162

When the natural world speaks, do you listen? You have great abilities, you are connected to the Divine, and serve as a messenger from the spirit world to those here on Earth. At times it may feel as if you're buried underneath the complexity of it all.

Messengers:

Animal: *Sun Bear*
Nature: *Avalanche*
Universe/Energy: *Appreciated (feeling)*

163

Losing your temper, taking out anger on those smaller than you, can lead to a road of self-destruction and pain. You have more control than you're allowing yourself. Step back. Take a breath. Really consider your words and actions before you do something you'll regret later. The power is within you to be reasonable. Let yourself.

Messengers:

Animal: *Titmouse (bird)*
Nature: *Limestone Halite Rock Salt*
Universe/Energy: *Ring (sound)*

164

Try walking in someone else's shoes today. Look at situations from their perspective. Examine how their views differ from your own and why. Great beauty can come from darkness. When you look at positions different from your own, you bring light through knowledge. Today is a wonderful day to cook a new dish for friends or family.

Messengers:

Animal: *Serval (feline)*
Nature: *Night Blooming Cereus (plant)*
Universe/Energy: *Cooking (action)*

165

If the energy is blocked, you'll have things going wrong, emotions running high, and, a difficult day. To free up the energy around you, realign how you're approaching people and situations. Declutter your personal or workspace. Be careful of what you throw away so something important isn't lost forever.

Messengers:

Animal: *Vaquita (marine mammal)*
Nature: *Diamond (gemstone)*
Universe/Energy: *Rearrange Your Furniture (action)*

166

Speed, stealth, and strength are needed now. Respond to situations and opportunities without hesitation. Understand priorities and stay grounded to face them quickly and with extreme focus. Remember to take some time to recharge daily, to slow down, and just enjoy the little things in life.

Messengers:

Animal: *Cheetah*
Nature: *Red Beryl (gemstone)*
Universe/Energy: *Pleasure*

167

You've got to fight for what you want without going on the attack and destroying your opponent. That will not end well, and you will not achieve the results you desire. Don't be heartless, instead approach from a place of solid surety and the knowledge that you will win the battle.

Messengers:

Animal: *Killer Bee*
Nature: *Yams (vegetable)*
Universe/Energy: *Share Your Possessions*

168

Negative experiences can ignite a fire inside you, so you learn from them. Change may be on the agenda, or you may need to stay the path. Either way, you're moving away from negativity into the light of possibilities.

Messengers:

Animal: *Red Panda (bear)*
Nature: *Prickly Pear Cactus*
Universe/Energy: *Investigate*

169

Itching and scratching, heat and sweat, it's just miserable when you're working outside in the middle of summer. There is no reason for you to lack confidence though. You've survived worse in your life and hard work is always good for you. Think of summer fun instead.

Messengers:

Animal: *Water Flea*
Nature: *Humidity*
Universe/Energy: *Secure (feeling)*

170

Find time to lay down and relax. Add some flowers to your living space and enjoy their scent filling the air. You ordinarily move so fast that others find it hard to keep up with you. Now is not the time for that. It may be difficult for you to relax but you can do it.

Messengers:

Animal: *Kinkajou (mammal)*
Nature: *Cyclone*
Universe/Energy: *Clicking (sound)*

171

Good fortune and luck surround you. Choices become easy to make, and abundance abounds. You're on a roll and everything you touch seems to turn to gold. Show great appreciation for all that is gifted to you both from others and the Universe.

Messengers:

Animal: *Ladybug*
Nature: *La Niña*
Universe/Energy: *Kelly Green (color)*

172

You're leaving dark times in the past. As you move forward into better situations think about the lessons you've learned. Let go of negative thoughts and opinions of others and as you do, forgive them for any hurt they may have caused you. When you take this type of action, you can move forward free from the pressure of the past.

Messengers:

Animal: *Wool Carder Bee*
Nature: *Biotite (mineral)*
Universe/Energy: *Forgiveness*

173

Just as a seed needs fertilizer to grow, you need the ability to take yourself lightly and to see your beauty within. Spiritual growth can be intense, and it can be light and airy, but it needs the fertilizer of your participation in order to feed the growth you are capable of achieving.

Messengers:

Animal: *Gopher Snake*
Nature: *Saffron (spice)*
Universe/Energy: *Playful (feeling)*

174

Connecting with others is imperative now. When you receive the blessings coming your way you will want the support of family and friends to celebrate your achievements. This is not the time to be alone. Happiness and joy are yours to share with those you love.

Messengers:

Animal: *Night Heron*
Nature: *Atemoya (fruit tree)*
Universe/Energy: *Receive*

175

Expect to turn a defeat into a victory. Someone out there thinks they've gotten one over on you, but they haven't. You're on top of your game. You are balanced and grounded and go after what you desire.

Messengers:

Animal: *Lake Trout (fish)*
Nature: *Chili Pepper*
Universe/Energy: *Slow concentrated breathing (action)*

176

You're determined and once you set your mind to something you don't give up. You may strut your stuff and let your vibrance and colors light up someone's day as part of your quest for success. Sometimes you must *fake it until you make it* in creative ways.

Messengers:

Animal: *Peacock*
Nature: *Quaternary Rainbow*
Universe/Energy: *Freshly Washed Sheets (Scent)*

177

Sweeping away dirt and grim is cleansing for the soul. A clean house allows heightened energetic waves to flow all around you. You can turn ashes into beautiful gems if you so desire. Do not let clutter and disarray overwhelm your living space because the positive energy flow will be disrupted.

Messengers:

Animal: *Zorilla (mammal/polecat)*
Nature: *Helenite (gemstone)*
Universe/Energy: *Sweeping (action)*

178

Beware of false friends hiding within your inner circle. You have had situations that seemed odd to you in the recent past, where you've questioned the motives of someone you're close to, even though they seemed sweet. Listen to those feelings.

Messengers:

Animal: *Hagfish*
Nature: *Natural Fault Line*
Universe/Energy: *Funnel Cakes (Scent)*

179

Abundance and prosperity abound but to achieve your desires you'll have to make sacrifices. Give from the heart and go out of your way for others. You've risen above doing things for your own self-gain and have moved into the higher levels of frequency where you strive to achieve universal oneness on the earthly plane.

Messengers:

Animal: *Turkey*
Nature: *Gazania (plant)*
Universe/Energy: *Mediumship*

180

Beneath the earth are gemstones that can help you in all aspects of your life. Learn about each of them and start to carry some with you so that you can glide through life filled with joy and hope. You are a natural when it comes to understanding how the gems of the Earth can enhance life for the people on the planet.

Messengers:

Animal: *Squirrel Glider (marsupial)*
Nature: *Soil*
Universe/Energy: *Crystals & Gemstones*

181

Good news is on the way. In the meantime, learn about things that you feel drawn to, whether it is history, current events, how to do something for yourself, or philosophical ideals. The more you know, the more you can grow within your spiritual self and share with others.

Messengers:

Animal: *Great Blue Heron*
Nature: *Coffee Plant*
Universe/Energy: *Learn something new*

182

Slow and steady wins the race. Keep moving forward with purpose and the knowledge that you can meet any challenges that cross your path. You'll be captivated by someone soon. There is a particularly good chance that this could lead to a long-term relationship.

Messengers:

Animal: *Painted Turtle*
Nature: *Youtan Poluo (rare flower)*
Universe/Energy: *Entrancement*

183

Stop resisting the inevitable. The situation you find yourself in requires you to make a choice. You already know what you want to do but you're not allowing yourself to have what you want. Look at the reasons why. Once you understand your resistance you can let it go and enjoy what you deserve.

Messengers:

Animal: *Skipjack (fish)*
Nature: *Veronica Flower*
Universe/Energy: *Spend time alone (action)*

184

Pay attention to what your body is telling you. If you need to start an exercise program this would be a good time. Don't let a cold turn into bronchitis because you're ignoring it. If you're running yourself ragged, get more sleep. It's time to take care of yourself.

Messengers:

Animal: *Magpie Moth*
Nature: *Smartweed (plant)*
Universe/Energy: *Alarm Going Off (Sound)*

185

Listen to your higher self. You've been ignoring the message for too long. The result, when you listen, will be rapid spiritual or personal growth that covers several different areas of your life. The more you enjoy yourself the more joy you'll discover. The more you discover, the more spiritual growth you'll experience.

Messengers:

Animal: *Anteater*
Nature: *Foam Flower*
Universe/Energy: *Bemusement*

186

Get ready to rebuild. It's time to remove what has become outdated and is no longer working properly. This can apply to both your physical surroundings or thoughts and ideals. Move forward slowly to make sure that when you're finished the result will be strong and beautiful.

Messengers:

Animal: *Slow Loris (primate)*
Nature: *Ponderosa Pine*
Universe/Energy: *Progressive relaxation (action)*

187

You are busy, busy, busy. With multiple projects going on all at once you'll barely have time to catch your breath. This is only for a brief time and the results will be amazing. Listen to what comes back to you because it will have an important effect on the things you're working on.

Messengers:

Animal: *Jumping Spider*
Nature: *Turritella Agate (gemstone)*
Universe/Energy: *Echo*

188

You prefer that others don't know the real you. Instead, you allow them to know what you want them to see about yourself. There is a fire in your heart that is very rarely shared with others. When it is, it's with inexplicable trust.

Messengers:

Animal: *King Cobra (snake)*
Nature: *Fire Opal (gemstone)*
Universe/Energy: *Cucumber (scent)*

189

When your empathic abilities are running in overdrive it feels much like a lightning strike. So overwhelming that you just want to hide away from the world. To get a handle on the emotional overload, use creative visualization to build a bubble around yourself that can block the emotions of others from reaching you.

Messengers:

Animal: *Hermit Crab*
Nature: *Lightning*
Universe/Energy: *Clairempathy*

190

You're being squeezed from all sides. There is so much going on in your life that it is extremely hard to handle. Protect your crown chakra, as it is the key to finding balance and peacefulness in the chaos. You can handle even the roughest storms.

Messengers:

Animal: *Green Anaconda (snake)*
Nature: *Fairy Chimneys (topography)*
Universe/Energy: *Thundersnow (natural phenomenon)*

191

Spice up your life a little by doing something out of character today. Splash in a fountain, run in a meadow, take a nap in the middle of the day. Pick something you'd never do in your daily routine and enjoy yourself while you're doing it.

Messengers:

Animal: *Moonrat (mammal)*
Nature: *Star Anise (spice)*
Universe/Energy: *Cleverness (action)*

192

When you look to the stars what do you see? The magic of the ages is up there, waiting for you to tap into its frequency, so you will bloom into the great being you have always been inside. Sometimes you have to settle within yourself to truly blossom into your true being.

Messengers:

Animal: *Bluefin Tuna*
Nature: *Blossom (flower)*
Universe/Energy: *Shooting Star*

193

You are the key. Always be the reason that others have a smile on their face, that they talk about their dreams, make plans, and seek your advice on how to achieve them. Never be the reason that a singer no longer has a song, a believer no longer believes, or an untamed spirit is tamed.

Messengers:

Animal: *Honey Possum (marsupial)*
Nature: *Blue Jacaranda (tree)*
Universe/Energy: *Chamomile (scent)*

194

You are surrounded with purity, beauty, and lightness of being. Spirituality filters through every part of yourself as you connect not only to Universal Conscious and your higher self, but to the Divine. This light shines from you to touch everyone you encounter. Embrace the true you.

Messengers:

Animal: *Fox Squirrel*
Nature: *Coconut*
Universe/Energy: *Magnolia Blossoms (Scent)*

195

Nourish your body. You must take care of yourself before you can offer support to others around you. Sharing, whether it's of your time, possessions, or knowledge is important now. This is also a time of spiritual growth. Don't doubt your experiences, accept them.

Messengers:

Animal: *Coral*
Nature: *Tundra*
Universe/Energy: *Transient Lunar Phenomenon*

196

It's time to go after what you want instead of waiting around for it to come to you. Decisions will be easier, and situations will seem less complex once you go after what you desire. You're highly intelligent but you don't have to overanalyze things for them to succeed. Sometimes the solution is simple.

Messengers:

Animal: *Rainbow Lory (bird)*
Nature: *Jadeite (mineral)*
Universe/Energy: *Elevator (sound)*

197

The Universe will not let you miss an opportunity because if you do, it will present it to you again and again. When you're ready, you'll reach out and grab it. Pay attention to beginnings and endings in your life. Spice up your day in flavorful ways.

Messengers:

Animal: *Cinnamon Teal (bird)*
Nature: *Sonora Sunrise (gemstone)*
Universe/Energy: *Flavorful (sensation)*

198

A sour face does not always mean a bitter person is behind it. Step out of your comfort zone to extend a friendly hand. You may be surprised at the results that happen and how a frown can turn into a smile. Love and kindness, even if it's for someone you don't really know, can bring about wonderful changes.

Messengers:

Animal: *Black Swift (bird)*
Nature: *Lemon*
Universe/Energy: *Gathering*

199

Color can inspire you. It can balance you and it can bring you out of hiding and into the light. If you've been surrounding yourself with drab colors now is the time to choose bright ones that energize and excite you. This will raise your frequency and bring you joy.

Messengers:

Animal: *Deer Mouse*
Nature: *Peacock Plant*
Universe/Energy: *Be an Inspiration*

200

Strength lives within you. There is a pure power inside of you that makes others want to be around you. Safety, pride, and passion color your energy. You are a hero to many, but you don't acknowledge that in yourself. To you, you help others because it's the right thing to do.

Messengers:

Animal: *Oil Fish*
Nature: *Ilmenite (mineral)*
Universe/Energy: *Auric Sight*

201

Find a way to evaluate your current situation in a relaxed state. The situation may be chaotic, so you need to look from an opposite perspective. Don't be lazy and lie around doing nothing all day. Get moving and spice things up a bit. Avoid doing anything in excess.

Messengers:

Animal: *Pot Belly Pig*
Nature: *Red Bell Pepper*
Universe/Energy: *Chimney Smoke (Scent)*

202

Instead of racing around trying to get everything done, slow it down. Plan your movements with care so you are continually going up. When you reach the top of the trees, when you ascend to the pinnacle of the mountain, you will be amazed and in awe of the view. For it is not just about the beauty you see, it is about the climb to get there.

Messengers:

Animal: *Spider Monkey*
Nature: *Mountain Top*
Universe/Energy: *Blood Moon (phenomenon)*

203

This is a time of new beginnings. Of keeping the home fires warm and bright while appreciating the energy surrounding you. It's a great time to start a new business or a relationship. Want to change? Make resolutions and keep them.

Messengers:

Animal: *Sperm Whale*
Nature: *Amphibolite Anthracite Coal*
Universe/Energy: *Aura*

204

Expect to travel soon. Stick by your decisions and don't second guess yourself. Protection of family is important. You're strong and will endure through adaptability and determination. Move forward with surefooted easiness and without limitation. Glimmer brightly and spread your happiness to others.

Messengers:

Animal: *Caribou*
Nature: *Aquamarine (gemstone)*
Universe/Energy: *Joviality*

205

Use your intuitive ability to seek out the truth of a matter so you can stabilize the sense of being overwhelmed by your circumstances. Pay attention to your dreams right now because the spirit world is helping you work though this situation for your greater good.

Messengers:

Animal: *Ringtail Cat (feline)*
Nature: *Gaspeite (mineral)*
Universe/Energy: *Cat's meow (sound)*

206

Something is irritating you, but you don't really know what it is. You may feel on edge, quick tempered, and irritable. It feels hard to focus and complete tasks. Take a step back from others and look at the situations you're in to discover the cause of what's bothering you.

Messengers:

Animal: *Flea*
Nature: *Heatwave*
Universe/Energy: *Maize (color)*

207

Keep your head up, hold yourself to a higher standard and listen to your intuition. You're a leader who is very aware of what's happening around you. Create long-range plans by looking further into the future. Plant positive seeds to grow in the minds of others.

Messengers:

Animal: *Sand Cat (feline)*
Nature: *Pickerel Plant*
Universe/Energy: *Mantra*

208

Have you confused yourself when it comes to reaching your goals because you've let that little voice in your head spout off a bunch of doubt and negativity? Now is the time to tell it to zip it shut. Move forward with positivity and a sure knowledge that all is as it should be. Still doubtful? Look for confirmation messages from the spiritual world.

Messengers:

Animal: *Green Jack (fish)*
Nature: *Acorn Squash*
Universe/Energy: *Cloud Messages*

209

Look to what is no more to find all that can be. New beginnings are present now. They may have a rough start, but they will be abundant and profitable in the future. There is a pathway to achieving your passion, but you'll need to look back to move ahead.

Messengers:

Animal: *White Tiger*
Nature: *Black Medic*
Universe/Energy: *Car Starting (Sound)*

210

There are times when you must advise yourself to achieve your goals. No one else knows as well as you do what needs to be addressed, what moves need to be made, and how you should go about accomplishing what it is that you're trying to do. True guidance comes from within in this case.

Messengers:

Animal: *Morgan (equine)*
Nature: *Buttercup*
Universe/Energy: *Guidance*

211

You may feel as if you're on the outside looking in more than being in the midst of what is happening. In your current situation, you're in the best position possible because something is going to happen that will directly affect those who are excluding you at this time. This is a time to be thankful that you're not in the middle of the situation. You are an integral part of another group where you feel included and important. Take a moment to think about who they are.

Messengers:

Animal: *Scimitar-horned Oryx (mammal)*
Nature: *Fossils*
Universe/Energy: *Included*

212

You have a voice that is well heard not because of the volume at which you talk, but because of what you say. People pay attention to you and respect your wisdom. Guide them wisely. Remember to eat well because you often forget. Take time to snuggle up and hibernate for a while.

Messengers:

Animal: *Howler Monkey*
Nature: *Fava Beans*
Universe/Energy: *Reflection (feeling)*

213

To draw prosperity to you, close your eyes and imagine your financial flow is like a river moving toward you. Imagine the water flowing over you. You can feel its force, but instinctively know there is beauty surrounding it, not violence.

Messengers:

Animal: *Grayling (fish)*
Nature: *Hyacinth (plant)*
Universe/Energy: *Charitable Giving (action)*

214

You are being healed from the inside out. You're growing and developing, transforming into your true spiritual self through faith, intuition, and the ability to find light in the darkness. You're connecting with the secrets of the Universe. Anything you attempt right now can be successful.

Messengers:

Animal: *Silkworm (insect)*
Nature: *Milfoil (aquatic plant)*
Universe/Energy: *Active Thought*

215

Excess could bring trouble your way so pay attention to how you're spending your money, how you're eating, and how you're interacting with others. It's one thing to have a good time. It's another thing completely to take that good time too far and end up with problems.

Messengers:

Animal: *Jack Fish*
Nature: *Queen Victoria Agave (succulent plant)*
Universe/Energy: *Massage your scalp (action)*

216

Being emotionally calm, feeling joy, and peacefulness within yourself will help you attract people with the same qualities. Building a rich foundation will help you grow in a variety of ways. Be careful of those whose words have bite. They don't have your best interest at heart.

Messengers:

Animal: *Saltwater Crocodile*
Nature: *Ugli Fruit*
Universe/Energy: *Rich Soil (Scent)*

217

When the warm winds blow, when the thunder booms and the lightning strikes, when you're soaked from the rains of life, know that this too shall pass. Write down your worries and then put them away. The sun will shine soon, with the rain leaves behind a wholesome scent of goodness.

Messengers:

Animal: *Fossa (mammal)*
Nature: *Thunderstorm*
Universe/Energy: *Sugar Cookies (Scent)*

218

Do not move aimlessly. Instead utilize swift and calculated movements that will target your prey. You can see what others don't, especially when it comes to seeing through lies and seeing what lives in the darkness. You tend to stay away from negative emotions, but they can still present themselves from time to time. Stand firm, do not slip in your beliefs.

Messengers:

Animal: *Nighthawk (bird)*
Nature: *Seabeach Sandwort (plant)*
Universe/Energy: *Welcoming (feeling)*

219

There are times when you want to burrow deep and hide. Other times you need to be out in the open to feel the strength of the wind blowing across your face and through your hair. There are always different experiences you will face as you raise the levels of your personal energy, your frequency. It is the continual growth process called life.

Messengers:

Animal: *Marmot (rodent)*
Nature: *Chinook Wind*
Universe/Energy: *Daydream (action)*

220

When you reach the bottom of your cup, do not see it as empty. Instead, look deeper into the residue and listen to the impressions you receive. Maybe it is time to leave the shell you have placed around yourself and instead stand tall for the world to see. Do not fear life. Live it.

Messengers:

Animal: *Loggerhead Turtle*
Nature: *Banyan Tree*
Universe/Energy: *Citrus (scent)*

221

You can always start over. There are no absolutes that say you can't. While you're brave, powerful, and strong, you still have weaknesses. That's human nature. Determine how you can make them stronger, then take the appropriate actions to do so.

Messengers:

Animal: *Blackbuck (mammal/antelope)*
Nature: *Wasabi (plant)*
Universe/Energy: *Slide (action)*

222

What could you do today to bring joy to someone else? When you can give to another you are spreading your own light and joy into the world, which will enable someone else to do the same. It will lift your mood and theirs.

Messengers:

Animal: *Red Jungle Fowl (bird)*
Nature: *Yellow Squash*
Universe/Energy: *Cuddle with a pet (action)*

223

Always mix up your activities. If you've been working on the computer for hours, take a break and go for a walk. If you've been talking on the phone all day, then turn it off for a couple of hours and do something completely different without interruption. Doing one thing for a prolonged period can drain your frequency and slow you down.

Messengers:

Animal: *Sea Cucumber (marine echinoderm)*
Nature: *Jade Vine (plant)*
Universe/Energy: *Mulberry (color)*

224

Every little effort you make will help you attain big results. Dig deep, work and rework all aspects of your environment to bring about enormous change. It's time to clean house and let go of what's not needed in every aspect of your life. Do for yourself instead of waiting for others to do for you.

Messengers:

Animal: *Earthworm*
Nature: *Sage (herb)*
Universe/Energy: *Doorbell (Sound)*

225

What you think you see may not always be what you're actually seeing. When in doubt, pay attention to your intuitive thoughts and impressions. Flow with the energy you're feeling. Listen to the sounds associated with the situation. Are there scents involved? Rule out logical reasons for what is happening before determining it to be of a paranormal nature.

Messengers:

Animal: *Pink Pigeon*
Nature: *American Beach Grass*
Universe/Energy: *Orbs*

226

Confusion abounds. The answer should be obvious, but it eludes you. Make sure you're not looking at the situation emotionally instead of rationally. Take a step back, analyze, and the solution will appear. Don't listen to the input of others but follow your own instincts.

Messengers:

Animal: *Platypus*
Nature: *Boniato*
Universe/Energy: *Clothes Right Out of the Dryer (Scent)*

227

While you may come across as quite prickly on the outside, you've extremely sweet on the inside. You stand tall and are proud of your accomplishments. You enjoy harmony and balance in your life so there is a smooth ebb and flow. This is a good time to strike out on a new adventure.

Messengers:

Animal: *Atlantic Salmon (fish)*
Nature: *Chinquapin Nut*
Universe/Energy: *Harmonica (sound)*

228

It's okay to be elusive and to stay to yourself but if you are letting yourself drown in the negatives in life, it's time to change and find a new perspective. Surround yourself with people who have a cheerful and outgoing outlook.

Messengers:

Animal: *Golden Cat*
Nature: *Virgin's Bower (plant/vine)*
Universe/Energy: *Be Aware of the Present Moment*

229

Bright colors, happy times, and feeling at peace within yourself is what you're all about right now. You're grounded, steady, and feel secure within yourself. Stay focused on all of that because there is a jealous person who will try to cause problems.

Messengers:

Animal: *Discus (fish)*
Nature: *Phyllite Quartzite (rock)*
Universe/Energy: *Pay Attention to Psychic Impressions*

230

To make great strides forward you need to acknowledge what is behind you. Is there something you can release that is holding you back? Or maybe there is something or someone you left behind that should be with you now as you continue your forward journey. Take some time to figure it out.

Messengers:

Animal: *Leaf Cutter Ant*
Nature: *Thyme (herb)*
Universe/Energy: *Exceed (action)*

231

Your dreams are not impossible to reach. Strive to reach them through little steps. One at a time, slow and sure. You're in a productive part of your life where you can achieve remarkable things. While you like to work alone, sometimes being part of a group will speed up your results and you'll have lots of fun along the way.

Messengers:

Animal: *Cebu Flowerpecker (bird)*
Nature: *Red Beans*
Universe/Energy: *Crop Circles*

232

Someone is trying to get a message to you from the spirit world. Pay attention to the signs and signals. This message may be one that is to be delivered to another person. You are flexible and bend with the winds of life. Know when to get out of the wind so it doesn't uproot you.

Messengers:

Animal: *Northern Cardinal*
Nature: *Weeping Willow*
Universe/Energy: *Pumpkin Spice (scent)*

233

If you have someone who is sucking the life out of you with outrageous demands on your time or emotional support, distance yourself from them. Sometimes looking at situations too closely can be like looking through distorted glass. Stay rooted in your beliefs and do what needs to be done to resolve the situation so you're free from the negative drains of another.

Messengers:

Animal: *Aphids (insect)*
Nature: *Yuca/Cassava (root)*
Universe/Energy: *Crackle (sound)*

234

This is a time of joyful rebirth. You have been going through changes and spiritual growth and were probably keeping to yourself while doing so. Now is the time to break through the confines of your nest and set your spirit free.

Messengers:

Animal: *Mason Wasp*
Nature: *Nuttall's Lotus (legume)*
Universe/Energy: *Joy*

235

Being true to your authentic self does not mean you're being any less true to those around you. If people understand that you're honest with your own self, then they'll know you'll be honest with them too.

Messengers:

Animal: *Potoroo (marsupial)*
Nature: *Tide*
Universe/Energy: *Authenticity*

236

Finesse is an art form with you. It's what makes you such a great leader. Remember that because you're in a situation where you could become too controlling with people. It's in your nature to pry things apart, see how it works, and put it back together in a better fashion. Just don't try to do that to people.

Messengers:

Animal: *Starfish (asteroidea)*
Nature: *Pond*
Universe/Energy: *Horse's Coat (Scent)*

237

Make sure you're not being wasteful, especially with food products. Only buy what you need instead of buying more than you can eat before it goes bad. There are many distractions around you right now so it's important to maintain your focus so that you don't stray off your path.

Messengers:

Animal: *Goshawk (bird)*
Nature: *Hot Springs*
Universe/Energy: *Focus (action)*

238

Instead of burrowing away to avoid the light, climb high and look at the expansive world around you. Listen for clarity. Each day is beautiful and filled with possibilities, a new adventure, a new place, and time spent on something you've never experienced.

Messengers:

Animal: *Ice Worm*
Nature: *Butte*
Universe/Energy: *Solar Plexus Chakra*

239

You're more connected to the Divine at this time and will receive great inspiration from the spiritual realm. Listen closely. Tune into the quiet peacefulness around you. Step outside at night, especially if you can do so in nature. Listen to the sounds around you, take comfort in the natural world.

Messengers:

Animal: *Moon Moth*
Nature: *Lake*
Universe/Energy: *Longevity*

240

You will step into the role of leader to guide others. Your visibility will increase as you dominate the situation to bring it to a positive resolution. Multitasking comes easily to you but delegate parts of the work to others to encourage their own growth.

Messengers:

Animal: *Lion*
Nature: *Peach*
Universe/Energy: *Ascended Masters*

241

There can't be joy in your life if there is hatred in your heart. Now is the time to send that negativity into the atmosphere. Imagine it moving away from you like a comet streaking across the night sky. Only then will you be free to swim in the waters of purity and love.

Messengers:

Animal: *Danio (fish)*
Nature: *Comet*
Universe/Energy: *Love*

242

You're entering a phase where you will be able to center your spiritual self, your chakras, and the positive and negative elements in your life both quickly and efficiently. You're a rare bird who might be misunderstood by others.

Messengers:

Animal: *Nene (bird)*
Nature: *Kyanite (mineral)*
Universe/Energy: *Summer Air (Scent)*

243

Higher thoughts and ideals should take center stage. Family or being part of a group is important for your personal growth. Take the higher road, the one less traveled, to find an abundance of riches for your spiritual self.

Messengers:

Animal: *House Sparrow*
Nature: *Fungus*
Universe/Energy: *Corona Effect (phenomenon)*

244

It's time to move quickly to where you want to go. Don't hold back. Don't second guess yourself. Let your mind and body flow free and just do what you want. When you second guess your first impressions and feelings you cause confusion in your life. Avoid this if possible so you have a clear path forward.

Messengers:

Animal: *Marmoset (primate)*
Nature: *Flying Duck Orchid (plant)*
Universe/Energy: *Intention (action)*

245

Sometimes growth can only come from looking into the past of your spiritual self, not your physical self in this lifetime. There you will have the ability to move smoothly though difficult waters as you understand what you've been though on a soul level to clarify where you're going in this lifetime. Emotions run deep but when you look to the past, you'll understand.

Messengers:

Animal: *Hooded Nudibranch (sea slug)*
Nature: *Palm Tree*
Universe/Energy: *Akashic Records*

246

Blend in and take a moment. Something or someone is holding you back from achieving what you truly desire. Evaluate the situation from the background, to discover what it is. Once you know, you can let it go, and move forward on your own path. Obstacles do not hold you back.

Messengers:

Animal: *Octopus*
Nature: *Leek (vegetable)*
Universe/Energy: *Old Books (Scent)*

247

Instead of limiting your view of things, take the time to visit the wide-open spaces and free your mind from clutter and noise. Consider your views on the topic again. Can you see it differently? Spend time toiling in the soil of the earth. Getting dirty oftentimes can bring the utmost clarity.

Messengers:

Animal: *Haflinger (equine)*
Nature: *Limonite (iron ore)*
Universe/Energy: *Plant a garden (action)*

248

What do your habits say about you? Are they causing you to ignore your feelings, your intuitive abilities or avoid change? It's easy to feel comfortable doing the same thing every day. Today is a good day to face what you *really* feel and to decide if you're stuck in old habits or if it's time to do something new.

Messengers:

Animal: *Hereford Cow*
Nature: *Common Eelgrass*
Universe/Energy: *Practice Gratitude (action)*

249

Are you in a situation where it would be healthier for you to let it go, leave it behind, or to walk away from it? Can you stay in the situation but make changes that will make it better? Think about it before you decide and then stick to that decision.

Messengers:

Animal: *Limpkin (bird)*
Nature: *Hyacinth Bean*
Universe/Energy: *Frangipani (scent)*

250

Be patient, persistent, and slow it down for a while. Really look at what you're doing and achieving in your life. Is there a change you'd like to make? Do it now. Use your resources wisely and make the most of what you have.

Messengers:

Animal: *Tortoise*
Nature: *Borage (plant)*
Universe/Energy: *Spontaneous Drawing*

251

You have so much to be grateful for today. There is more that surrounds you that you can't see at this moment but that will be revealed soon. Show your appreciation and gratitude, because in showing it, and acknowledging what has come to you and those who brought it, you will bring more goodness into your life.

Messengers:

Animal: *Oriole (bird)*
Nature: *Majesty Palm (tree)*
Universe/Energy: *Cedar (Scent)*

252

To reclaim your inner strength, you must first attain peace of mind. Have compassion and understanding for your spiritual self as you go through this process. Don't make it any harder than it must be.

Messengers:

Animal: *American Saddlebred (equine)*
Nature: *Lady Slipper (plant)*
Universe/Energy: *Self-discovery (action)*

253

Your stress is elevated. Being on edge and anxious will make you quick to anger, which is not your normal way of being. A connection to water, earth, and air is needed now to help you find balance.

Messengers:

Animal: *Duck*
Nature: *Butternut White Walnut*
Universe/Energy: *Ask a question (action)*

254

If you can't teach others, then learn more for yourself. You have a thirst for knowledge about everything. The more you know, the more you understand. Your memory is long, and you don't often forget.

Messengers:

Animal: *Indian Elephant*
Nature: *Starfruit*
Universe/Energy: *Teach*

255

As you increase your frequency to greater heights you may discover that the people who are around you now, no longer resonate with your new frequency levels. You may realize that you no longer feel as close to them as you once did. Expect new people to come into your life.

Messengers:

Animal: *Falcon*
Nature: *Pomelo (fruit)*
Universe/Energy: *Apple Cinnamon (scent)*

256

Each morning pick something to focus on for the day. This goes a long way in helping you grow spiritually and eliminating any uneasiness you may feel. When you have a plan, even if it's a little plan, you will feel a sense of accomplishment when it's complete.

Messengers:

Animal: *Shad (fish)*
Nature: *Elderberry*
Universe/Energy: *Affectionate (feeling)*

257

Are you not sure where to step to stay on solid ground? Do you feel like you're sinking no matter what you try to do? Then stop for a second, take a step back and look around. Consider what you're doing and why. Look for the rocks around you that will support your weight. Plant seeds and then test your footing again. Grow stronger.

Messengers:

Animal: *Pompano (fish)*
Nature: *Quicksand*
Universe/Energy: *Cultivate*

258

Energize your intentions in unusual and creative ways. Make a plan and follow it through. Instead of blocking yourself, allow yourself to attain what you desire. Make sure you're getting enough rest and eating lots of greens. You're going to be remarkably busy soon and it will be exciting and fun.

Messengers:

Animal: *Black Molly (fish)*
Nature: *Mud volcano*
Universe/Energy: *Creation*

259

It's a thin line between offering your assistance and taking over another person's project. Know the difference. Don't overreact and take things too seriously when they were meant in a fun and playful manner. You don't let opportunities pass you by but reach out and grab them with both hands. The time is now, don't procrastinate.

Messengers:

Animal: *Bohar Reedbuck (antelope)*
Nature: *Clover*
Universe/Energy: *Leap of Faith*

260

Don't be surprised when you attract the interest of people who could help put you on the map. Whether your goal is to be a popular singer, or if you've created a product that you plan to launch, the right people will be drawn to you soon. Whatever you do, don't give up on your dream. Success is right around the corner.

Messengers:

Animal: *Long Tail Skipper (butterfly)*
Nature: *Chives*
Universe/Energy: *Fascinated*

261

Watch your bite. Negative emotions are pulling you down and creating a massive amount of emotional confusion. Don't say things you'll regret later. Speak from a place of kindness and positivity. If you can't think of something that fits those guidelines, it may be best to remain silent. Remember the saying, *if you can't say something nice, don't say anything at all.*

Messengers:

Animal: *Barracuda (fish)*
Nature: *Lentils (legumes)*
Universe/Energy: *Ball Lightning (phenomenon)*

262

You'll meet your long-term goals through small steps and consistent pacing. Listen to those who are guiding you from the other side. The message is important. Your intuitive frequency is very elevated, and others are drawn to you because of it.

Messengers:

Animal: *Prairie Chicken*
Nature: *Morganite (gemstone)*
Universe/Energy: *Past Life*

263

You may feel like you have no direction, as if you're wandering and don't know which way to go. It's time to simplify your life, to be focused and aware of both your inner self and the way you live.

Messengers:

Animal: *Deer*
Nature: *Rhododendron (plant)*
Universe/Energy: *Telepathy*

264

Do not be shocked by the little things in life, let situations scare you, or cause you to fall out on the floor in hysterics. Smell the sweetness of nature's perfume. If you need direction, ask your guides to show you what you need to know.

Messengers:

Animal: *Fainting Goat*
Nature: *Wisteria (plant/vine)*
Universe/Energy: *Read Random Book Text for inspiration (action)*

265

Sometimes you must be sneaky to accomplish a task. You do not need to hide or be embarrassed by what you're doing. Some people are extremely hard to surprise. Keep things to yourself for the time being because there's a big mouth in your midst who could ruin your plans if they know about them.

Messengers:

Animal: *Black Footed Ferret*
Nature: *Chlorite (mineral)*
Universe/Energy: *Embarrassment*

266

When you think of what you want in the wrong way, you can bring what you don't want to you. Be clear and concise in what you ask of the Universe. Be focused but not so focused that you are too single minded. Balance is needed.

Messengers:

Animal: *Pig*
Nature: *Ginkgo Nut*
Universe/Energy: *Discretion*

267

Someone close to you may be going through a crisis and trying hard to hide it from everyone around them. Take time to be there for others so you may help to lift them up from the problems they're facing. A helping hand goes a long way to healing the heart.

Messengers:

Animal: *Goby (fish)*
Nature: *Heather (plant)*
Universe/Energy: *Apple Pie (Scent)*

268

Silence your mind. As you sink into a peaceful, meditative state, listen closely to the sounds around you. Pay attention to your breathing. Feel the beat of your heart. Do you hear the hum of the air conditioner? Are birds singing outside of your window? Just listen. Now think of the situation you face. The answer is right in front of you. Listen.

Messengers:

Animal: *Tarpon (fish)*
Nature: *Aster (plant)*
Universe/Energy: *Crunch of Walking on Snow (Sound)*

269

Arguments don't really get you anywhere or solve anything, especially if you're fighting with someone who is right and you're in the wrong. Arguing just elevates stress, causes tension, and other problems. Consider your options before jumping into an argument with someone. Can the situation be resolved through discussion and not a fight? Try that first.

Messengers:

Animal: *Golden Pheasant*
Nature: *Marsh*
Universe/Energy: *Tyndall effect (phenomenon)*

270

You are a person with vision. You can see what has not happened yet. You see the potential in people and in situations. You're the kind of person who takes the reins and makes things happen. Luck and fortune follow you.

Messengers:

Animal: *Ring-necked Pheasant*
Nature: *Golden Alexander (plant)*
Universe/Energy: *Luck*

271

Now is not the time to look at a situation as all or nothing. There are varying shades of gray that need to be considered. Nothing is absolute. This is a time for balance, seeing individuality, and maintaining a sense of community.

Messengers:

Animal: *Zebra*
Nature: *Arid (Dry) Climate*
Universe/Energy: *Graceful (feeling)*

272

When you let a situation get blown out of proportion, then you've allowed a mole hill to become a mountain. This can lead to feelings of stress, guilt, and wishing you'd done something different in the beginning. Relax, take a breath, let yourself deflate for a minute. Now approach the situation with the attitude of resolving it.

Messengers:

Animal: *Spiny Pufferfish*
Nature: *Key Lime*
Universe/Energy: *Remembrance*

273

If someone or something is important to you do not ignore it or them. When you spend too much time away or are not involved in the project or in someone else's life, then you become expendable. This will lead to regret.

Messengers:

Animal: *Red Salamander*
Nature: *Date Fruit*
Universe/Energy: *Carefree*

274

Decide now. Don't wait, don't second guess. Make up your mind, take charge, and go for what you want. You are full of courage and determination which will bring success in all ventures. Naysayers abound but bring them into your circle. Befriend your enemies, for they too will help you succeed.

Messengers:

Animal: *Cougar*
Nature: *Bloodstone (mineral)*
Universe/Energy: *Togetherness*

275

When you keep yourself busy you don't have the time to get involved in drama and trivial things like *he said, she said*. Instead of spreading gossip keep yourself busy with situations and people who make your life feel more productive.

Messengers:

Animal: *Alligator Gar (fish)*
Nature: *Common Opal (gemstone)*
Universe/Energy: *Uplifting (emotion)*

276

Hope doesn't die. It may feel like it dwindles down to a very small speck of light in the distance at different times in your life but it's still there in your heart. Let that little glow of hope grow in you until you are beaming with it for all to see.

Messengers:

Animal: *Flying Squirrel*
Nature: *Daffodil*
Universe/Energy: *Hope*

277

If you have something to say about someone, always make sure you say something good. Good news travels just as fast as bad news. If what you said gets back to the person you said it about, wouldn't you prefer to make them feel happy and uplifted instead of sad or mad?

Messengers:

Animal: *Sea Bass (fish)*
Nature: *Ice Jam*
Universe/Energy: *Juniper (Scent)*

278

Are you a risk taker? An adrenaline junkie? It's one thing to take risks for a reason. It's another thing entirely to take unnecessary, dangerous risks. Weigh the outcome of your actions and decide if the risk is necessary or if you're just seeking a thrill. Don't put your life in danger just for a quick thrill.

Messengers:

Animal: *Humpback Whale*
Nature: *Jade (gemstone)*
Universe/Energy: *Lemon (Scent)*

279

The doors of communication open both ways. To understand one another you have to make an effort to talk. Instead of laying in the sun to bask, avoiding one another, or ignoring the situation between you and someone else, take a stand. Make an effort with a phone call or visit.

Messengers:

Animal: *Tegu Lizard*
Nature: *Red Algae*
Universe/Energy: *Communication*

280

If you're faced with a situation where you don't know what to do, one that is difficult to understand or resolve, then set it aside for a while. You may need to distance yourself from the situation for a bit so you can see though the undergrowth to the real issue at hand.

Messengers:

Animal: *Uromastyx (reptile)*
Nature: *Sago Pondweed*
Universe/Energy: *Set a Goal (action)*

281

Get busy with your hands. You need to make something physical using your creativity. A hobby could turn into a full-time business for you so don't be afraid to put your designs out there. It will be easy to become obsessed so make sure you treat it like a business and not let it consume all your time.

Messengers:

Animal: *Raccoon*
Nature: *Black Ice*
Universe/Energy: *Epiphany*

282

It's time to unlock what has kept you from reaching your potential. It's hard to let go because you may feel that others will make fun of you or not understand your beliefs. Instead of worrying about what someone else will think, stay true to yourself and swim in the depth of your soul while floating free of what has encased you.

Messengers:

Animal: *Lake Sturgeon (fish)*
Nature: *Butterfly Milkweed (plant)*
Universe/Energy: *Bergamot (scent)*

283

Do not let tough times make you bitter. Instead learn from it and move on. Enjoy the chip of the crickets, relax on the beach in a tide pool, or spend time with others. You'll gain support for any innovative ideas you have and will be able to easily overcome obstacles.

Messengers:

Animal: *Marlin (fish)*
Nature: *Tide Pool*
Universe/Energy: *Chirping (Sound)*

284

If you enjoy watching a bruise turn from black to blue to yellow and green, then you just may have a bit of a morbid curiosity about things. Gross things don't freak you out instead you find them interesting. This is a good time to browse around in a forest to gain a deeper connection to nature.

Messengers:

Animal: *Okapi (mammal)*
Nature: *Unakite (rock)*
Universe/Energy: *Mustard (color)*

285

Get ready because there are a lot of little projects coming your way that will lead to prosperity if you can handle them all. Quick reactions and decisions are important now. Do not allow past hurts to hold you back.

Messengers:

Animal: *Rabbit*
Nature: *Orange*
Universe/Energy: *Jubilation*

286

Change what you're doing today. If you've been stuck in the same routine day in and day out, then doing something different is just as invigorating as getting rest. Take a swim, or a different route to work, anything that will make your day amazing.

Messengers:

Animal: *Dipper (bird)*
Nature: *Chocolate Cosmos (plant)*
Universe/Energy: *Beep (Sound)*

287

Don't overthink things. That's exactly how you can create an aversion to what you want to do by *what if-ing* it to death. Then you end up not doing it at all. Any number of things can feel like gravel under bare feet when you're overthinking. Decide and go with it.

Messengers:

Animal: *Natal Duiker (antelope)*
Nature: *Gravel*
Universe/Energy: *Spellbound (feeling)*

288

You are a light in the darkness, hope when all seems lost, a guide for the weary and a shoulder for someone to cry on, even if that someone is yourself. Listen to your spiritual self and let your innate knowledge of the Universe guide you.

Messengers:

Animal: *Firefly*
Nature: *Phragmites (plant/reed)*
Universe/Energy: *Silliness (feeling)*

289

There are many spiritual resources that will benefit your growth. These may be in the form of books, group meetings, other people who are on a similar path. Gather them around you to learn from their experience.

Messengers:

Animal: *Kingsnake*
Nature: *Sandstone Arches*
Universe/Energy: *Hay (Scent)*

290

You know what they say about opinions. Everyone has one. That doesn't mean that you need to force your opinions down someone else's throat. Instead, let your opinions be a beautiful song that you put out into the world. For those it resonates with, they will agree with you. The others will ignore it.

Messengers:

Animal: *Mountain Bluebird*
Nature: *Soursop (fruit)*
Universe/Energy: *Examine Your Opinions (action)*

291

You have strengths you haven't discovered yet. The time is coming when you will be put to a test. Pay attention to the instructions so you don't fail. This is a good time to write down what you're doing and how your projects are progressing.

Messengers:

Animal: *Hercules Beetle*
Nature: *Pomegranate (fruit)*
Universe/Energy: *Greater Good*

292

You are directly linked to the magical and mystical part of life. You see deeply into the spiritual realms and are happily at peace within yourself. You understand dreams and how to use light for protection and growth.

Messengers:

Animal: *Damselfly*
Nature: *Quince (fruit)*
Universe/Energy: *Bliss*

293

Protect yourself from negative energy. It's time to look for negative attachments and cut them loose from your spiritual self. It's pulling you down, and to rise to greater heights, you must release it. Clear up clutter so energy flows freely through your living space.

Messengers:

Animal: *Ostrich*
Nature: *Sugarcane (plant)*
Universe/Energy: *Divine Connections*

294

You can bring light and love to those around you just by being yourself. Showing your truth of being, your inner spirit, your hopes, and dreams, to others will have a positive effect. When you embrace and manifest your inner spirit you will help others grow on their own paths.

Messengers:

Animal: *Mud Turtle*
Nature: *Cardón Cactus*
Universe/Energy: *Musk (Scent)*

295

Blocking out sound can help you get more work done, however, if you block out too much, then you may miss something important. You're able to change as needed to fit into your surroundings, job description, or to wear as many hats in your life. Just don't forget to take some time for yourself to relax amid the busy parts of your day.

Messengers:

Animal: *Jackson's Chameleon*
Nature: *Soybean*
Universe/Energy: *Barking (Sound)*

296

Allow universal energy to bring concepts to you as you embrace your creativity. Spirituality, inner wisdom, and mindfulness are important now. Take time to just be. Listen to soothing music, soak in a hot bath, go for a walk on the beach or in nature.

Messengers:

Animal: *Praying Mantis*
Nature: *Radicchio (vegetable)*
Universe/Energy: *Byzantine (color)*

297

Try not to be unaware or oblivious of what happens around you. This is a time when you must be observant and have an investigative mind. Look at all levels, all possibilities. And then, once you have figured it all out, you can rest and relax or take a mud bath.

Messengers:

Animal: *Kune Kune (mammal/pig)*
Nature: *Biosphere*
Universe/Energy: *Ignore (action)*

298

Longing for what you don't have but someone else has attained will only make you a jealous, bitter person. Don't hold it against someone because they've worked hard and are successful. Strive to make your own mark in the world and create your own success.

Messengers:

Animal: *Black Rail (bird)*
Nature: *Licorice*
Universe/Energy: *Engagement (action)*

299

Express yourself in vivid and vibrant ways. Be vocal so you're heard and understood. This is a time to clear the air, start new adventures, and show appreciation for those close to you. You're friendly and outgoing but quick to rip into someone who threatens you or talks bad about you or anyone close to you. Watch that temper.

Messengers:

Animal: *Baboon*
Nature: *Romaine Lettuce*
Universe/Energy: *Clairgustance*

300

There's an old saying that one person's trash is another's treasure. Look through your trash and see if you can donate it to a good cause. It may just be exactly what someone else needs. Watch out for overgrowth in your life. Does your yard need weeding? Do the trees need to be pruned back? Have you accumulated a mess? Trim back the excess.

Messengers:

Animal: *Arapaima (fish)*
Nature: *Sugilite (gemstone)*
Universe/Energy: *Citrine (color)*

301

When you give love, do you feel it back? If you're only giving and not receiving love, then the relationship isn't going to work out. It's time to really look at your relationships and see if they are healthy or if someone is just taking advantage of you and the love you feel for them.

Messengers:

Animal: *Garter Snake*
Nature: *Grassland*
Universe/Energy: *Take in the View Around You*

302

Family is at the forefront right now. Pay special attention to both your immediate and extended family. Reconnect with those you haven't spoken to in a while to establish harmony and balance within your family. You will also discover that you have a new creative talent.

Messengers:

Animal: *Daddy Longlegs (arachnid)*
Nature: *Condensation*
Universe/Energy: *Horse walking (sound)*

303

You may feel out of control right now. Like everything you do is chaotic and running rampart without any organization or purpose, as if you're being herded down a path and you don't know why you're on it. Avoid negative thinking at this time because it will only make you feel angry and disappointed in the situation. Go with the flow for a positive outcome.

Messengers:

Animal: *Wildebeest*
Nature: *Orchid*
Universe/Energy: *Saw (sound)*

304

Keeping your composure in tough situations comes naturally to you. People trust you to keep calm when they're losing it. They gravitate to you because of this strength of character. What they may not know is that you sometimes tend to come undone when the tough situation is over. Even you have a breaking point.

Messengers:

Animal: *European Starling (bird)*
Nature: *Hot Pepper*
Universe/Energy: *Consequence (action)*

305

Do you feel stuck and discouraged because you're not moving forward in life? Look to the glorious lights in the sky to feel more comfortable in your skin. You're full of energy and life even though it might be tough to get into the waters where you can move swiftly and gracefully.

Messengers:

Animal: *Antarctic Fur Seal*
Nature: *Ice Circles*
Universe/Energy: *Russian Light Pillars (phenomenon)*

306

Your principles are a core part of your being. It's your moral code, your spiritual essence. Never compromise these things or sacrifice your beliefs just to please someone else. If the other person cannot accept you as you are, then they aren't the right person for you to be involved with. Stay true to yourself.

Messengers:

Animal: *Leaf Hopper (insect)*
Nature: *Mimosa Pudica (herb)*
Universe/Energy: *Catatumbo lightning(phenomenon)*

307

Get busy and create some brilliant magic! It's prime time for whatever you're attempting in your work or business, but you've got to get moving. Opportunities are all around you just waiting for you to grab hold of them. They are striking fast. What are you waiting for?

Messengers:

Animal: *Grebe (bird)*
Nature: *White Rainbow*
Universe/Energy: *Heat Lightning (phenomenon)*

308

To climb the ladder of success, or to climb to greater spiritual evolvement, you must know when to step and when to balance. Do not attempt to flatten your personality into something you're not, but instead shine like the artistic person that you are. When you do, you'll move up all ladders with ease.

Messengers:

Animal: *Bluegill Sunfish*
Nature: *Jacob's Ladder (plant)*
Universe/Energy: *Art*

309

Move slowly, carefully, and follow a well laid out plan. You are connected to the Divine and your inner spirituality and intuition at this time. Avoid holding on too tightly, being too possessive or insecure.

Messengers:

Animal: *Boa Constrictor*
Nature: *Lagoon*
Universe/Energy: *Belief (action)*

310

Vibrancy is an essential part of your being. You are highly intelligent, a clear communicator, and give outstanding advice. You enjoy collecting things. You get bored easily so it's important to have varied interests. You need time to fly, to get away from the everyday work needed to survive.

Messengers:

Animal: *Cockatiel (bird)*
Nature: *Atoll (land/sea formation)*
Universe/Energy: *Gasoline (Scent)*

311

If you feel like you need a break from your daily life, go to a world map online, and pick a place at random. Imagine what that place looks like, how the air feels, and what kinds of plants and animals do you see? Let yourself have a little private getaway in your mind, just to give yourself a break, by creating an image of this place in your mind. When you're done, look it up and compare what you imagined with what you discover about the place. If it's so far away that it will be impossible to visit, then take a trip to the local library and find a documentary about the place.

Messengers:

Animal: *Haddock (fish)*
Nature: *Chokecherry (plant)*
Universe/Energy: *Pick a place on a map and go there (action)*

312

Live with gusto. Spin a web of your desires and catch everything you ever wanted in it. You move slowly at times because you're contemplating your steps along the way. It's fine to move quickly too if necessary. Have your shoulder available because someone may need it to cry on soon.

Messengers:

Animal: *Nursery Web Spider*
Nature: *Living Rocks (succulent plant)*
Universe/Energy: *Comforting Someone*

313

Be as specific as possible when you're putting your intentions out into the Universe. If you're looking to make more money, how much do you need or want? If you want more opportunities in life, what kind? Remember to think and project your desires with positive words and intentions. It will come back to you.

Messengers:

Animal: *Sand Dollar (sea urchin)*
Nature: *Lamb's Quarter (plant)*
Universe/Energy: *Sailing Stone (phenomenon)*

314

Do what you need to do to survive. It may seem like life is falling apart around you, but you see things from angles that others miss. Make the most out of this ability and be quick to make changes needed to move forward. Don't let pride get in your way. Clear the air, be graceful and remain calm.

Messengers:

Animal: *Fruit Fly*
Nature: *Money Tree Plant*
Universe/Energy: *Throat Chakra*

315

You are fearless and excel when challenged. Back down against an opponent? No way! You go after what you want in life whether it's related to work, your personal or love life, and you don't give up until you get it.

Messengers:

Animal: *Honey Badger*
Nature: *Rhodochrosite (gemstone)*
Universe/Energy: *Honor*

316

Your brain is in overdrive and needs a rest. You're creative and have lots of great ideas but you can't do everything all at once. Prioritize. Right now, you need grounding and balance before you get overwhelmed and burned out.

Messengers:

Animal: *Narwhal (mammal/whale)*
Nature: *Gray-head Coneflower*
Universe/Energy: *Ker-ching (sound)*

317

It makes you uncomfortable when the spotlight is on you, and you tend to shift the focus to someone else as quickly as possible. Part of your growth in this lifetime is to learn to accept compliments for what you do.

Messengers:
Animal: *African Wild Ass*
Nature: *Stratocumulus Clouds*
Universe/Energy: *Cobalt Blue (color)*

318

You are a powerful person who can be persistent in getting what you want, yet on the inside you question yourself and have doubts. You can be easily irritated by what you feel is silly, wrong, or biased. Use creative visualization to elevate your frequency during these times or irritation or doubt to keep balance within your spiritual self.

Messengers:

Animal: *Hornet*
Nature: *Four O'clock Flower*
Universe/Energy: *Sky Punch (phenomenon)*

319

It's time to look at the big picture and see everything around you prior to acting. There is a community dependent upon what you do so make the right choice. Take everything in stride with joy in your heart.

Messengers:

Animal: *Prairie Dog*
Nature: *Conglomerate Diatomite (rock)*
Universe/Energy: *Cold Wind*

320

Birth and rebirth are central to you as you create a deeper connection to your core spiritual self and the higher realms. It's time to test your limits of your intuitive abilities so you can break free of any restraints you've put on yourself. You may feel alone during this process. Some frequency work can only be done by yourself.

Messengers:

Animal: *Moon Fish*
Nature: *Phlox (plant)*
Universe/Energy: *Pineapple (scent)*

321

You have a sense of purpose and drive. You aren't easily bored because you keep yourself busy. You like rearranging things or decorating. If you're the one instigating the change, you're incredibly happy. But when change happens that wasn't your idea you can become moody and sulk about it.

Messengers:

Animal: *Oscar Fish*
Nature: *Realgar (gemstone)*
Universe/Energy: *Grape (Scent)*

322

You always have the right to make your own decisions. You are a colorful individual who follows the beat of your own drum. Your energy is peaceful, loving, inquisitive, and free. You might do things differently than others, but you always achieve the results you want.

Messengers:

Animal: *Painted Bunting (bird)*
Nature: *Peace Lily (plant)*
Universe/Energy: *Free Will*

323

Sex is at the forefront. Now is the time to strut your stuff and find a new mate. You're like a magnet, drawing your perfect partner to you. If you're with a long-term partner, it's time to spice up your love life.

Messengers:

Animal: *Pheasant (bird)*
Nature: *Magnetite (iron ore)*
Universe/Energy: *Effervescence*

324

Are you doing something to just be along for the ride? Could your time be spent better elsewhere? Look at what you're doing to see if it's truly something productive or if you're wasting time. Soon you'll have an event that will require you to build something or hold something together. Be prepared.

Messengers:

Animal: *Shark Sucker (fish)*
Nature: *Coneflower (plant/daisy)*
Universe/Energy: *Lightness of Being*

325

It's time to move! Get those feet going and pursue your dreams. Get organized, find the balance within yourself, and forge ahead with plans to accomplish your dreams. Be clear to avoid misinterpretation. Soon you'll meet someone with whom you'll have a close psychic connection, or you'll remember them from a past life.

Messengers:

Animal: *Centipede (arthropod)*
Nature: *Radish*
Universe/Energy: *Pepper (Scent)*

326

Instead of singing to the world what you're working on, you should keep your projects secret. Don't talk about them and guard them. This is also a time to look for inspiration. Think of the things you admire most in your life and consider how those can motivate you in your current work.

Messengers:

Animal: *Killdeer (bird)*
Nature: *Ozone Layer*
Universe/Energy: *Admiration*

327

If you're sitting around hoping that something great will happen to you, then you're wasting time. Instead take action to get what you want. It's important to be transparent in your actions instead of hiding your true intentions. Be aware of the spirit world at this time because you are in tune with the paranormal and will probably encounter spirit.

Messengers:

Animal: *Turtle Dove (bird)*
Nature: *Phlogopite (mineral)*
Universe/Energy: *Poltergeist (phenomenon)*

328

Withdraw completely and spend some time alone just for a little while. You are off balance and need to decide what you want to attach yourself to in life. Do you want to start a business? Go to school? Become a painter? The possibilities are endless and it's something you need to decide on your own. Don't let others judgement alter your belief in yourself.

Messengers:

Animal: *Spirula spirula (mollusk)*
Nature: *Polka Dot Agate (gemstone)*
Universe/Energy: *Run (action)*

329

Something is puzzling you and needs to be figured out. This is the time to act instead of waiting for something to happen. Have fun but be careful in your activities. Be resourceful, flexible, and nimble and the solution will come to you quickly. Then, when you listen to that quiet still voice, you'll realize you just discovered a universal truth.

Messengers:

Animal: *Monkey*
Nature: *Bladderwort (plant)*
Universe/Energy: *Divination*

330

How spontaneous are you? Can you take off and do something without overanalyzing and talking yourself out of it? If life is lacking an adventurous spontaneous frequency, now is the time to add it. Be wary of becoming too possessive of your material possessions or the people in your life.

Messengers:

Animal: *Flying Lizard*
Nature: *Pachira Plant*
Universe/Energy: *Sort through your closet (action)*

331

How full is your cup of life? Intention and hard work will fill it to the rim. When it's too full and runs over, then you have more than you need. Consider helping others who are lacking in abundance with your excess.

Messengers:

Animal: *Lyrebird*
Nature: *Fire Agate (gemstone)*
Universe/Energy: *Wolf Howl (sound)*

332

Acknowledging the things happening in your current lifetime which point directly to events in past lives can help you with problems you're facing now. As spirit, all lessons are cumulative and enhance our overall eternal growth. You started small but when you finish in the spiritual plane, your knowledge and wisdom will be unlimited.

Messengers:

Animal: *Tadpole Shrimp (crustacean)*
Nature: *Gas Fire*
Universe/Energy: *Consider your past (action)*

333

Loyalty, friendship, and trust surround you now. You'll work together with others on a project that will jumpstart itself. If you're feeling confined, then make some time to run free. Work out any restlessness you're feeling through exercise. Feel the wind in your face, the sun on your back. Work your muscles until they burn. Bet on something for the win.

Messengers:

Animal: *Horse*
Nature: *Nickel*
Universe/Energy: *Mellow*

334

It's time to get your negative emotions under control. Anger, rage, and a quick temper are getting the best of you because you are hurt and feel betrayed. As hard as it might be, forgiveness and getting yourself out of the situation and away from the people involved will help you.

Messengers:

Animal: *Tasmanian Devil (marsupial)*
Nature: *Bay*
Universe/Energy: *Kindness*

335

Many hands make light work. When you can get everyone to help then the project moves faster, and one person isn't completely worn out at the end. Pitch in, do your share instead of standing around and watching. When everyone has finished, sit back, and relax for a while with a snack and a drink and pride yourself on a job well done.

Messengers:

Animal: *Millipede (arthropod)*
Nature: *Glade Coneflower (plant)*
Universe/Energy: *Relax in a Hammock (action)*

336

Common sense and good judgment are an integral part of your frequency. You are serene and see what others ignore. At times you need to move slowly to be sure that what you're doing is correct and will result in the outcome you seek.

Messengers:

Animal: *Slug (terrestrial mollusk)*
Nature: *Christmas Fern*
Universe/Energy: *Deep fuchsia (color)*

337

The wildness of nature is calling you. There is freedom in its fast-moving hooves. You've felt held down for too long and now is the time to break free and run wild. You will rest when your soul fills complete and full. There has been something missing for a while. Now is the time to find yourself again.

Messengers:

Animal: *Mustang (equine)*
Nature: *Hosta (plant)*
Universe/Energy: *Bike ride (action)*

338

You are covered and safe from that which you fear. Anxiety and stress surround you. To find peace again you must be stubborn and resist what others are trying to make you believe. Seek out the truth because lies abound. Once accomplished, the anxiety and stress will dissipate.

Messengers:

Animal: *Onager (equine)*
Nature: *Duckweed (aquatic plant)*
Universe/Energy: *Merriment (emotion)*

339

The love of sun and surf, of basking in the heat of the day, brings you a sense of calm peacefulness. Being outside is invigorating and you do your best thinking while listening to the sound of the water lapping against the shores. If you can't physically visit the beach, get a recording or audio file and listen to it.

Messengers:

Animal: *Lemming (rodent)*
Nature: *Ghost Plant*
Universe/Energy: *Pamper yourself (action)*

340

This is a time of protection and discovery so you may understand your path in life. You've been out of balance and unsure of where to go. The right choice will be illuminated now so you can clearly see the way.

Messengers:

Animal: *Lobster*
Nature: *Coontail (aquatic plant)*
Universe/Energy: *Centering*

341

You're about to open new spiritual doors and windows all around you. There is so much information coming at you from all directions you're not sure which to absorb first. Take your time and be disciplined in your approach.

Messengers:

Animal: *Margay (feline)*
Nature: *Full Circle Rainbow*
Universe/Energy: *Disciplined*

342

Do not hold others in disrespect. You may not agree with their beliefs or actions. What they choose to do is what is right for their path—not your path. You must stay true to yourself. Do not become a pest by trying to convince them that they are in the wrong. What is wrong for you may be exactly right for them.

Messengers:

Animal: *Dog Tick*
Nature: *Birch (tree)*
Universe/Energy: *Pardon (feeling)*

343

When you bare your soul self you may feel naked and exposed. It is when you are aware, brave, and confident in yourself that you can do this with wisdom and humility. Sometimes letting others see your true spiritual self can be illuminating for them and enable them to see their true spirit as well. The result can be a burst of joy from within.

Messengers:

Animal: *Naked Mole Rat (rodent)*
Nature: *Emerald (gemstone)*
Universe/Energy: *Boom (Sound)*

344

Your intuition is at an all-time high. You're very aware of the messages being sent from the spiritual realm and are in tune with everything and everyone around you. This high level of frequency can be disconcerting at times.

Messengers:

Animal: *Alpine Newt (amphibian)*
Nature: *Bornite (mineral)*
Universe/Energy: *Appreciation*

345

The unexpected awaits. This could be in the form of a new job, travel, a marriage, the birth of a baby or any other dramatic life change. Positivity and forward motion surround you. Now is not the time for moodiness but to grasp all that is offered with a happy smile. The unexpected may mean walking away and starting over on your own.

Messengers:

Animal: *Jackal (mammal)*
Nature: *Opalized Wood*
Universe/Energy: *Harp (sound)*

346

Prepare to be offered a position where you will take charge of a project that requires you to manage workers. You are a born leader who has the uncanny ability to know what needs to be done and when to keep you ahead of schedule.

Messengers:

Animal: *Grizzly Bear*
Nature: *Nutmeg (spice)*
Universe/Energy: *Mingle (action)*

347

Keep your vision as wide as it is high. Don't limit yourself by narrowing the scope of what you do. You're an enlightened individual who is continuously awakening to deeper levels of spirituality. You seek a more involved relationship with your higher self and the Divine.

Messengers:

Animal: *Permit Fish*
Nature: *Leatherwood (plant)*
Universe/Energy: *Reaffirm (action)*

348

Your curious nature opens the doors to so many opportunities that you seem to be the luckiest person around. You have the unique ability to edge out the competition through your vibrant and eager personality. While you don't show aggression, you have the tenacity to achieve what you want by following routes not often taken by others.

Messengers:

Animal: *Bull Shark*
Nature: *Chromite (mineral)*
Universe/Energy: *Alluring (feeling)*

349

A simple, uncomplicated life can be the change you need. While the world around you may seem to be spinning out of control, you can make the decision to remove yourself from the chaos and create a different adventure for yourself. People may see you as naïve, but you are in fact aware and making controlled, focused decisions that are right for you.

Messengers:

Animal: *Blond Capuchin (primate)*
Nature: *Ice Pellets*
Universe/Energy: *Rejoice (action)*

350

You glitter and glow in the sun. You are a rare individual who radiates positivity and light. Others are captivated by your energy. Spending time in your presence is a blessing to them. Don't let this go to your head though.

Messengers:

Animal: *Akhal-Teke (equine)*
Nature: *Heliodor (gemstone)*
Universe/Energy: *Pizza (Scent)*

351

Let go of any negative feelings and try to understand why you're having them. Once you release them, the root cause will be displayed. You're undergoing a spiritual awakening and will experience connections with and messages from your guides, masters, and the angelic realm.

Messengers:

Animal: *Siamese Fighting Fish*
Nature: *Bamboo*
Universe/Energy: *See a Plan to Completion (action)*

352

You can reach great heights in both your personal and work life by standing out from the crowd. Make sure you aren't looking down on others but are instead being a nurturing, helpful person. Don't overdo that either or you'll be seen as invading another person's space. Create balance.

Messengers:

Animal: *Giraffe*
Nature: *Bindweed*
Universe/Energy: *Brown (Color)*

353

An alluring mystery awaits you. Tread carefully as you unravel the cords holding it together. For when you discover what is within, you will be embraced by its brilliance. New relationships are being formed at this time. It just might be the love of your lifetime. Don't give up.

Messengers:

Animal: *Black Swan*
Nature: *Cardinal Flower*
Universe/Energy: *Illumination*

354

You are blanketed in warmth although the cold surrounds you. This is a good time for contemplation, meditation, and reflection. You will awaken to a new realization that will be life changing in a positive way. This may be a new attitude on your part, the offer of a new job, or a move.

Messengers:

Animal: *Icelandic Horse*
Nature: *Davidor (vegetable/shallot)*
Universe/Energy: *Contemplation*

355

You are a secretive person who is also a healer. You can protect yourself and others from psychic attacks and can stop one if it has already started. You're very spiritually aware and have heightened intuition. You can do hands-on healing and distance healing with your abilities. You often help others who have experienced loss in their lives.

Messengers:

Animal: *Pitta (bird)*
Nature: *Amethyst (gemstone)*
Universe/Energy: *Black (color)*

356

Live simply and with purpose. Sometimes change comes in swarms, with one happening right behind the other. Now is the time to boost your immune system. To keep a head cold from progressing to something worse make sure you're taking care of yourself in the beginning.

Messengers:

Animal: *Locust (insect)*
Nature: *Fire Rainbow*
Universe/Energy: *Simplicity*

357

Don't waste time. Get busy working on ideas that have been percolating in your mind, now is when you can bring them to fruition. Keep your secrets and pay special attention to how others speak, they will show their true intentions in the inflections of their voice. New ventures will be successful at this time.

Messengers:

Animal: *Chipmunk*
Nature: *Gold*
Universe/Energy: *Birds Tweeting (sound)*

358

You're attuned to the beauty around you, your sexuality, control, and inner strength. You avoid jealousy, are fair, and don't give up on what you want. You have a very high vibration and are sensitive to the frequency of others, places, and things. You have a keen alertness to all types of changes whether it's in the environment, relationships, or intuitive messages.

Messengers:

Animal: *Scorpion*
Nature: *Carnation (plant/flower)*
Universe/Energy: *Guardian*

359

You have the power of vibrational energy at your fingertips. Your connection to spirit and the Divine is exceptionally strong. Transformation and enlightenment surround you. You are balanced, grounded, and in tune with your spiritual self. This is a time of exponential spiritual growth, of understanding ancient truths, and uncovering hidden knowledge from the Divine. Connect very closely with your intuition during this time.

Messengers:

Animal: *Whale*
Nature: *Autumn*
Universe/Energy: *Bay rum (scent)*

360

An exciting new arrival is coming your way and with it will bring extreme happiness to your life. This doesn't mean it is a human baby, but it might be. You may be resolving issues from your childhood. This is a happy time of rebirth, financial gain, and unparalleled opportunity.

Messengers:

Animal: *Stork (bird)*
Nature: *Oregano (herb)*
Universe/Energy: *Exuberance*

361

Feeling emotional pain will help you get through it. When you block it, push it deep down inside and don't let your emotions flow, then you're blocking your frequency. It will get to a point where you will not be able to hold it back and you'll break. Don't let yourself get to this point.

Messengers:

Animal: *Shearwater (bird)*
Nature: *Cannellini Beans*
Universe/Energy: *Cat purring (sound)*

362

Maintain focus. Avoid being distracted by trivial things. You're connected to the higher realms and are embarking on a spiritual quest for enlightenment and personal growth. You'll reach great heights in everything you set out to do. Be honest with yourself first and then with the people around you.

Messengers:

Animal: *Hawk*
Nature: *Plains (landform)*
Universe/Energy: *Amber (scent)*

363

Plan ahead instead of waiting until the last minute, which could result in disappointments and regret. Invest in a copper bracelet to help boost your frequency to give you more stabilized energy so you're not feeling restless or on edge.

Messengers:

Animal: *Sea Dragon (fish)*
Nature: *Copper*
Universe/Energy: *Stretch (action)*

364

Gentleness, strength, and protection during difficult times are yours. Now is the time to connect with the calming energy of water. Look deep inside to explore the hidden power within you and make your current situation work for your benefit. Look at your behavior. If you're being devious, ruthless, or unprincipled then make a change from the negative to the positive.

Messengers:

Animal: *Capybara (rodent)*
Nature: *Sea Thrift (plant)*
Universe/Energy: *Go Canoeing*

365

Promote healthy living for its therapeutic value. This is a suitable time for cleaning your house of cobwebs and dust, to change your air filters and burn some scented candles. Clearing the air aids in raising frequency.

Messengers:

Animal: *Arthropod*
Nature: *Endive (vegetable)*
Universe/Energy: *Sincerity*

366

Have you ever thought about creating pottery? You could make interesting designs that you paint in colorful hues. They could be small and easy to display or large enough to hold plants. Your designs will help others feel better about themselves. Don't follow the same patterns that others follow but instead make something unique and totally your own.

Messengers:

Animal: *Small-toothed Harvest Mouse*
Nature: *Sandstone (rock)*
Universe/Energy: *Connected (feeling)*

367

Live wholeheartedly, in full awareness, and present in the moment. Be nonjudgmental, patient, trusting, and accepting of others and of yourself. Leave doubts, stress, and burdens by the wayside. They are weighing you down from living a full and spectacular life.

Messengers:

Animal: *Tench (fish)*
Nature: *Elder Wood (tree)*
Universe/Energy: *Release doubt*

368

From the biggest to the smallest, from the loudest to the softest sound, there is beauty all around you. Open your heart and mind in appreciation of it all. Sadness can turn to joy, boredom to fun times, and indifference to feeling accepted.

Messengers:

Animal: *Gaur (mammal/bison)*
Nature: *Pea (vegetable)*
Universe/Energy: *Wood Burning in a Fireplace (sound)*

369

There is a place for everything, and everything belongs in its place. When you leave things scattered around your house or your work area it can be annoying, confusing, and frustrating because now it's just clutter. Put things back where they belong when you're finished with them.

Messengers:

Animal: *Lesser Wanderer (butterfly)*
Nature: *Coal Conglomerate (rock)*
Universe/Energy: *Rejuvenated*

370

When you have nothing to really do, but want to keep busy, try puttering around or tinkering with something. Puttering is the act of doing little things that don't have much importance but that keep you busy, and tinkering is fixing things that need repair. This is a great time to let your mind wander and come up with solutions and ideas to other issues.

Messengers:

Animal: *Bream (fish)*
Nature: *Russian Sage (plant)*
Universe/Energy: *Clove (Scent)*

371

To be truly awake means to be connected to the Divine, to the power within yourself, and to higher consciousness through your own ideals, thoughts and spiritual truths, not those of other people. It is understanding the world you live in from the smallest animals to the grandest galaxies. When you have awakened within, it shows on the outside.

Messengers:

Animal: *Key Deer*
Nature: *Armillaria Ostoyae Mushroom*
Universe/Energy: *Awaken*

372

Get moving! It's time to increase your physical activity. When you're too placid, you can get agitated and frenzied and take your frustration out on others lightning fast. Even if you move slowly, just move. You tend to work too much and not take enough time for the fun adventures in life.

Messengers:

Animal: *Shark*
Nature: *Boneset (herb)*
Universe/Energy: *Wind through the trees (sound)*

373

Worrying about money has the opposite effect than what you may be trying to achieve. When you worry, the emotions of fear, deprivation, lack, and poverty override your attempts to manifest money. Instead, you're indirectly manifesting the negativity you're worrying about. Create a budget. Any time you have extra, that is abundance. Appreciate it and it will continue to come to you.

Messengers:

Animal: *Bonefish*
Nature: *Canal*
Universe/Energy: *Cool Fall Air (Scent)*

374

Magical energy surrounds you; but you still need to be on the lookout for predators. Surround yourself with protective light to keep them at bay. Your ability to share your spiritual enlightenment with others is at the forefront now. You have help from the elemental world, so share what you know with those who ask.

Messengers:

Animal: *Escolar (fish)*
Nature: *Four-leaf clover*
Universe/Energy: *Electric guitar (sound)*

375

There are abundant opportunities in your life. The more forward movement you have, the more of them you will discover. Instead of waiting, do something which will move energy around you and within yourself. You might need a kickstart to get going but afterwards you'll be able to enjoy the fruits of your labor.

Messengers:

Animal: *Goblin Shark*
Nature: *Jackfruit*
Universe/Energy: *Freshly Baked Bread (Scent)*

376

Are you having a tough time adjusting to something like a new job, a new home, or any major life change? You have all the tools you need for this to be a success, but something is holding you back. Consider how you're reacting. Are you overreacting or resisting for some reason? Seek a bit of solitude until you figure it out.

Messengers:

Animal: *Gray Fox*
Nature: *Baseball Plant*
Universe/Energy: *Denim (color)*

377

Even the smallest birds can have a big song. Sing yours proudly and loudly. Romance and love are in the forefront for you now. You tend to be interested in the feelings of others and uplifting those who are down in the dumps. This time, someone will be there to lift you up. Be careful of scratching an itch that shouldn't be scratched.

Messengers:

Animal: *Plain Chachalaca (bird)*
Nature: *Poison Oak*
Universe/Energy: *Be Romantic (action)*

378

Direct, clear, and concise communication is needed now. Otherwise, confusion and chaos could result. It's a time to do things with vibrancy and with your own unique flair. Be inspiring and be inspired. Push fear aside and let yourself shine. You're a loyal friend, a kindhearted person, who goes the extra mile. Now is the time to get in touch with your inner self.

Messengers:

Animal: *Toucan (bird)*
Nature: *Beryllium (metal)*
Universe/Energy: *Bubble wrap popping (Sound)*

379

Be very clear in your choices. One single action or wrong decision will have powerful consequences and can put you on a completely different path immediately. It may not be a path you would choose. Think before doing.

Messengers:

Animal: *Sprat (fish)*
Nature: *Black Currant (plant)*
Universe/Energy: *Tree bark (color)*

380

If you've made a mistake, it's time to learn from it. Take a calm, unbiased approach to the situation. Look at it objectively and truthfully using your intuition to guide you. Don't think about how you wish the situation had turned out, but the reality of it.

Messengers:

Animal: *Rice Weevil (insect)*
Nature: *Sodalite (gemstone)*
Universe/Energy: *Airy (sensation)*

381

Create ambience in your group settings. You work well in groups and tend to become the leader of group projects. Just make sure you don't get pulled under and end up doing all the work yourself. Everyone should carry their own weight even if they sulk about it.

Messengers:

Animal: *Scarlet Ibis (bird)*
Nature: *Liquid Asphalt*
Universe/Energy: *Vibrant (feeling)*

382

There's nothing more important than staying true to your own colors. You may need to blend in at times or change to fit your surroundings. Other times you will need to take center stage. You'll know which to do. You are a surprise because although you move slowly you can be lightning fast when necessary.

Messengers:

Animal: *Chameleon*
Nature: *Beet*
Universe/Energy: *Tears of Joy (Sound)*

383

Don't let your anger get out of control. If you feel negative emotions building up, then get outside and run it off or take a long walk until you settle. Look at the flowers and beauty of nature along the way. Fury can come in all sizes. You must tame the anger within to enjoy the beauty without.

Messengers:

Animal: *Miniature Horse*
Nature: *Petunia*
Universe/Energy: *Rosewood (scent)*

384

Let each day be its own. Do not let what happened yesterday continue to affect you today. At the end of each day take a few moments before bed to go over your experiences. Appreciate the good, come to terms with the bad, and then put everything away. In the morning you can start fresh without being unclear about how your day will go.

Messengers:

Animal: *Dace (fish)*
Nature: *Oak Tree*
Universe/Energy: *Certainty (feeling)*

385

If you're feeling out of sorts, make yourself move around. This could be doing a mundane task such as cleaning or taking a walk. By doing something mundane, you free your mind to come up with new ideas and solutions to problems you may have been stressing over. Consider all the thoughts that come to you because one of them will be the solution, an inspiration, or maybe even a new business idea.

Messengers:

Animal: *Lake Whitefish*
Nature: *Nutsedge (plant/weed)*
Universe/Energy: *Chocolate (Scent)*

386

Are you blocking your guides? If you are, they may send information in your dreams, signs in the clouds, on billboards, or on television. They may even shout out your name to get your attention. Be aware of the subtle signs around you.

Messengers:

Animal: *Gourami (fish)*
Nature: *Thermal Energy*
Universe/Energy: *Spirit Guides*

387

Revive an old hobby or project. Be curious and resourceful. There is something you can investigate that has spiked your interest. Get involved. The sweet smell of success awaits you. Look deeper beneath the surface for clues. Through language and communication, you will enjoy the adventure of discovery.

Messengers:

Animal: *Cicada (insect)*
Nature: *Kohlrabi (vegetable)*
Universe/Energy: *Honeysuckle (Scent)*

388

Keep secrets close, assess situations, and wait for the right time to act. Your intuition and creativity are at elevated levels. Be fearless, acknowledge deep emotions, and remain ethical to grow on your spiritual path. There is also a friend who could benefit from your guidance in these areas. Bring them along on the journey.

Messengers:

Animal: *Alligator*
Nature: *Burnet (plant)*
Universe/Energy: *Caring*

389

Trust your methods. You have the time you need to successfully complete what you're attempting to do. Don't feel rushed. Follow your instincts as you move forward. When rushed, you can make mistakes. Don't let someone else's hyper energy get you off track. You prefer to be sure before jumping ahead. Stick with that.

Messengers:

Animal: *Bar Jack (fish)*
Nature: *Coral Bells (plant)*
Universe/Energy: *Clock ticking (sound)*

390

Timelessness surrounds you. Pay attention to what people say, to repeating numbers, to things that happen again and again. Learn from them. Age is but a number. Do not let it affect how you see yourself. There is birth and rebirth happening in your life. Embrace the happiness it brings.

Messengers:

Animal: *Galapagos Tortoise*
Nature: *Raspberry*
Universe/Energy: *Recurring Words / Phrase*

391

You are incredibly lucky lately. You're coming into your own, opening to higher frequencies, and embracing your inner song. Align with your spiritual self to gain a deeper understanding of the path you must take. Doors are being opened for you on a regular basis. Take the time to step though them and make the most of the opportunities given.

Messengers:

Animal: *Cricket*
Nature: *Rose*
Universe/Energy: *Worthy (feeling)*

392

Something or someone is irritating you, causing your happiness to turn to anxiety and stress. The problem needs to be addressed face-to-face and then released. You can pinpoint problems and strike quickly to resolve them. Expect a social gathering and a feast in the near future.

Messengers:

Animal: *Alder Flycatcher (bird)*
Nature: *Ragweed*
Universe/Energy: *Gaiety*

393

A diplomatic stance is needed to keep a situation at work under control. Emotions are taunt and others around you are grasping on to whatever they can find to find balance. Whatever the cause—company buyouts, change in direction, cancelled contracts—try to stay grounded. This will resolve itself as all the kinks are worked out.

Messengers:

Animal: *Sea Lamprey (fish)*
Nature: *Great Northern Beans*
Universe/Energy: *Diplomacy*

394

Be aware of your position in life. Plan and take action to achieve new goals or to move up to higher positions. You are a natural leader so don't get bogged down by what others may say. You know your own strengths and weaknesses. Act upon them accordingly to achieve all you desire.

Messengers:

Animal: *Meerkat*
Nature: *Green Ash Tree*
Universe/Energy: *Opening a can of carbonated beverage (sound)*

395

This is a good time to reawaken old desires. If there is something that you always wanted to do but never got around to it, try it now. You're creative and beautiful in spirit. There isn't anything you can't accomplish once you set your mind to it.

Messengers:

Animal: *Apollo Butterfly*
Nature: *Methane Gas*
Universe/Energy: *Cerulean (Color)*

396

The Divine is speaking to you, are you listening? The energy around you is elevated and is drawing a powerful strength from beyond. You are in tune with your intuition and are ready for what is in store for you. This is a time of great transformation, of an even deeper awareness, and of spiritual growth.

Messengers:

Animal: *Barn Swallow (bird)*
Nature: *Glory of the Snow (plant)*
Universe/Energy: *Oracle*

397

Instead of getting on the telephone and venting with a friend, try writing down your frustrations so you can go back and look at them later. There are many ways to relieve feelings of anxiousness without talking about it. Writing it down is a reliable way to get it out without leaving words in the Universe to be shared with others without your knowledge.

Messengers:

Animal: *Milk Snake*
Nature: *Hematite (gemstone)*
Universe/Energy: *Reliable*

398

Look deep within to find the truth for it lies within you, not with another. Once found, balance will be restored. Stop fighting your intuitive abilities. It is part of you and it's time to embrace all parts of your true self.

Messengers:

Animal: *Loon (bird)*
Nature: *Dust Storm*
Universe/Energy: *Seagulls calling (sound)*

399

Calmness is needed at this moment. Looking at both sides of a problem and rationally figuring out a resolution is much better than speaking with a sharp, snarky bite that stings. Be smart as you approach the issue because there is an easy solution.

Messengers:

Animal: *Black Fly*
Nature: *Amazonite (gemstone)*
Universe/Energy: *Intelligence*

400

You are the first to arrive, the first to jump right in, and the first to apologize when you're wrong. You live life with leaps and bounds. You love challenges because you want to meet them, which brings out the best in you.

Messengers:

Animal: *Gazelle*
Nature: *Early Dog Violet*
Universe/Energy: *Fire Brick (color)*

401

The Aka is the cord between the physical and astral bodies. You are being drawn to research more about astral travel at this time. Pay attention to the role the aka plays during traveling in the astral plane. This is a time to take firm steps in your approach.

Messengers:

Animal: *Clydesdale (equine)*
Nature: *Boston Fern (plant)*
Universe/Energy: *Novaya Zemlya Effect (mirage phenomenon)*

402

Have you stopped chasing your dreams? Has life got you down? Are you hiding out in your house instead of getting out and about? It's time to toughen up your outer layers and start over. Don't let past circumstances keep you from excelling and pursuing your dreams. You've got this, you just have to give yourself a reboot.

Messengers:

Animal: *Horny Toad Lizard (reptile)*
Nature: *Cordierite (gemstone)*
Universe/Energy: *Present (feeling)*

403

Don't take things for granted. Give thanks for the unexpected gifts that fall into your lap instead of questioning why you're receiving them. Not everything in life has an ulterior motive. Waste less, work hard, and support others. What's good for everyone as a group is good for you as an individual.

Messengers:

Animal: *Piranha (fish)*
Nature: *Salt*
Universe/Energy: *Write a letter (action)*

404

Give your motivation a jumpstart if you're feeling sluggish. There's a lot you need to do and putting it off isn't going to get it done. Add some sweetness to your life. Try something you've never had or done before. Don't hold on to resentments or plan revenge on someone else. It will only come back to hurt you.

Messengers:

Animal: *Mountain Beaver*
Nature: *Sapodilla (tree)*
Universe/Energy: *Geranium (scent)*

405

Your vision for the future is phenomenal. You're tuned in and are acting on your insights, which causes you to flourish. If you're in sales, you may find it quite easy to close deal after deal. The possibilities are endless for you. When you feel chills unexpectedly and you're not ill, that's the Universe telling you that you're on the right track.

Messengers:

Animal: *Mudpuppy (fish)*
Nature: *Black Mustard*
Universe/Energy: *Chills of Universal Truth*

406

Communication is key. Understanding is necessary. Keep your temper in check as you observe. Business dealings are of utmost importance now so make sure you're being diplomatic yet firm, so you're not taken advantage of. Expect great rewards from your current situation or endeavor.

Messengers:

Animal: *Chimpanzee*
Nature: *Lava hair*
Universe/Energy: *Second Summer (weather phenomenon)*

407

You do your best work at night. The darkness and quiet heightens your senses and your frequency. You've learned to control yourself and listen to what your body needs. Now is a wonderful time to draw up new plans for yourself. Go big with your ideas.

Messengers:

Animal: *Kultarr (marsupial)*
Nature: *Graphite (mineral)*
Universe/Energy: *Challenge Yourself*

408

You have a tough outer shell that often protects you from emotional hurt. But watch what you say so you don't hurt someone else without realizing it. It's time to address your fears and move forward. Be aware of any illegal activity happening around you. Remove yourself from dicey situations or report something you see happening to the authorities.

Messengers:

Animal: *Pangolin (mammal)*
Nature: *Carrot*
Universe/Energy: *Baking (Scent)*

409

Your energy is endless, and you can go for an exceptionally long time before you get tired. But when fatigue hits you, it hits you hard. Understanding this about yourself will help you avoid the point of exhaustion. Schedule time for rest.

Messengers:

Animal: *Frigate Bird*
Nature: *Wahoo Elm Tree*
Universe/Energy: *Understanding*

410

Do your actions match your words? Your aura is the energy that surrounds your body. If you're actions and words aren't the same, then it will lower your frequency and change your aura. To keep your energy levels high, always live and speak in harmony.

Messengers:

Animal: *Quarter Horse*
Nature: *Sky*
Universe/Energy: *Take a photo (action)*

411

There are some days when clumsiness rules. Today might be one of them. Pay attention to where you're stepping and hold tightly to objects, so you don't drop them. Look around your home. Are you hoarding anything? If you are, take time to sort through it and let part of it go.

Messengers:

Animal: *Greater Glider (marsupial)*
Nature: *Bearberry (plant)*
Universe/Energy: *Your Favorite Perfume/Cologne (Scent)*

412

If you catch a whiff of a smell that reminds you of a loved one that has passed, then it may be a message from the other side. First, rule out any physical source of the scent. This is a time when you must be very adaptable because you're going to experience some positive changes and will need to flow with them.

Messengers:

Animal: *Dingo (canine)*
Nature: *Nettle (plant)*
Universe/Energy: *Clairscent*

413

Primal instincts, unconscious drives, and the energetic life force of the Earth are all at work now. Recent gains and losses may have you emotionally spent. Do not drown in sadness but instead lift yourself up. The sun will shine through the rain to change your luck for the better.

Messengers:

Animal: *Golden Tree Snake*
Nature: *Sun shower*
Universe/Energy: *Lemon chiffon (color)*

414

Are you trying to cover a lot of ground or climb to new heights? Don't flounder along the way but stay tenacious in all that you do. Right now, you are relying on yourself and don't need additional support from others. This is important for your spiritual and personal growth. Some things must be done alone.

Messengers:

Animal: *Flounder (fish)*
Nature: *Virginia Creeper (plant)*
Universe/Energy: *Tenacity*

415

Do not ruin the innocence of others by being too harsh and dampening their dreams. This is especially true if you're dealing with children. They are more vulnerable to even helpful criticism so always be kind in the way you phrase your words. Something lost will be found.

Messengers:

Animal: *Mountain Sheep*
Nature: *Jerusalem Artichoke*
Universe/Energy: *Rejoice (feeling)*

416

It's time to be a team player due to deadlines or group activities. Make sure you have time alone to recharge and energize yourself. It's important to rest as much as possible when you must push hard to meet goals.

Messengers:

Animal: *Flamingo (bird)*
Nature: *Lily of the Valley (plant)*
Universe/Energy: *Spoon clinking in cup (sound)*

417

Being territorial is important to protect your own. Take extra precautions to protect what is yours. If you're feeling trapped in or upset about a relationship that you no longer want to be in, then gather your courage and walk away. It's your life and your choices. Choose what you desire.

Messengers:

Animal: *Black Widow Spider*
Nature: *Coriander (herb)*
Universe/Energy: *Cologne (Scent)*

418

Reversal of your emotions is happening now. If you are sad about a situation, it will start to turn so more joy is brought into your life. This is an excellent time for manifestation work. You will also be able to gather a clearer understanding of your life purpose and releasing negative energies that may have clung to you from a past lifetime.

Messengers:

Animal: *Moon Bear*
Nature: *Andalusite (gemstone)*
Universe/Energy: *Capable (feeling)*

419

The thoughts that you think and the words that you say will go out into the Universe and come back to you in abundance. It's important that your thoughts and words are clear, precise, positive, and loving. Just as there can be a quick change in the weather, your experiences can change just as fast when negativity you previously put out comes home. Stay positive.

Messengers:

Animal: *American Kestrel (bird)*
Nature: *Stratus Clouds*
Universe/Energy: *Thought Forms*

420

Watch out for toxicity around you. The emotions of others may be pulling on your empathic abilities making it hard for you to concentrate. Find the source and cut it out of your life. You're highly sensitive, graceful, and have strong intuition. Because of this you can move quickly and get out of difficult and tricky situations.

Messengers:

Animal: *Fallow Deer*
Nature: *Arsenopyrite (rock)*
Universe/Energy: *Yoga (action)*

421

Do not try to force spiritual growth on yourself or on the people around you. It will only come to you when your spiritual self is ready to learn. Trying to force your intuition will only cause you frustration. Instead, read as much as you can, spend time in nature, around water, and animals to see what messages you receive.

Messengers:

Animal: *Brook Trout (fish)*
Nature: *Sesame Seed*
Universe/Energy: *Popping popcorn (sound)*

422

Keep your guard up at work because a tricky situation is about to arise. Make sure you're able to move and adapt quickly to whatever happens. Acknowledge your true nature. Look to ancient mythology to discover something that will resonate with your spiritual nature.

Messengers:

Animal: *Dik Dik (mammal/antelope)*
Nature: *Alfalfa Sprouts*
Universe/Energy: *Volunteer (action)*

423

Use your instinct and intuition to uncover lies that are being told to you by someone you trust. When you do, you may feel hurt, but you can also choose to be free from this person in the future. Care for that which you have created including your children, projects, animals, or anything that is yours.

Messengers:

Animal: *Mallee Fowl*
Nature: *Wasatch Wind*
Universe/Energy: *Breathless (sensation)*

424

Look past outward appearances to see the spirit of the person. There may be a strong, giving person behind the scars on their body. You may lose a wonderful opportunity to know them if you evaluate them by appearance alone. This is a time of rejuvenation, cleansing, and letting go.

Messengers:

Animal: *Vulture*
Nature: *Birdsfoot Trefoil (plant)*
Universe/Energy: *Third Eye Chakra*

425

Hunker down and study even if you're not in school. This is the time to learn as much as possible. The results will be impressive, and you'll experience good fortune. Be noble and pure in your interactions with others. Untruths told now will come back to you ten-fold and cause destruction. Be prepared so you don't run out of gas.

Messengers:

Animal: *Great Egret (bird)*
Nature: *Petroleum*
Universe/Energy: *Whisper (sound)*

426

You're a survivor who can overcome obstacles that stand in your way. Look for the natural gems around you for inspiration. Pearls of wisdom from those older than you should not be ignored. Business dealings started at this time will be a success. Be elusive when it comes to disclosing details in the beginning.

Messengers:

Animal: *Kowari (marsupial)*
Nature: *Mahogany Tree*
Universe/Energy: *Worn Leather (Scent)*

427

You've labored intensely and enjoyed your hard-earned success. Now look towards a large body of water where you can relax and enjoy yourself for a while. After toiling to complete a task, always take time to replenish your energy before embarking on something new.

Messengers:

Animal: *African Spoonbill (bird)*
Nature: *Pawpaw (tree)*
Universe/Energy: *Rustling (sound)*

428

It's time to do some spring cleaning regardless of the season. Clean the house, clear out accumulated messes, donate what you no longer need. Give yourself a makeover and take more time with your personal hygiene. If you've been putting off a dental cleaning or haircut, now's the time to get it done.

Messengers:

Animal: *Silverfish (insect)*
Nature: *Zircon (mineral)*
Universe/Energy: *Jubilant (feeling)*

429

Acknowledge when you're out of control. Instead of letting yourself become hot-headed, take a deep breath, and balance your energy. Once grounded, allow feelings of calmness to flow over you. Give yourself a mini timeout to regain control of your emotions. Find a quiet place where you can identify solutions to what has you so worked up.

Messengers:

Animal: *Jack Dempsey (fish)*
Nature: *Silt*
Universe/Energy: *Smooth (sensation)*

430

You're a little shark in a big ocean but that doesn't mean you can't rise to the top and soar over the water like a dolphin. Moving in offsetting motions keeps the competition guessing at what you're doing. This is an excellent ploy to make sure you're winning year after year.

Messengers:

Animal: *Dogfish*
Nature: *Campion Flower*
Universe/Energy: *Blender (sound)*

431

Clearing the energy of past traumas will help you to heal old wounds and release any fear associated with past events. Keeping with family traditions will also help you to heal from the past. This is a fertile time for you, a time of transforming the past as you look to the future.

Messengers:

Animal: *Green Jay (bird)*
Nature: *River Birch (tree)*
Universe/Energy: *Tradition*

432

You may discover that a dry climate is good for you in the winter and a tropical climate is better for you in the summer. To gain more enlightenment on your spiritual journey try adding essential oils. They are good for what ails you and can help you accept all that the Universe has to give.

Messengers:

Animal: *Indigo Snake*
Nature: *Chromium (mineral)*
Universe/Energy: *Magenta (color)*

433

Take the time to feel your emotions deep in your soul. Don't just casually think about how you're feeling emotionally but *really feel* them inside you. This is an excellent way to deepen your relationship with yourself and others so you can understand and support one another.

Messengers:

Animal: *Blue Duck*
Nature: *Aventurine (gemstone)*
Universe/Energy: *Companionship*

434

When it comes to work, it's time to circle and pursue, to watch the actions of the competition so you can choose marketing tactics that will enable you to rise above them. Listen to the rhythms of the energy and sounds around you. Patterns are repeating. If you're aware of them, then you'll be able to taste the sweetness of success.

Messengers:

Animal: *Hen Harrier (birds of prey)*
Nature: *Casaba Melon*
Universe/Energy: *Biorhythm*

435

Trust in the sharpness of your vision to see future results. Be assertive in your search for prosperity. Opt for new growth in all areas of your life to bring beauty to you. You are bold and resourceful, which enables you to achieve your goals with ease.

Messengers:

Animal: *American Wigeon (duck)*
Nature: *Parrot's Beak Flower*
Universe/Energy: *Take a Nap (action)*

436

You're on the hunt and nothing is stopping you from achieving what you desire. Losing is not an option because the stakes are high. In the end you'll be successful and extremely happy. Look to the light for guidance. When you manifest the spiritual within you, realization becomes clear.

Messengers:

Animal: *Huntsman Spider*
Nature: *Durian (plant)*
Universe/Energy: *Labdanum (scent)*

437

It's time to make your way out of the tunnels you've dug for yourself. There is a deep connection to the Divine and an increase of frequencies. It's time to move forward with your inner song to guide you. Self-expression is important as is intent focus.

Messengers:

Animal: *Mole Cricket*
Nature: *Basil*
Universe/Energy: *Look for a Divine Sign (action)*

438

You're fitting in with a new group of people instead of working one-on-one. You have an amazing sense of observation which is beneficial now. You're able to blend in and able to go unnoticed, which benefits your goal. You have the tools to turn a situation around to your benefit if necessary. Be careful that you don't flood others with too much personal information.

Messengers:

Animal: *Flying Fox*
Nature: *Monsoon*
Universe/Energy: *Ride a Bike (action)*

439

Prepare to travel with a group. Fill yourself with optimism. There's nothing you can do about a certain situation except to let the other people involved straighten it out. It's out of your hands. You've done what you could to help create a bridge between others. Now it's up to them.

Messengers:

Animal: *Chukar (bird)*
Nature: *Land Bridge*
Universe/Energy: *Optimism (feeling)*

440

You need to listen very closely to what is being said to you instead of ignoring the signs. Don't be superstitious at this time, instead, think clearly and consider all options. You have the inner strength and dignity to handle any circumstances that come your way.

Messengers:

Animal: *Kamori (mammal/goat)*
Nature: *Dahlia (plant/flower)*
Universe/Energy: *Superstition*

441

If you've felt like you've been dealing with a storm in your life, it is ending or is over. Now you can swim in the gentleness of life's water and bask in the warmth of the sun. You have learned lessons and will no longer intentionally release something or someone that is important to you or take things for granted.

Messengers:

Animal: *Leatherback Sea Turtle*
Nature: *Ivy (plant)*
Universe/Energy: *Mooing (Sound)*

442

Family, friends, and deep connections are of a high priority. You may be celebrating with lots of food and drink. Really enjoy being with those you care about while listening to what others want to discuss instead of just talking about things that are important to you. Take time each day to practice manifesting your desires.

Messengers:

Animal: *Brant (bird)*
Nature: *Henna (tree)*
Universe/Energy: *Mint (color)*

443

In the horse world you are what would be known as an *easy keeper*. Intelligent, quiet, dependable, and strong. It doesn't take much to meet your needs. You enjoy your work and do your best at your job. You have excellent vision for the future and long-range goals. You plan and act in a way that enables you to move forward with strength and dignity.

Messengers:

Animal: *Gypsy Vanner (equine)*
Nature: *Mung Bean*
Universe/Energy: *Value*

444

Pick something you're passionate about and weave a web to manifest it in your life. Be careful of getting caught up in a web of lies, either of your own making or someone else's. It will be hard to get out of it later. Everything is going to be all right, you just have to give it time.

Messengers:

Animal: *Orb Weaver (spider)*
Nature: *Belgian Endive*
Universe/Energy: *Passion*

445

Hyperactivity is prevalent now. You may feel hyped up to get a project finished or to start something new. Whatever you desire, you must actively make it happen. Respect other people's opinions along the way through open communication and expression of ideas. Wash off any negative energy surrounding you that is holding you back from flowing with the underlying positive currents.

Messengers:

Animal: *Lorikeet (bird)*
Nature: *Seaweed*
Universe/Energy: *Play in a sprinkler (action)*

446

Are you having enough fun in your life? Or are you busy getting errands done like shopping in the market, cleaning the house or taking care of family when you have free time? Instead of only doing what you *have* to do, try doing something fun that you *want* to do.

Messengers:

Animal: *Red Squirrel*
Nature: *Lithop (plant/succulent)*
Universe/Energy: *Visit a Farmer's Market (action)*

447

You are nurturing and care deeply about others. Make sure you're caring the same way about yourself instead of putting your needs last or ignoring them altogether. Don't ignore potential danger that may be around you, instead, take action to keep you and your family safe. Be aware of toxic people.

Messengers:

Animal: *Orca (whale)*
Nature: *Willow Oak (tree)*
Universe/Energy: *Squish (sound)*

448

Are you being nosy? Trying to find out gossip about people you know? Back up and pay attention to your own life instead. Be wise and avoid getting pulled into a gossip circle. This is a good time to focus on working on opening your third eye to increase your higher consciousness, frequency, and enlightenment.

Messengers:

Animal: *Proboscis Monkey*
Nature: *Tephra (rock)*
Universe/Energy: *Karma*

449

You have a strong bite and are quick to defend yourself and others. You're a hunter who can find what is hiding. Your intuition is keen, and you use it on a daily basis. You're coming into a time of financial growth and opportunity. Pay attention and be highly motivated to make the changes needed in your life to be successful. Someone may disagree with your choices.

Messengers:

Animal: *Ferret*
Nature: *Tiffany Stone*
Universe/Energy: *Ginger (scent)*

450

Get outside and enjoy the energy and high frequency created by the next full moon. This is also a good time to practice dowsing. Balance is important now. Are you closing yourself off from other people too much and hiding inside your shell?

Messengers:

Animal: *Scallops (mollusk)*
Nature: *Watercress*
Universe/Energy: *Dowsing*

451

Keep your mind occupied so you don't get bored or feel sluggish. The greatest gains can be made with your mind. Ideas can be sparked by unrelated actions. Make note of and follow up on them. Many successful ventures start when one recognizes a need they can fill.

Messengers:

Animal: *Bonito (fish)*
Nature: *Rutabaga (vegetable)*
Universe/Energy: *Cranberry (color)*

452

If you had to describe your essential nature, what would you say? Write it down. How do the choices you make affect you? Are you running free or are you entwined so deeply around something else that you can't break loose? Examine yourself closely and then change what you want to be different in your life.

Messengers:

Animal: *Andalusian (equine)*
Nature: *Running Cedar*
Universe/Energy: *Bake Cookies*

453

You tend to shy away from others and keep to yourself and prefer to just be left alone. You're peaceful and calm yet when provoked your bite can be deadly. You're highly intelligent and are often in a position of power in your work.

Messengers:

Animal: *Black Mamba (snake)*
Nature: *Fluorite (gemstone)*
Universe/Energy: *Alone Time*

454

You're in a cycle of rebirth. During this time, you may be more susceptible to allergies or colds so make sure you're boosting your immune system. Anything you've been working on that has stagnated will now flourish. Your spiritual self has transformed, and your new way of thinking gives a new energy to all that you do.

Messengers:

Animal: *Sand Scarab (insect)*
Nature: *Yellow Sweet Clover*
Universe/Energy: *Coughing (Sound)*

455

Climb, step by step, to fulfill your destiny. You have a great connection to the Divine through your intuition and increased frequency. Just when you think you know all there is to know about a topic, you'll discover new information. Learning never stops. Do not accept what others say, but instead listen to your own truth.

Messengers:

Animal: *Katydid (insect)*
Nature: *Wonderstone (rock)*
Universe/Energy: *Soft (sensation)*

456

It's time to create your best laid plans. Don't look at the final product just yet. You've got to get all the ingredients into the pot before you can see the outcome. Regardless of the type of project you're working on, look at the journey, the steps needed along the way, instead of solely focusing on the result.

Messengers:

Animal: *Horse Fly*
Nature: *Spinach*
Universe/Energy: *Owl hooting (sound)*

457

Even in difficult and intense conditions, you manage to not only survive, but to thrive. You know how to store things for a rainy day, how to stay strong to endure challenging times, and what to say to those around you to encourage them to do the same. You take the time to calculate what is needed in the long run, not just for today.

Messengers:

Animal: *Common Goldeneye (bird)*
Nature: *Bunny Ear Cactus*
Universe/Energy: *Electric (sensation)*

458

Pay attention to your dreams. If you are having a tough time remembering them, keep a journal on your nightstand so you can write down everything you remember upon waking. There are messages and purpose behind what you're dreaming right now. An event will set off feelings of fight-or-flight within you. Stay calm and evaluate before acting.

Messengers:

Animal: *Gecko (reptile)*
Nature: *Raisin*
Universe/Energy: *Om (sound)*

459

You like maintaining control in all you do. Safety is a number one priority in your life, and you will seek out places where you feel the safest. You're also concerned with financial safety and are working to secure a bright financial future. It is not unusual for you to seek alone time often where you can work on your spiritual self in seclusion.

Messengers:

Animal: *Mink (mammal)*
Nature: *Chrysoberyl (gemstone)*
Universe/Energy: *Red (Color)*

460

Do not be blinded by parasites clinging to you. When you look deeply at others and their motives, you may realize that all isn't as it first seems. It's easy to be blindsided by others when you trust completely. In this case a surprise is not what you need right now.

Messengers:

Animal: *Greenland Shark*
Nature: *English Walnut*
Universe/Energy: *Surprise*

461

Your senses are very accurate and heightened, especially your sixth sense. Look, listen, and act on them. If you receive a vague or unclear impression, you can use oracle or tarot cards as a means of confirming what you've received when you aren't completely sure of its accuracy. Pull the card. Avoid second guessing yourself.

Messengers:

Animal: *Impala (antelope)*
Nature: *Canada Thistle*
Universe/Energy: *Clatter of coins (sound)*

462

Live in appreciation and gratitude of what you've been given in life as you strive to become even more successful. Look to the past for encouragement. You tend to be more active during the day than night. Rising early helps you accomplish more.

Messengers:

Animal: *Chuckwalla (reptile)*
Nature: *Ayre (landform)*
Universe/Energy: *Gratitude*

463

Make a decision and see it through. Expect the unexpected. Exciting changes are on the horizon. Seize sudden opportunities. It's not going to happen without your participation. Stop putting things off and just get the work done. You'll resolve any problems that arise with ease.

Messengers:

Animal: *Antelope*
Nature: *Lime (fruit)*
Universe/Energy: *Ambition*

464

Don't get too big for your britches. Don't think you're so important that others must treat you in special ways. Conceit is a negative energy that sets you apart from others because they will not like you or enjoy being in your company. Instead, ground yourself and take a good, hard look at how you interact with others and how you present yourself to the world.

Messengers:

Animal: *Milk Fish*
Nature: *Blackthorn (tree)*
Universe/Energy: *Dew (Scent)*

465

Prepare to look at something in a new way. There are important things happening to you right now, surprising things, and they will bring about joy and happiness. You may discover that you're more emotionally intense, more positive and elated. Your life has been painted in colors that you embrace. Enjoy!

Messengers:

Animal: *Paint Horse*
Nature: *Rose Mallow (plant)*
Universe/Energy: *Gasp of Surprise (Sound)*

466

It's important to be adaptable and to move with the winds of change. You're a survivor so this will be easy. You will find happiness in places you least expected it. Be aware that someone is trying to be sneaky, but you'll see what's really going on. Just don't ruin a surprise that is for you by letting others know you already figured it out.

Messengers:

Animal: *Cuttlefish*
Nature: *Wind*
Universe/Energy: *Happiness*

467

You have the ability to open your mouth so wide that your foot fits in there with ease. If you keep speaking before you think you could be in for quite the shock. There is a lot of interest in something you're doing so pay close attention. You may have the opportunity to sell something you've created, start a business, or become partners with someone.

Messengers:

Animal: *Marbled Electric Ray*
Nature: *Petrified Wood*
Universe/Energy: *Interest*

468

Become more sensitive to what makes you feel vulnerable. When you do, your survival instincts kick in and show you how to make positive changes. Understanding the why behind the reasons for these feelings helps strengthen you. Feel the positive energy around you and draw it into you, allowing it to move through your body and soul.

Messengers:

Animal: *Rainbow Lizard*
Nature: *Tomatillo (fruit)*
Universe/Energy: *Thunder (sound)*

469

A spiritual quest is in your near future where you will discover a deeper connection to your inner strength and universal wisdom. Expect the experience to bring about profound changes. There will be like-minded souls involved whose knowledge will aid in your spiritual growth. Stop and pay attention to the details.

Messengers:

Animal: *Emu (bird)*
Nature: *Rain*
Universe/Energy: *Settled (feeling)*

470

Behind the beauty is poison. This is a time to tread carefully. Be careful what you touch and who you trust. Some mysteries are easy to uncover if you look close enough and do research. You may need to take quick action if you're fooled or don't realize the danger at first. Be careful.

Messengers:

Animal: *Gnu (mammal)*
Nature: *Foxglove*
Universe/Energy: *Menthol (scent)*

471

Your soul is craving a connection to water. If you haven't visited a lake or beach in a while, this is a good time to do so. Soak in a tub, visit a swimming pool, or just sit by a creek. The high frequency of water will soothe you and satisfy your spiritual self.

Messengers:

Animal: *Merganser (bird)*
Nature: *Swiss Cheese Plant*
Universe/Energy: *Metallic bronze (color)*

472

Part of your life purpose is to engage others in the act of increasing their frequency and understanding their responsibilities to bring light and love to the earthly plane. You are divine, you are enlightened, and you share this with others without feeling that you are above or better than anyone else. You are light.

Messengers:

Animal: *Plains Wanderer (bird)*
Nature: *Corn*
Universe/Energy: *Midnight Sun (phenomenon)*

473

Taking the blame when things fall apart and giving credit to others when things go right is the sign of a great leader. You're able to hold people together in good times and bad. They look up to you for your fairness and honesty. Stay the path because you're helping more people than you even realize through your actions.

Messengers:

Animal: *Cairns Birdwing Butterfly*
Nature: *Hazelnut*
Universe/Energy: *Prowess (action)*

474

Something is causing an itch that you just can't get to go away. Take a minute to seek validation from the Universe to uncover what it is. If you need to take some time off work because you've been burning the candle at both ends, then do it.

Messengers:

Animal: *Lice (parasite)*
Nature: *Okra (vegetable)*
Universe/Energy: *Validation*

475

Adaptation is at the forefront now. You may need to make changes that you weren't anticipating, but they will be beneficial in the end. This is a time of walking between worlds, of showing others how to access their true spiritual being in order to grow on their own paths. You are the teacher who comes when the student is ready.

Messengers:

Animal: *Holstein Cow*
Nature: *Hydrillia (plant)*
Universe/Energy: *Notice your world (action)*

476

Use imagery to create a visual landscape in your mind of what you want to accomplish today. When you can create pictures with words you enable yourself to see things you might have overlooked. Write it down, then read it aloud to yourself. Doing this exercise in the early morning will help you stay on track all day.

Messengers:

Animal: *Frilled Lizard*
Nature: *Dawn*
Universe/Energy: *Imagery*

477

Slow it down, you're moving too fast. It's fine to be persistent and determined but when you fly through life at a breakneck speed, you miss the little things that make memorable moments. You're connected to ancient wisdom, so you know what to do.

Messengers:

Animal: *Turtle*
Nature: *Shagbark Hickory Tree*
Universe/Energy: *Originality*

478

Some physical work is hard. Some spiritual work is even harder. Don't give up but stay true in your determination to understand your spiritual self. Facing your fears, inadequacies, or other negative feelings takes a brave and caring attitude.

Messengers:

Animal: *Kelp Gull*
Nature: *Cascade (topography)*
Universe/Energy: *Perseverance*

479

Your words reach a wide range of people. Don't underestimate the importance of what you have to say. Are you terrified of speaking to groups? That may be exactly what you need to do to get over your fear and to reach more people. Your words can be transformational to others because you are able to touch the light within them.

Messengers:

Animal: *Bufo Toad*
Nature: *Glen (topography)*
Universe/Energy: *Buoyant (sensation)*

480

Blend in instead of drawing attention to yourself. Now is the time to be unnoticed and to stay in the background. Spend some time alone. Reconnect with your energy by connecting to the energy of water. Try to be consistent in your actions.

Messengers:

Animal: *Moose*
Nature: *Rock Pit*
Universe/Energy: *Leaves crunching under your feet (sound)*

481

You can intuitively see things in the past as they truly were and not as those involved thought they were at the time. You may feel hunted or as if others are out to get you when they're not. This is a time of revitalization, of letting go.

Messengers:

Animal: *Caracal (feline)*
Nature: *Black Beans*
Universe/Energy: *Retrocognition*

482

Be on alert for a negative verbal or psychic attack. Stand your ground. Now is also the time to venture out and see more of the world either by yourself or with a small group. This will renew your sense of awe and wonder and will help you to no longer take things, or people, for granted.

Messengers:

Animal: *Porcupine*
Nature: *Titan Arum (plant)*
Universe/Energy: *Grounded (feeling)*

483

To find the frequency within you, seek that which compels, intrigues, and excites you. These are spiritual treasures that will open a new world of knowledge for you. As your frequency increases, you'll find that you'll lead others through your actions.

Messengers:

Animal: *Mule Deer*
Nature: *Water Vapor*
Universe/Energy: *Discovery*

484

In today's technology age, unplugging from your phone for a while is necessary. When you're constantly on the phone your expectations of yourself and of others can get skewed. Just because someone doesn't answer you immediately should not affect your self-esteem in any way. Instant gratification can become a negative energy if you let it.

Messengers:

Animal: *Saiga Antelope*
Nature: *Tomato*
Universe/Energy: *Expectation (feeling)*

485

Free your creative energy though art. You can make beautiful sculptures, paintings, or statures using interesting materials and your hands. There's no need to barricade yourself inside a room to do this. Instead, find a place outside where the sun can reflect your energy as you create a masterpiece of your own design.

Messengers:

Animal: *Blue Whale*
Nature: *Sea Cave*
Universe/Energy: *Turquoise Ice (phenomenon at Lake Baikal)*

486

You're carrying a load that is too heavy, irritating, and taking a toll on you. Eventually you'll collapse under its weight. It's time to set it aside for a minute. Consider why you're carrying this burden. Is there any of it that you can leave behind? Can you share it with someone else to ease the weight? Keeping things inside isn't always the best idea.

Messengers:

Animal: *Alpaca*
Nature: *Meadow*
Universe/Energy: *Pale blue (color)*

487

Hold your head up in trying times. Let the lightning around you energize and lift you up instead of sending you running out of the storm. Face what is happening with a fresh enthusiasm and optimism. Spots are not stains; they are delightful patterns that bring joy.

Messengers:

Animal: *Appaloosa (equine)*
Nature: *Volcanic Lightning*
Universe/Energy: *Palo Santo (scent)*

488

Humor can diffuse a tense situation. Awareness of the sharks in your midst will help you keep the advantage. Sometimes a lighter approach will work best when emotions are running high instead of questioning in a defensive manner. Don't take yourself too seriously either. What's good for others is also good for you.

Messengers:

Animal: *Lemon Shark*
Nature: *Static Electricity*
Universe/Energy: *Aware*

489

You're a social person but haven't been spending much time with friends lately. Let healing energy move over you to help you find the centered balance that you need. Emotional thinking can drain you. This is a time for new beginnings and letting go of emotional and physical things that are no longer serving your greater good.

Messengers:

Animal: *Black Rat*
Nature: *Cornflower*
Universe/Energy: *Healing*

490

Don't hold anger in your heart. Forgive and move on. When your song is bright and cheerful, then your draw more goodness to you. You may have the opportunity to sell something you've created or become partners with someone. Look at all options before making a decision.

Messengers:

Animal: *Eastern Bluebird*
Nature: *Switch Grass*
Universe/Energy: *Frankincense (scent)*

491

Right now, it seems like you have your hands in everything. Super busy doesn't even begin to describe your day. It feels as if there is a flurry of motion going on constantly. It's time to slow things down otherwise you'll start to dread the work you do. Look to the future because positive energy is headed your way and opportunities along with it.

Messengers:

Animal: *Feather Star (marine invertebrate)*
Nature: *Twinned Rainbow*
Universe/Energy: *Crisp Linen (scent)*

492

You may not want to hear it, you may not want to change, but someone is about to give you some very sound advice. Pay attention to their words. This is someone who you respect and who you look up too. They're not going to guide you down the wrong path. What they're saying to you is with your best interest in mind.

Messengers:

Animal: *Leopard Cat (feline)*
Nature: *Hibiscus (plant)*
Universe/Energy: *Respect*

493

Good fortune, joy, and abundance surround you. You may be on the receiving end of someone else's generosity. Be thankful and appreciative if you are. The energy surrounding you is very potent and is filled with positivity and light. This is the perfect time to create new affirmations, visualizations, and for connecting to the wisdom of the Divine.

Messengers:

Animal: *Black Angus (cattle)*
Nature: *Topaz (gemstone)*
Universe/Energy: *Cinnamon (Scent)*

494

Look for messages in nature and in the weather patterns. Spend time along the coast enjoying the connection to the water and the animals that live nearby. It's time for you to wander a while, to really relate to the solitude of being alone. Paint what you see and feel on a canvas or with words in a journal.

Messengers:

Animal: *Albatross (bird)*
Nature: *Coast*
Universe/Energy: *Painting*

495

Opportunity is knocking. Open the door. Look at life from a new perspective. Change, growth, quick decisions, and persistence in reaching goals is important now. You could be easily irritated, which could also cause you to be annoying to others, so stay focused and don't get distracted by little things.

Messengers:

Animal: *Fly (insect)*
Nature: *Gneiss Hornfels (rock)*
Universe/Energy: *Pine green (color)*

496

You are built for speed and don't hesitate to act quickly. Be vigilant. Sometimes waiting is the hardest part. Seeds need to grow before they can be harvested and that applies to what you're going through right now. Yes, it's a waiting game but the benefits will be a blessing to you.

Messengers:

Animal: *Merlin (bird/falcon)*
Nature: *Hogback (topography)*
Universe/Energy: *Birds Singing (Sound)*

497

Are you disappointed or overwhelmed? Maybe you've just gotten out of a difficult situation and haven't bounced back yet. It takes some time to adjust to a new way of being after overcoming obstacles. If you can't fly yet, you can still climb, you can still walk and talk. Little by little you'll find your song again. Give it time.

Messengers:

Animal: *Kakapo (bird/parrot)*
Nature: *Tornado*
Universe/Energy: *Melon (Color)*

498

If you find yourself in a group situation keep a physical distance that is slightly apart until you can understand the current group dynamics. Only then can you plan accordingly for your own future. Others might object to your plans, but you must do what you feel is right for yourself and your own spiritual path.

Messengers:

Animal: *Patagonian Mara (rodent)*
Nature: *Leaf*
Universe/Energy: *Bubblegum (Scent)*

499

Your intuition needs your attention. Listen to the impressions you receive. This is not a time for doubt but instead a time for trusting your inner self. Look for meaning in everything to learn more about your abilities. This is a time of discovering balance and harmony and the freedom that being grounded within your spirituality brings to you. Bloom in your belief.

Messengers:

Animal: *Dolphin*
Nature: *Water Poppy (plant)*
Universe/Energy: *Purity*

500

Plant now so you can reap and sow in preparation for the winter. This isn't the time to leech off someone else. You must prepare your own stores for your table. Don't expect others to take care of you if you're not trying to take care of yourself.

Messengers:

Animal: *Jaeger (sea bird)*
Nature: *Rhodonite (gemstone)*
Universe/Energy: *Quiet (sound)*

501

One of your intuitive abilities is clairsentience which means clear feeling. It is the ability to connect to energetic vibrations and obtain information about the past, present, or future. As you feel the energy flowing through you pay special attention to any visions that may come along with the message which will clarify the meaning.

Messengers:

Animal: *Blind Snake*
Nature: *Sundew (plants)*
Universe/Energy: *Clairsentience*

502

It's time to get back to your intuitive roots. You've strayed away from your beliefs and have sometimes felt like a fish out of water because of it. Ignoring your abilities will not make them go away. Acceptance and understanding of yourself and your connection to the Divine is necessary. It doesn't matter if other people don't believe your intuition, you must believe in them yourself.

Messengers:

Animal: *Arowana (fish)*
Nature: *Malanga (vegetable)*
Universe/Energy: *Propose a new concept (action)*

503

Your friendly and mystical nature draws people to you. A lot of people. They sense your inner light and want to be where you are. Just remember that your interaction with them and the words spoken may be exactly what they need at this moment in time.

Messengers:

Animal: *Seal (mammal)*
Nature: *Aspen (tree)*
Universe/Energy: *Amber (Color)*

504

You're raising your frequency! Your energy is moving in an upward motion, and you may feel as if you're lagging behind. Have a keen focus to engage with the higher levels of energy that you're connecting to on your path. You're courageous and are no longer hiding behind the masks you used to wear. You're leaving behind negative thinking and bad habits or patterns.

Messengers:

Animal: *Lionfish*
Nature: *Epidote (mineral)*
Universe/Energy: *Evaluate your frequency (action)*

505

Lighten up. You're coming across as defensive and arrogant when you're not that way at all. Look at your actions. Don't take yourself so seriously because you're making your stress levels go through the roof. Take a moment to step back, relax, and organize your thoughts.

Messengers:

Animal: *Skunk*
Nature: *Morning Glory (plant)*
Universe/Energy: *Basketball Bouncing (Sound)*

506

Are you coming across as too abrasive? This is not a time for bluntness but a time for choosing your words wisely. You want to be helpful, not disregarded because your attitude is too strong. If you've been separated from family for too long, it's time for a visit home.

Messengers:

Animal: *Pacman Frog*
Nature: *Corundum (gemstone)*
Universe/Energy: *Intimate (feeling)*

507

With the help of nature spirits, you have a sacred connection to the Divine. You are surrounded with light, positivity, and goodness. You make the most of every situation you're involved in and often lift others up along the way. For you it's not just about bringing out the best in yourself, but it is just as important to bring out the best in others.

Messengers:

Animal: *Quetzal (bird)*
Nature: *Hickory Nut*
Universe/Energy: *Nature Spirits*

508

This is a happy time in your life and you're often just chattering away without realizing how much you're talking. It's hard to contain so much joyful excitement. You stay away from those who have an irritable or angry attitude just because you just don't want that negativity in your life right now.

Messengers:

Animal: *Grackle (bird)*
Nature: *Chrysoprase (gemstone)*
Universe/Energy: *People laughing (sound)*

509

If it feels like your space has been invaded by a plethora of people lately then it's time to get away for a while. Take an impromptu weekend vacation. Or jump in the car and drive. There will be many opportunities to see beauty along the way. You need time to rest, relax, and to center yourself without too many people around.

Messengers:

Animal: *Nutria Rat*
Nature: *Camellia (plant)*
Universe/Energy: *Devotion*

510

When it comes to understanding your spirituality, there are many gateways through which you will pass. Each of these are steppingstones to getting closer to your true spirituality. The more you know, the more want to know. In the ice storms of life there is still beauty shimmering and reflecting in all that you see.

Messengers:

Animal: *Sanderling (bird)*
Nature: *Ice Storm*
Universe/Energy: *Connect with your soul song (action)*

511

You live in the moment with boldness, patience, and persistence. Courage, strength, and beauty embrace you and embolden you. Accept your uniqueness for your power runs deep. You know yourself well and see others for who they truly are. Be aware of the effect you have on others for your strength makes them nervous and uncomfortable at times.

Messengers:

Animal: *Leopard (feline)*
Nature: *Petal*
Universe/Energy: *Black Spruce (scent)*

512

Good fortune is yours. Your frequency is sparking, jolting, and rapidly increasing. Hang on for an interesting ride. Find a power spot near you where you can hang out and purposefully increase your frequency even more. This is also a time of reconnecting to things from your youth, being part of a group yet maintaining your individuality, and not yielding to peer pressure.

Messengers:

Animal: *Minnow*
Nature: *Sand boil (topography)*
Universe/Energy: *St. Elmo's Fire (phenomenon)*

513

You're a social bird who loves to flitter from place to place just for the sheer enjoyment of it. This isn't a time to be content to hide within your shell, instead get out and about and have fun. Skiing, whether in snow or water, will be exhilarating and exciting. Or choose a different sport to enjoy. Be independent instead of becoming too dependent or clinging on someone else.

Messengers:

Animal: *Northern Bobwhite Quail (bird)*
Nature: *Pistachio*
Universe/Energy: *Winter Sky (color)*

514

You're aware that time is passing by and it's kind of freaking you out a little bit. Don't worry, it'll be all right. You'll be able to accomplish what you need to do within your deadline. Just take a deep breath, keep *to do* lists in your mind, and stay the course. Occasionally take a break, have some strawberries, or pet a pony or other animal. You're okay.

Messengers:

Animal: *Shetland Pony*
Nature: *Strawberry*
Universe/Energy: *Gallant*

515

You're the life of the party, enjoying fun times. Good things are flowing to you in waves right now. Enjoy it! You've been through a few difficulties in the recent past and now you're getting a welcome reprieve from those times. If you find things are slipping your mind, make a list.

Messengers:

Animal: *Dory (fish)*
Nature: *Mint*
Universe/Energy: *Cotton Candy (Scent)*

516

Be bold, brash, and sure of yourself. You're moving rapidly and juggling several things at once. Pay attention to details, they are important and if you miss something it could throw a wrench in your plans. Brainstorming and working together for a quick result are important.

Messengers:

Animal: *Ermine (mammal/weasel)*
Nature: *Golden Pothos (plant)*
Universe/Energy: *Heartbeat (Sound)*

517

Teasing, cheekiness, playfulness, and a light and airy energy is around you. You're living in the moment and having a wonderful time. You are experiencing new things and enjoying every minute of it. Being a little nutty is a welcome stress reliever. Make sure to take some quiet time to recharge and then get back to the festivities.

Messengers:

Animal: *Kea (bird/parrot)*
Nature: *Cashew*
Universe/Energy: *Stillness after a Snowstorm (Sound)*

518

Money matters are taking center stage. Make sure you're budgeting and not overspending. Put money away for a rainy day. There is balance between what you have, what you need, and what you want. Find that to add security. You may feel a little isolated because you need to save, but it will pass.

Messengers:

Animal: *Cowries (mollusk)*
Nature: *Island*
Universe/Energy: *Chakras*

519

You are a seer who has blocked your abilities or who is denying them. It's time to cut open the barriers you've created and embrace your ability. You're graceful, intelligent, and very powerful. You may not feel it is your right to have this ability, but it is your destiny. You will help many when you embrace your gift.

Messengers:

Animal: *Lechwe (mammal/antelope)*
Nature: *Beryl (gemstone)*
Universe/Energy: *Define Yourself*

520

Fill the lightness of your spiritual being. Enjoy life to the fullest with friends and family. Avoid confrontation but stand up for yourself if needed. Avoid burning out by doing too much at once. Take some time to recharge even if it means just slowing down for a bit. Look for areas in your life that are stagnant and refresh them.

Messengers:

Animal: *Hummingbird*
Nature: *Standing Water*
Universe/Energy: *Carnations (Scent)*

521

Are you acting like a scavenger and looking for treasures? Have fun searching because you just might find something valuable that can spice up your bank account. A situation may arise where you need to remain impartial and refrain from passing judgment. Justice will be served but not by you. There are things happening in the background that you're not aware of.

Messengers:

Animal: *Snowy Sheathbill (bird)*
Nature: *Cardamom (spice)*
Universe/Energy: *Unity (feeling)*

522

Do you like the colors of yourself that are being reflected to the world? Are you bright and light or dark and dreary? It's time to put a little antiseptic on your wounds and change the dark to light. It may take some acceptance of yourself, some time spent basking in the sun to cleanse away the darkness, but you will shine brightly.

Messengers:

Animal: *Green Iguana*
Nature: *Witch Hazel*
Universe/Energy: *Engaged (feeling)*

523

There's a restlessness going on within you. It's burning and has you yearning for something, but you aren't sure what that something is. You are free to choose the direction you take once you settle. Be patient, it will come to you. Unexpected things are happening now.

Messengers:

Animal: *Gray Crowned Crane*
Nature: *Poison Ivy*
Universe/Energy: *The Unexpected*

524

Spread your wings wide to fly on your own. You have the confidence and belief in yourself to fly as high as you desire and to accomplish every goal you've set. Abundance and prosperity are around you now. Have faith that you will receive what is meant for you.

Messengers:

Animal: *Kori Bustard (bird)*
Nature: *Sunflower*
Universe/Energy: *Radiance (feeling)*

525

Life is what you interpret it to be. What is right for you may be wrong for someone else. It all depends on your perspective and understanding of the way your own spirituality works in the physical world. Smell the aromatic fragrances around you, let them become part of your essence. The energy of safety is abundant at this time.

Messengers:

Animal: *Arctic Tern (bird)*
Nature: *Cicely (herb)*
Universe/Energy: *Interpretation*

526

If you can't swim, you can still reach your destination by walking on your fins. There's always a way to get around something if you need to. Be inventive, creative, and think outside of the box. Listen for sounds that will signal messages from the other side. You'll be victorious on your journey.

Messengers:

Animal: *Monkfish*
Nature: *Cycad Plant*
Universe/Energy: *Take a step out of your comfort zone (action)*

527

You have a fighting spirit. You never give up even under the harshest criticism. You strive to stay connected to your emotions without losing control of them. You're linked to the Divine, to healing from within, and to moving forward with purpose.

Messengers:

Animal: *Cobia (fish)*
Nature: *Lizard's Tail (plant)*
Universe/Energy: *Complimentary*

528

Listen to your intuition to manifest your destiny. There is a wind blowing positive opportunities your way. Revel in its energy as it moves over you. Remain grounded and centered so you make the right moves. It will be easy to get caught up in the excitement of what is happening, which is fine, just don't lose your direction.

Messengers:

Animal: *Kingfisher (bird)*
Nature: *Gale Wind*
Universe/Energy: *Excitement*

529

You are connected to the spiritual realm and are receiving messages from those who have passed and your spirit guides. Pay close attention because you are on the path of hope, love, and renewal. Part of your path is that of teacher and caregiver, even if you don't realize that's what you're doing at the time.

Messengers:

Animal: *Cardinal*
Nature: *Giant Baobabs (tree)*
Universe/Energy: *Baby Laughing (Sound)*

530

You may think you are indestructible. That nothing can touch you, harm you, or cause you distress. Don't get too caught up in thinking you're a superhero with supreme powers. There is magick around you and in you, but you must balance it with the reality that you are a human living on the earthly plane. Proceed with caution.

Messengers:

Animal: *Tardigrade (micro-animal)*
Nature: *Exotic Angel Plant*
Universe/Energy: *Tea Tree (scent)*

531

You understand deep subject matters that others may find a bit hard to grasp. Sometimes a simple explanation is better but other times a well exampled description gives a clearer picture. If it's still not understood, try again at a different time. Be careful of poisonous plants and remove any that you find.

Messengers:

Animal: *Frilled Shark*
Nature: *Black Nightshade (plant)*
Universe/Energy: *Timer Beeping (Sound)*

532

There's a tendency to be loud and annoying lately. Whether that tendency is within you or is coming from someone else, it needs to stop. Instead of circling around your intention just come right out and say it. Make sure to be proactive when it comes to protecting yourself from injury. It's best to be safe now than sorry later.

Messengers:

Animal: *Guinea Fowl*
Nature: *Avocado*
Universe/Energy: *Apricot (scent)*

533

This is a time for studying, taking exams, and using your imagination to produce creative solutions to problems. Yes, you're working hard right now and have little time for socializing or goofing off. That will come later. Don't waste time on negative thoughts but instead be enthusiastic, lively, and excited about the life you're living.

Messengers:

Animal: *American Goldfinch (bird)*
Nature: *Muscovite (mineral)*
Universe/Energy: *Imagination*

534

Are you adapting to the changes happening in your life or are you holding back because you're afraid? Transformation is happening now so you might as well accept that the energy around you is elevating. Motivate yourself to match your frequency with the frequency around you to raise it and gain a clear insight into your own spiritual essence.

Messengers:

Animal: *Leopard Gecko*
Nature: *Parsley*
Universe/Energy: *Motivation*

535

Are you swimming on the bottom of the pond and ignoring what's going on in the world around you? Caution is necessary so you don't get caught out of your waters. But being overly cautious will have negative results. You're going through a time of self-discovery and positive change. Look at all aspects of your world as you learn more about yourself.

Messengers:

Animal: *Channel Catfish*
Nature: *Green Beans*
Universe/Energy: *Fluid (sensation)*

536

Are you breaking the speed of sound with your thoughts? Is there so much going on in your mind that you just feel overwhelmed and anxious? Find a quiet place where you can compartmentalize your thoughts and get organized. If you need to write down notes, then do so. Find a place to sit where there are plants because their energy will stabilize yours.

Messengers:

Animal: *Mulgara (marsupial)*
Nature: *Ficus Lyrata Plant*
Universe/Energy: *Airplane taking off / landing (Sound)*

537

Connecting to the Divine through an interaction with nature will enable you to not only raise your frequency but to use your own internal vibrations to heal what distresses you. Your higher self is reaching out to you to show you the way. Raise your voice in song to enhance the Divine link. You will grow stronger now.

Messengers:

Animal: *Rock Dove (bird)*
Nature: *Wilderness*
Universe/Energy: *Vibrational Healing*

538

If you never let anything, go, then nothing new can come into your life. To live to your fullest potential there must always be an ebb and flow where you collect things and then let them go when they're no longer needed. Light a fire within yourself to get started.

Messengers:

Animal: *Pack Rat*
Nature: *Andesite Basalt (volcanic rock)*
Universe/Energy: *Lighting A Match (Sound)*

539

The bigger your aspirations, the better. There is no limit to what you can achieve. Remain calm and have a soothing manner with those around you. Speak softly and embrace silences in the conversations. Innovative ideas will pop up unexpectedly. Write them down so you don't forget them.

Messengers:

Animal: *Percheron (equine)*
Nature: *Calm Air*
Universe/Energy: *Glorious (feeling)*

540

You can dominate a room with your presence. Every eye seems to be on you as soon as you walk through the door. You radiate power and strength, which causes people to look up to you and seek your advice. You're a skilled conversationalist. Listen to the words in your dreams. There's a message there that is being repeated. Pay attention.

Messengers:

Animal: *Blue Bull (mammal/antelope)*
Nature: *Costmary (plant)*
Universe/Energy: *Dream*

541

Choose a spiritual wellness system to participate in that will help you distribute energy throughout your body. Consider reflexology, reiki, acupuncture, crystal healing, yoga, or another system to help you. It is important to engage yourself at all levels to jump to great heights.

Messengers:

Animal: *Lipizzan (equine)*
Nature: *Tangelo (fruit)*
Universe/Energy: *Spacious (feeling)*

542

It is especially important to ground yourself, find your center and learn from whatever is affecting your emotions so deeply at this time. If the emotion is negative, release it in a controlled way, not in an explosion. If you explode, you may experience the end of something that you don't really want to end.

Messengers:

Animal: *Gelada Baboon*
Nature: *Volcano*
Universe/Energy: *Near Death Experience*

543

Discretion is needed now. Keep your mouth closed instead of blabbing all you know. Some stories are not yours to tell. Leave those stories to the people who experienced it to tell the tale. You're wise and people often come to you for advice, but it is imperative that you keep the secrets of others just as you would keep your own.

Messengers:

Animal: *Crane (bird)*
Nature: *Wheat*
Universe/Energy: *Warm Apple Cider (Scent)*

544

Your inner self knows the path you must take, all you have to do is walk it. Intuitive visions are strong so be attentive to what you see. Find balance between your spiritual and physical worlds. Live a better life by being wise and making well thought out decisions.

Messengers:

Animal: *Great White Shark*
Nature: *Desert Rose (mineral)*
Universe/Energy: *Contribution*

545

Fiercely loyal, you'll never give up on others. Love, tenderness, and your supportive nature draw people to you. Look to the innocence of your youth to maintain control over the present. Some solutions need extra thinking time to produce the right answer. Don't decide just yet.

Messengers:

Animal: *Kawakawa Looper (Insect)*
Nature: *Dusk*
Universe/Energy: *Alternative*

546

This is a time to further develop your intuitive abilities. You're a fast learner who needs the stimulation of constant education. You've grown so much spiritually that now you can shine for others to see. Nurture others but don't forget to nurture yourself.

Messengers:

Animal: *Caiman (reptile)*
Nature: *Butternut Squash*
Universe/Energy: *Enlightened*

547

You're hard to catch, a mystery to unravel, and easy to love. This is a time to move slowly and with deliberate action. People will speak freely because they forget you're right there listening. Valuable information can be discovered through your silence.

Messengers:

Animal: *Pintail (duck)*
Nature: *Cove*
Universe/Energy: *Tolerance*

548

Push any obstacles out of your way. They may bind you, keep you at arm's length and prevent you from attaining what you desire. You have the strength to overcome and move forward to your goal. Trust your own judgement and stand on your own two feet.

Messengers:

Animal: *Elephant*
Nature: *Wetlands*
Universe/Energy: *Veil to the Other Side*

549

Majestic, bold, and brave. Your energy is at a high frequency which enables you to fly to great heights. You represent authority, daring, and can rise above difficulties. You have excellent organizational, communication, and people skills. Prosperity and well-being are prevalent now.

Messengers:

Animal: *Sea Eagle (bird)*
Nature: *Pumpkin*
Universe/Energy: *Microburst (phenomenon)*

550

Sometimes you must take the good with the bad. A situation may have turned and is no longer beneficial to your life. This could be a job or relationship. Look at it calmly and decide if it's time to let it go. Be diligent, keep your workspace orderly, and increase communication to progress toward your goals.

Messengers:

Animal: *Tarantula Hawk (wasp)*
Nature: *Rhubarb (vegetable)*
Universe/Energy: *Calmness*

551

Endurance and persistence are two of your top qualities. Giving up isn't an option. You don't hesitate to jump right into work, to help even if it's something not assigned to you. Mental stimulation is necessary to keep you grounded because you get bored easily. You're always up for a challenge.

Messengers:

Animal: *Arabian (equine)*
Nature: *Shale (rock)*
Universe/Energy: *Daring (feeling)*

552

You are the foundation of your family, what holds it all together during tough times and good times. Your patience, kindness and caring nature go a long way to making others feel at home in your life. You'll pull someone under your wing in a minute if you can help them in some way.

Messengers:

Animal: *Belgian (equine)*
Nature: *Bedrock*
Universe/Energy: *Wisteria (Scent)*

553

You often take matters into your own hands and deal with problems alone. You're confident, a fighter who doesn't give up without a struggle, and you have lots of stamina. You're not easily embarrassed and will put yourself out there without worrying about how you appear to others. With you, what they see is what they get and that's just the way you like it.

Messengers:

Animal: *Yellowfin Tuna*
Nature: *Tea Plant*
Universe/Energy: *Citronella (scent)*

554

Your adventurous spirit makes you want to wander. You feel driven to explore the world, to travel to distant shores, or visit a place that's a short car drive away. This is your inner spirit needing time to be set free in the natural world to experience the beauty of a waterfall or mountain. Explore phenomenon occurring in space through media.

Messengers:

Animal: *Smelt (fish)*
Nature: *Waterfall*
Universe/Energy: *Nebula*

555

Someone close to you needs you. Remember you can be kind and tough at the same time and that's what is needed now. Intuitive visions guide you. Pay attention to them. A fierce gentleness is necessary. Find your balance, know your true self. Instead of hibernating step out into the world and experience life to the fullest.

Messengers:

Animal: *Bear*
Nature: *Persimmon*
Universe/Energy: *Muse*

556

To feel a sense of deep accomplishment, you must first be in harmony with yourself. Honesty and a profound sense of moral responsibility guide you. Expressing your inner truth by living it is the best way to inspire self-confidence. You'll be successful through perseverance.

Messengers:

Animal: *African Wild Dog*
Nature: *Poinsettia (plant)*
Universe/Energy: *Pride (emotion)*

557

Study your situation and make a plan of action before taking flight so you don't find yourself in an embarrassing or compromising position. Taking time to relax instead of constantly working or doing for others is a priority now. Spend some time doing nothing to revitalize your body, mind, and spirit.

Messengers:

Animal: *Flying Dragon (reptile)*
Nature: *Cilantro*
Universe/Energy: *Hot Cocoa (Scent)*

558

Invasive and intimidating. Are you being this way lately? Are you being nosy, gossiping, or just putting yourself in other people's situations when you don't really belong there? If you are, then it's time to stop. Think about what is really going on in your life that is making you invade other people's lives. Let go of negative behavior to raise your frequency.

Messengers:

Animal: *Snakehead (fish)*
Nature: *Mamey Sapote (fruit)*
Universe/Energy*: Rosewood (color)*

559

Take things at face value instead of looking for a hidden agenda. Reclaim your inner power by fine-tuning your intuitive abilities and let them guide you. Being secure, self-confident, and independent is important at this time. Do not be afraid to take a risk and go after what you want.

Messengers:

Animal: *Jaguar (feline)*
Nature: *Hill*
Universe/Energy: *Sienna (color)*

560

If things are changing and you don't know how to handle them, then it's time to sit down and look at the reasons you may feel stressed and anxious. When you're afraid of change, you are only seeing the bad things that could happen, not the good. Look for the positives instead.

Messengers:

Animal: *Shire (equine)*
Nature: *Tourmaline (gemstone)*
Universe/Energy: *Industrious*

561

If your life has gotten out of control with too many bills, too much clutter, and too many events that you must attend, then it's time to simplify. Sell whatever you don't need that's eating up your money, say no to invitations, and throw away or donate the clutter around you. When you're finished, you'll feel lighter and happier.

Messengers:

Animal: *Tadpole*
Nature: *Pummelo (fruit)*
Universe/Energy: *Perspective*

562

For you, the veil between worlds is thinning. Your intuition is growing by leaps and bounds. Awareness of those with a cold nature is imperative. Don't believe everything they say. You're intelligent, shrewd, and it's hard to trick you. That doesn't mean people aren't going to try. Show compassion but let them know, in a subtle way, that what they're trying to do isn't working.

Messengers:

Animal: *Arctic Wolf*
Nature: *Winter*
Universe/Energy: *Intuition*

563

You're going through a period of highs and lows. Don't feel sorry for yourself. You are bright, ambitious, and have a lot to offer. You have the courage to bravely fight for what you believe in even in precarious conditions. The situation will stabilize soon. Remain loyal to those around you and avoid conspiring against others. You know the truth in your heart. Follow it.

Messengers:

Animal: *Hake (fish)*
Nature: *Glade Thistle (plant)*
Universe/Energy: *Luminous (feeling)*

564

You're extremely sensitive to the energy around you, especially the energy of others. You don't have to see what is happening because you have an innate knowing through energy. Touching objects gives even more intuitive insight and can help uncover hidden information. To find balance, work in the soil, plant a garden, or pull weeds.

Messengers:

Animal: *Mole Shrew*
Nature: *Log Fern*
Universe/Energy: *Piano playing (sound)*

565

Your leadership skills are at the forefront. There is turbulence at your job and it's up to you to straighten out the problem. Ideas come to you in abundance. Enjoy the sounds of a bubbling brook. It's time to look through the haze to see what is really happening deep down. This may mean spending hours going over books and talking to people. Conduct your own investigation.

Messengers:

Animal: *Kaka (bird/parrot)*
Nature: *Haze (weather)*
Universe/Energy: *Bubbling (Sound)*

566

This is a time of new beginnings, spiritual renewal, to let go of what's holding you back to embrace the positivity coming to you. Sometimes you just have to dive right in to get what you want. And when you get it, realize that it's enough instead of always looking toward greener pastures. Matters of the heart are prevalent at this time.

Messengers:

Animal: *Osprey (bird)*
Nature: *Rose Quartz (gemstone)*
Universe/Energy: *Beginnings*

567

An opportunity to uncover hidden information is presenting itself. You tend to be a loner but sometimes you need the input of others. Everyone knows you're a strong person who can hold their own, you don't have to tell everyone all the time. There is someone close to you who can get underneath the persona you present to the world. Hold that person close.

Messengers:

Animal: *Walrus*
Nature: *Monstera Plant*
Universe/Energy: *Blue Green (Color)*

568

You have the spirit of royalty. Noble, fair, and wise. Beauty radiates all around you and from within your essence. You are on a journey of discovering the wisdom within your spiritual self. This is a lifelong journey that will take some time. . Be patient, listen to your inner self and your guides along the way.

Messengers:

Animal: *Madagascan Sunset Moth*
Nature: *Stream*
Universe/Energy: *Creative Expression*

569

Suppressing your intuitive abilities due to fear of being judged by others will only have a negative effect on you in the long run. When your intuitive abilities come knocking, if you don't open the door and let them in, they'll just keep knocking until you do. It's time to rub away all the dead weight and open to the brightness that acceptance brings.

Messengers:

Animal: *Crayfish (crustacean)*
Nature: *Bahia Grass*
Universe/Energy: *Knocking (Sound)*

570

Your mouth can be sharp as a blade if you're not watching what you say. Instead of skimming the top, dig deep into the things that interest you. Make memories with family and friends. Make minor changes to create larger ones. Sometimes you need to take baby steps before you can take off running.

Messengers:

Animal: *Skimmer (bird)*
Nature: *Rock Salt Sandstone*
Universe/Energy: *Memories*

571

Don't be surprised to discover that you're going through a time of transformation again. You may have experienced spiritual enlightenment recently but get ready for more. You're like a ball rolling downhill building momentum. More information and abilities are opening to you at a rapid pace. Hold on, the fun is just beginning.

Messengers:

Animal: *Diamondback Rattlesnake*
Nature: *Cassava (vegetable)*
Universe/Energy: *Amazement*

572

The gift of gab is yours. Praising others, motivating them to achieve their dreams, and offering encouragement are some of the things that make you such a special person. At times, you need to take a moment for a deep breath to center yourself. The devotion you show others is a reminder to all that love should be a part of everything in life.

Messengers:

Animal: *Fin Whale*
Nature: *Frangipani (plant)*
Universe/Energy: *Praise*

573

n't forget to eat! You're so energetic and move from one thing to the other throughout the day that you often forget to take the time for a meal. It's easy to become so immersed in the work you're doing and the new discoveries you're making that time flies by. Fuel yourself to keep the fires burning throughout the day.

Messengers:

Animal: *Salmon (fish)*
Nature: *Crabgrass*
Universe/Energy: *Integrate opposites*

574

What have you been neglecting? Is there a gray cover of dust in your home? It's time to make your living area shine. If you've been putting off something, now is the time to do it. Or there may be things from your past that you need to reconnect with for the present. Climb high for clarity of thought and to accomplish greatness.

Messengers:

Animal: *Chamois (goat-antelope)*
Nature: *Dust*
Universe/Energy: *Gray (Color)*

575

Impatience isn't an emotion that resonates with you. Instead, you can wait for a long time if needed. You're a specialist in your field and are sensitive to your surroundings. If you're feeling out of sorts look at how the energy is flowing around you. This could be a suitable time to move furniture or buy something new to enhance your space.

Messengers:

Animal: *Weaver (bird)*
Nature: *Rhyolite (rock)*
Universe/Energy: *Allow yourself to receive (action)*

576

You're hungry for some solitary time where you can spend some time just hanging around. There's nothing specific you want to do except rest, eat, and sleep. While you do, consider the areas of your life that are filled with irregularities. How can you find ways to fill the gaps or repair holes?

Messengers:

Animal: *Cobweb Spider*
Nature: *Sea Rocket (plant)*
Universe/Energy: *Freshly Popped Popcorn (Scent)*

577

Look into the eyes to discover the truth of the soul behind the mask. Some people try to hide who they really are, but you have the distinct ability to see them on a spiritual level. They say the eyes are the window to the soul and for you that is the truth. You can also see their past lives and how you two were connected in those lives if you look hard enough.

Messengers:

Animal: *Barred Owl*
Nature: *Cinnabar (mineral)*
Universe/Energy: *Unveil your spiritual truth (action)*

578

Look at the layers of your spirituality instead of hiding behind them. When you peel back layer after layer you discover so much about yourself. Sometimes it's hard to lay yourself bare like that but it can be very healing. This also gives you the ability to get in touch with your inner child and the innocence you have left behind.

Messengers:

Animal: *Pampas Deer*
Nature: *Red Cabbage*
Universe/Energy: *Giant permafrost explosions (phenomenon)*

579

If you're not paying attention, you could miss opportunities. Something may be puzzling you. It's time to figure it out on your own, without help from others. You are creative and imaginative and will find a distinctive and unique way to solve the puzzle. Take action, pay attention to details, but avoid repetition. Something you've been working on is coming to fruition. Enjoy the rewards.

Messengers:

Animal: *Woodpecker*
Nature: *Equator*
Universe/Energy: *Relate (action)*

580

Turn that frown into a smile and stop being hardheaded. Your nerves are frayed yet you still are holding your own and not changing your mind. In this case, it is beneficial to look at all points of view instead of being stuck on what you want. There is a glow of positivity all around you. This will work out if you just let it.

Messengers:

Animal: *Rockfish*
Nature: *Victoria Amazonica (plant)*
Universe/Energy: *Moon Dog (phenomenon)*

581

You're adventurous and daring, which draws people to you. Your insightfulness helps them to understand their own purpose. Dig in and seek out information. Diligence and focused attention are needed. Don't give up. It might take manual labor to accomplish your task but you're up to the job.

Messengers:

Animal: *Gopher*
Nature: *Giant Cliff*
Universe/Energy: *Sage (Scent)*

582

Is your intelligence being questioned? Your ability to do your job? This is a good time to take a deep breath and stand up for yourself. Even the smallest good deed can go unnoticed if others aren't aware of it. Typically, you wouldn't brag but, in this case, your deeds and actions need to be known.

Messengers:

Animal: *Krill (crustacean)*
Nature: *Caliche Chalk (rock)*
Universe/Energy: *Azure (color)*

583

Stand up and let the focus be on you. This is your moment. The culmination of what you've been trying to attain through hard work, diligent study, and resourcefulness. Enjoy being in the limelight for a little while because it is well deserved. You've carved out a niche for yourself which will be beneficial for years to come.

Messengers:

Animal: *Brown Bear*
Nature: *Green Bell Pepper*
Universe/Energy: *Resourceful*

584

To touch is to know. To hear is to see. You have access to ancient knowledge, to the Akashic Records, and to the past of people and things. Dive deeply into your impressions to obtain a clear view of the people and events involved. Mysteries can be solved through the images received.

Messengers:

Animal: *Florida Pompano (fish)*
Nature: *Baby toes (succulent plant)*
Universe/Energy: *Clairtangency (Psychometry)*

585

When everything is speeding by you, just stop. Wait. Listen. You are like a vine that grows to great heights and then blooms with wonderous beauty. Protection is abundant and you're safe in the arms of others. Accept the help offered. Abundance, passion, and prosperity are waiting for you.

Messengers:

Animal: *Cottontail (mammal/rabbit)*
Nature: *Bougainvillea (plant)*
Universe/Energy: *Stop and Consider (action)*

586

Did you know that you're an artist at heart? Now is the time to move into new artistic endeavors. You're very crafty and create objects with intricate details. What may start as a hobby could turn into a full-time job. Along the way you may discover that others aren't as interested in what you're doing as you think they should be. That's okay. You do you.

Messengers:

Animal: *Gerbil*
Nature: *Devil's Thorn (plant)*
Universe/Energy: *Ping Pong Ball Bouncing (Sound)*

587

It's time to plant. Seek out a place that is moisture rich, fertile, and has good sunlight. Stay out of dark or shady places to ensure the production of a good crop. While you're at it, add some sweet-smelling plants just for the sheer enjoyment of them. There is much to learn from this season of growing and harvest.

Messengers:

Animal: *Earwig (insect)*
Nature: *Pitaya (fruit)*
Universe/Energy: *Lilacs (Scent)*

588

If you don't learn from your current situation, you're bound to repeat it until you do, even if that means it follows you to a future lifetime. Instead of letting the lessons slip away, create a detailed account of the "what and why" of the situation for further examination. Write all the details down so you can go over it thoroughly later.

Messengers:

Animal: *Bongo (mammal/antelope)*
Nature: *Happy Alien Flower*
Universe/Energy: *Mirage (phenomenon)*

589

Are you discriminating against someone and not realizing it? Are they closed off, quiet, and shy so you feel as if they're indifferent when maybe they're just nervous about coming out of their shell? This is a good time to practice what you preach and to reach out and embrace those who may not know what to do to be included.

Messengers:

Animal: *Mussel (mollusk)*
Nature: *Hyssop (plant)*
Universe/Energy: *Clover (scent)*

590

There is power in stillness. Make use of it by being still, watching, and waiting until the course of action you should take is revealed to you. Now is the time to build up your defenses, to be independently productive, and to do the unexpected. Keep things hidden for now. Blend in. Don't cause too much excitement around yourself.

Messengers:

Animal: *Stick Insect*
Nature: *Mushroom*
Universe/Energy: *Listen to the sea in a conch shell (sound)*

591

Trust among friends is important. Pay attention to any small irritations so they don't blow up into something that causes a big problem. You may feel frustrated, so communication is key to keep the flow of energy between everyone moving in a positive manner.

Messengers:

Animal: *Mite (arachnid)*
Nature: *Cranberry*
Universe/Energy: *Camaraderie*

592

If you're broken-hearted, you may find that you want to rebel in every aspect of your life. Some of this rebellion is negative while other rebellious streaks have positive results. Acting out will not heal the hurt you're feeling. Be courageous and strong. Stand tall and with dignity. Soon you will be feeling back to your normal self.

Messengers:

Animal: *Black-billed Magpie (bird)*
Nature: *Coast Redwood (tree)*
Universe/Energy: *Discover your life purpose (action)*

593

Be a good person who is responsible, loyal, and honest instead of seeking power, prestige, and a following. The more honest and down to earth you are, the more powerful your energy. Being in the public eye brings with it a plethora of problems you may not expect or enjoy.

Messengers:

Animal: *Black Sole (fish)*
Nature: *Daisy*
Universe/Energy: *Release Control*

594

What big ears you have! Are you snooping around listening to other people's conversations just to get the scoop on someone else? What do you plan to do with any information you discover? Are your thoughts positive and pure or do you have other intentions? Be honest with yourself.

Messengers:

Animal: *Fennec Fox*
Nature: *Obsidian Pegmatite (rock)*
Universe/Energy: *White Sage (scent)*

595

You may experience a case of mistaken identity that could lead to a new opportunity. Play around with the colors in your home. Paint some walls to brighten up your living space. An uncertain situation will solidify and bring about great news you've been waiting for.

Messengers:

Animal: *Bullsnake*
Nature: *Crystallization*
Universe/Energy: *Color Healing*

596

Look for ways you can control your emotions while asserting your feelings in a calm way. Maybe you need to focus on your own private issues instead of causing problems for someone else. Clear thinking is needed now as well as open communication.

Messengers:

Animal: *Basking Shark*
Nature: *Daikon (vegetable)*
Universe/Energy: *Examine your inner self (action)*

597

Everyone has an interesting life. It is up to you to decide whether or not you are interested in what makes other people interesting. If you are, ask questions, listen to their stories, engage with them regularly, and genuinely care about the fireworks happening in their lives. You are not the only one who glows.

Messengers:

Animal: *Glow Worm*
Nature: *Holly*
Universe/Energy: *Fireworks*

598

Spending time in the forest to experience a deep connection to nature, to the animals living in a forest, and the climate among the trees is needed. Leave behind any negative energy bothering you. Stripping away the old to reveal the new, colorful you underneath is appropriate now.

Messengers:

Animal: *Mountain Pademelon (marsupial)*
Nature: *Rainbow Eucalyptus Tree*
Universe/Energy: *Sparkly (sensation)*

599

Regardless of what is happening around you it is important to stay calm, remain quiet, and think logically. Secrets are coming to the surface and some people aren't going to like being outed and others are going to be shocked at the news. Stay rooted where you are. Don't let yourself get engaged in their issues.

Messengers:

Animal: *Bullfrog*
Nature: *Rutile (mineral)*
Universe/Energy: *Black Hole*

600

The position of protector is yours. You watch over those in your care and have a clear, far-reaching vision for them. You are enthusiastic and spending time in the sun only strengthens your resolve. You would give someone the shirt off your back if they needed it.

Messengers:

Animal: *California Condor (bird)*
Nature: *Puddle*
Universe/Energy: *Grapefruit (scent)*

601

You are often so busy it's hard to find time for yourself, but you must. To prevent yourself from being burned out because you work too much, find some solitude. It may be as simple as taking a walk or soaking in the bath after everyone in your family has gone to sleep. You need some *me time*. Take it.

Messengers:

Animal: *Black Rhinoceros*
Nature: *Middlemist Red (flower)*
Universe/Energy: *Sky Blue (Color)*

602

Do you walk away or try harder? You have a talent for understanding the rare things in life, embracing them, and feeling compassion. You tend to be a worrywart and that means you will debate this question to death. The solution is simple. Read it again and then listen to the first thing your intuition says back to you. That's what you need to do.

Messengers:

Animal: *Merino Sheep*
Nature: *Morel Mushroom*
Universe/Energy: *Astonishment (emotion)*

603

Look for the meaning in the little things in life. Notice what you often ignore. Instead of blending in, rise to the forefront and speak up. Pay attention to inspiration and ideas received at night because they will be the most successful. Pursue it to become successful and fulfilled.

Messengers:

Animal: *Jerboa (rodent)*
Nature: *Daytime*
Universe/Energy: *Determination*

604

It's time to push past barriers that you've set up for yourself or that other people keep placing in front of you. Don't give up. You will reach your goal. You may take a fall on the way and skin a knee but put some salve on it and keep on pushing forward. You'll be rewarded with the sweet joy of success.

Messengers:

Animal: *Agouti (rodent)*
Nature: *Fuchsite (gemstone)*
Universe/Energy: *Look for the lesson (action)*

605

If you feel you're being held captive by life and aren't moving forward, it's easy to let it get the best of you. Don't turn to negative behaviors at this time because that will only make things worse. Surrounding yourself in negativity or participating in negative behaviors to escape situations doesn't solve problems but can exacerbate them. Look for ways to release yourself from the ties binding you to your current situation.

Messengers:

Animal: *Capuchin (primate)*
Nature: S*afflower*
Universe/Energy: *Stillness (sensation)*

606

You're receiving messages from spirit in an abundance of forms. Animals, spirit guides, angels, and those who have passed are all talking to you now. It's time to pay attention. Not only will the messages you receive bring clarity to your life and situations you're dealing with, but they will also help you acknowledge the magick inside of you.

Messengers:

Animal: *Marbled Cat*
Nature: *Slush*
Universe/Energy: *Spirit Messengers*

607

It's time to start something new. This could be a new business, a new family, or a move to a new place. Paying it forward to other people is important now as well. Do a good deed today for someone who doesn't know you and who isn't expecting anything. Be productive because time is money.

Messengers:

Animal: *Anole (reptile)*
Nature: *Goldenrod (herb)*
Universe/Energy: *Pleased (feeling)*

608

Are you overworked and feel like you're underpaid? Are you happy with what you have? This is a time to be comfortable at home. To appreciate the hearth fires. Love, passion, and equality are at the center of your current situation. You have realistic expectations but are holding back on sharing them with your significant other.

Messengers:

Animal: *Genet (mammal/cat-like)*
Nature: *Cinnamon*
Universe/Energy: *Earth rhythms*

609

You are surrounded by unconditional love yet you're rejecting it at every turn. People adore you; they want what's best for you, yet you still push them away. To overcome the problem, you're currently facing you must accept the help of those who love you. They only have your best interests at heart.

Messengers:

Animal: *Muntjac (mammal/deer)*
Nature: *Jet (gemstone)*
Universe/Energy: *Adoration*

610

There's a time to speak and a time to stay quiet. Now is your time to speak. You'll need to be truthful about your feelings. It may feel like you're exposing the deepest part of yourself to someone else. It's because you are. Good things will come out of the situation.

Messengers:

Animal: *Raven (bird)*
Nature: *Crater*
Universe/Energy: *Relief*

611

Sit a spell and enjoy the sweetness of an orange. Rest now because you're going to be busy soon. Changes are coming that are going to be good for you in many ways. Don't resist but gladly accept what is offered. You will be surprised and thankful. If you're feeling pressure from someone at work, leave those feelings at the job.

Messengers:

Animal: *Pike (fish)*
Nature: *Mandarin Orange*
Universe/Energy: *Sweetness*

612

This is a time of expansion, of new birth, and new ventures. Success surrounds all endeavors. You often ignore negativity but for the moment pay attention to it because it will show you the truth someone is trying to hide from you. You're generous and put family first. Creativity is in abundance.

Messengers:

Animal: *Chicken*
Nature: *Blazing Star (plant)*
Universe/Energy: *Spruce (scent)*

613

You're extraordinary and can accomplish an impressive number of tasks in a day. People respect your uniqueness and strive to emulate you. Watch for changes in people's words and actions. There may be deceit underneath. Keep your secrets close. You have a lot going for you and you always seem to be in the right place at the right time.

Messengers:

Animal: *Barnacle (crustacean)*
Nature: *Iceberg*
Universe/Energy: *Bounce a Ball (action)*

614

Are you wearing your heart on your sleeve? You are filled with inner joy, and you readily share it with everyone around you. You don't hide your feelings from others. You may cry like a waterfall one day and be happy as a lark on another. Sharing your feelings is simply part of who you are.

Messengers:

Animal: *Crested Caracara (bird/falcon)*
Nature: *Dayflower*
Universe/Energy: *Examine your Multifaceted Self (action)*

615

Be aware of your reputation. Watch your words and actions so you are not misinterpreted. Problems arising now based on your actions could follow you for the rest of your life. Darkness can funnel you into its depths if you let it.

Messengers:

Animal: *Funnel Web Spider*
Nature: *Cassia (spice)*
Universe/Energy: *Sense Connections Around You*

616

Challenging times require faith and persistence. Transformation is upon you. Divine wisdom comes through making you notice specific details, which will be enlightening and uplifting. You possess sacred knowledge of spiritual ideas that should be shared with others. Use these talents to help others as well as yourself to get things to work out in everyone's favor.

Messengers:

Animal: *Beetle*
Nature: *Fescue Grass*
Universe/Energy: *Toasted Coconut (Scent)*

617

Is your heart stained from past hurts? Start the healing of your emotions by listening to soothing sounds. Let go of the past through laughter and turn the hurt into happiness. Live your own truths, not the truth someone in the past wanted you to believe.

Messengers:

Animal: *Kookaburra (bird)*
Nature: *Black Walnut*
Universe/Energy: *Liquid Being Poured (Sound)*

618

If you're stubborn, protective streak is getting in the way of your relationships, it's time to be agile and turn your way of thinking around. People need to stand on their own without someone else hovering over them. Watch from afar and if there's a fire, then rush to put it out. Otherwise, stand back.

Messengers:

Animal: *American Bison*
Nature: *Bee Orchid*
Universe/Energy: *Burning Wood (Scent)*

619

Even the slightest tinkling sound will grab your attention. You feel like prey but you're not. Calm down, don't be tempted to run away from things that put you on high alert. Your energy is powerful. Share it.

Messengers:

Animal: *Kudu (mammal/antelope)*
Nature: *Telegraph Plant*
Universe/Energy: *Ice Dropped into a Glass (Sound)*

620

You can grab the attention of others quickly and easily because of your unique appearance and skills. You're adventurous, independent, and take risks, which draws people to you. You're exciting and fun, outgoing and energetic, highly intelligent, and work well under pressure.

Messengers:

Animal: *Swordfish*
Nature: *Rue (herb)*
Universe/Energy: *Patchouli (Scent)*

621

Good news is on its way. You've been waiting for an answer to a situation, and it will come soon. It may not be exactly what you wanted but it's a good start to getting what you need. You're working hard and it shows.

Messengers:

Animal: *Grass Snake*
Nature: *String Bean*
Universe/Energy: *Relaxation*

622

There are many layers to understand in the messages you're getting from the spiritual world. You must not skim over them but look deeper into what they mean. Sitting by the ocean and listening to the tranquility there will help you realize these greater meanings. If you can't get to the ocean, find a quiet place to reflect.

Messengers:

Animal: *Red Tailed Hawk*
Nature: *Ocean*
Universe/Energy: *Appetizing (feeling)*

623

If you're in hot water, shower off, cool down, and look at the situation without fear. Your personal and spiritual power is very elevated, and you know more than you say. Use this power wisely as you face the situation. You will need to be competitive and prepared to move forward.

Messengers:

Animal: *Mako Shark*
Nature: *Temperature*
Universe/Energy: *Shower Fresh (Scent)*

624

Make time to get your footing back on solid ground. Approach problems with thick skin and keep emotions out of your current situation. You must be true to yourself even if it means you defy others who may try to sway you to a different path.

Messengers:

Animal: *Rhinoceros*
Nature: *Staurolite (gemstone)*
Universe/Energy: *Pouring a beverage (sound)*

625

The shimmering glow of clouds at sunrise or sunset will help you connect to the transformational ancient energy of the Universe. Let it wrap around you, strengthen you from within so that you know your true value lies in what you believe and not what others say or tell you to believe.

Messengers:

Animal: *Cottonmouth (snake)*
Nature: *Noctilucent Clouds*
Universe/Energy: *Goodness*

626

You may be feeling trapped in your current lifestyle and desperately want to do something different. Using clear vision and trusting your intuition, look for the path you should take. You can see clearly even in darkness. The answer will appear when you are ready.

Messengers:

Animal: *Peruvian Night Monkey*
Nature: *Beach Bur (plant)*
Universe/Energy: *Clairvoyance*

627

Contrasting colors will brighten your day. Fertility, abundance, and blessings are significant now. You have feelings of contentment and happiness in your life. Create a home cooked dinner with your family, or have a barbeque, to spend quality time together.

Messengers:

Animal: *Cacique (bird)*
Nature: *Hominy (vegetable/grain)*
Universe/Energy: *Crickets Chirping (sound)*

628

Getting tied up in the negativity surrounding you can make you feel as if you don't matter. It's time to disassociate yourself from the people who are making you feel this way. They are a bad influence and what they're representing isn't right for you. Lift yourself up so you can smile again.

Messengers:

Animal: *Ribbon Fish*
Nature: *Cassiterite (mineral)*
Universe/Energy: *Cornsilk (color)*

629

Your popularity is high right now. You give great advice, and it seems like everyone needs some. You're in a time of transformation and growth. Do your work at night for the best outcome. Listen closely to what's going on around you.

Messengers:

Animal: *Moth*
Nature: *Sulfur*
Universe/Energy: *Travel (action)*

630

When you can't sleep, when the path feels stony and harsh, look inward for discovery. There is a deep awareness of your spiritual self that you have yet to figure out. Now is the time to be alone and attempt to listen to both your inner self and guides to make progression.

Messengers:

Animal: *Halibut (fish)*
Nature: *Diorite Gabbro (rock)*
Universe/Energy: *Apricot (Color)*

631

The shadows speak. Their message isn't clear, but it is continuous. Listen closely to gain understanding. Look to the upper corners of rooms for there is where the answer lies. Do not fear that which you cannot see. The spirits around you want to help, not harm.

Messengers:

Animal: *House Fly*
Nature: *Creek*
Universe/Energy: *Phantoms*

632

Your determination is at an all-time high which makes sleeping difficult. Your mind will not shut down but is continually planning and considering different options. Make a solid plan and stick with it to reach your goals instead of going back and forth between multiple scenarios.

Messengers:

Animal: *Brown Jay (bird)*
Nature: *Titanite (mineral)*
Universe/Energy: *Sleep (action)*

633

Trust your instincts and let them guide you through the various levels of energy you're about to face. You are going to encounter some people who will drain your energy and others who want to boost you up. Both can be overwhelming. Protect your energy to keep others from affecting you.

Messengers:

Animal: *Pronghorn (mammal)*
Nature: *Cat Palm (tree)*
Universe/Energy: *Vortex Energy*

634

Being at one with your intuition and spirituality, being deeply connected to the energy of the earth, and following your heart is of utmost importance right now. Your visions and prophetic dreams are increasing. Use all your senses and abilities to create an easy flow in life.

Messengers:

Animal: *Hedgehog*
Nature: *Rose-Apple*
Universe/Energy: *Emerald (color)*

635

Sharpen up your mental skills because you're about to head into some negotiations at work that will be tough and time consuming. Be analytical, logical, and stay on point. You may have to concede some points to obtain what you want.

Messengers:

Animal: *Red Fox*
Nature: *Musk Thistle*
Universe/Energy: *Scarlet (Color)*

636

This is a time of warmth and celebration, of birth, or rebirth. There is joy to be found in the anticipation as much as in the arrival. Friends and family are important at this time and will join in your happiness.

Messengers:

Animal: *Amazon Parrot*
Nature: *Dogwood Tree*
Universe/Energy: *Warmth*

637

Monotony is dragging you down. Doing the same thing day in and day out is boring. Change it up a bit. Watch a new television show, read a book, or talk on the phone to someone you haven't spoken to in a while. Break the monotony to get yourself out of a rut.

Messengers:

Animal: *Pacific Gull*
Nature: *Kiwifruit*
Universe/Energy: *Sacral Chakra*

638

Challenging your brain by using it to figure out complex ideas will strengthen it just as much as hard physical labor strengthens your body. To grow in mind, body, and spirit, all need to be pushed to their limits sometimes.

Messengers:

Animal: *Ibex (mammal)*
Nature: *Prune*
Universe/Energy: *Lime (scent)*

639

Keep your friends close and enemies closer. If provoked it's time to fight and stand up for yourself, your family, or your friends. Not much gets by you and you're quick to see right through people who want to use you to attain their own goals. Listen to your intuition, it's not going to lead you wrong.

Messengers:

Animal: *Warthog*
Nature: *Peach Tree*
Universe/Energy: *Mercury Retrograde*

640

How often are you acting on your impulses? This is a time to picture yourself in a new situation of your choosing. Embarking on this adventure will be fulfilling and will stimulate your thirst for knowledge. Be pure in thought to help someone who is having personal drama.

Messengers:

Animal: *Cockatoo (bird)*
Nature: *Algae (plant)*
Universe/Energy: *Shimmering (sensation)*

641

Sometimes it's hard to know what the right thing to do is. You may feel like you're being pulled in several different directions at once. The lack of warmth and lack of declarations of support should help you decide the path to take. Be aware of people who might be trying to take advantage of you.

Messengers:

Animal: *Loris (primate)*
Nature: *Arctic Air*
Universe/Energy: *Trumpets (sound)*

642

It's time to dig in the dirt and remove the invasive things around you. While they may be beautiful on the outside, they may be deceptive and manipulative on the inside. Clearly seeing the truth in someone's spirit will allow you to heal from hurts they have caused. Dig them up and dispose of them to be free of their negativity.

Messengers:

Animal: *Axolotl (amphibian)*
Nature: *Creeping Charlie (plant)*
Universe/Energy: *Insightfulness*

643

You're a social butterfly that everyone loves. It's important to know when to retreat from the limelight so you can find your true place in the world. You were meant for greater things than partying and having a good time. You've yet to recognize the power of your spirit and intuitive abilities.

Messengers:

Animal: *Hyrax (mammal)*
Nature: *Mist Flower*
Universe/Energy: *Well-being*

644

There is always light even in the darkest of times. Beware of toxic individuals who are looking to swindle you out of your money, time or possessions. They may stubbornly refuse the *no* that you tell them, but don't let them back you into a corner. Shine brightly my friend.

Messengers:

Animal: *Lightning Bug*
Nature: *Orpiment (mineral)*
Universe/Energy: *Tenderness*

645

Now is the time to sing. Be vocal, be excited about new ideas and projects, be truthful to those around you and most importantly to yourself. Positivity abounds. You are unique and easily remembered. Make a great impression to accomplish great strides. Make sure you're not confusing feeling comfortable in a situation with true happiness.

Messengers:

Animal: *Boreal Chickadee (bird)*
Nature: *Periwinkle (plant)*
Universe/Energy: *Knowledge*

646

Guidance is what you need. There are situations that feel like they're out of your control and you just don't know which way to turn. Look to both outside sources and to messages from your higher self, guides, and the Universe for answers.

Messengers:

Animal: *Leopard Shark*
Nature: *Green Beryl (gemstone)*
Universe/Energy: *Green (Color)*

647

Stealth, courage, and diversity are needed now. You're ambitious and often bite off more than you can chew but you are still able to handle it. Uplifting energy will aid you during any mini crisis that occurs. You're full of vitality which helps you through all situations.

Messengers:

Animal: *Black Dragonfish*
Nature: *Cavern*
Universe/Energy: *Lion's Roar (sound)*

648

Instead of trusting your inner self, you're looking for signs but not seeing them, which is confusing. The signs are right in front of you but you're looking so hard they evade you. Don't focus so intently. Just let things happen. Once you relax into this mindset, you'll see the signs and hear your inner self.

Messengers:

Animal: *Meadowlark*
Nature: *Cirrocumulus Clouds*
Universe/Energy: *Puzzled (feeling)*

649

You are an open book and people can see deeply into your spirit. You don't try to hide things from people and are about as honest as you can get regarding everything in your life. You don't like keeping secrets. Expect delays in some of your plans. They're going to take longer than expected.

Messengers:

Animal: *Glass Frog*
Nature: *Coast Wallflower*
Universe/Energy: *Detour*

650

Remain calm, step with care, and keep your balance. Connect to your higher self as you rejuvenate physically to help you heal emotionally. Don't hesitate. Now is the time for quick action and to fight for what you want. Be courageous, determined, and powerful. Don't doubt yourself but be clear a clear communicator to achieve your desires.

Messengers:

Animal: *Badger*
Nature: *Montana Moss Agate (gemstone)*
Universe/Energy: *Trust*

651

Love and luck are coming your way. This is a time for big life changes. You may also be breaking away from relationships you thought were permanent but are now in ruins. This change is for the best even though it may feel like you're slipping on ice as you're going through it.

Messengers:

Animal: *Mandarin Duck*
Nature: *Ice*
Universe/Energy: *Jackhammer (sound)*

652

If you feel like you've been misled, head back to the family unit. It's important to be levelheaded and to embrace the support of those closest to you. The issue isn't as bad as you initially thought and through brainstorming, you'll discover a way to attain your goals anyway.

Messengers:

Animal: *Emperor Penguin*
Nature: *Key Lime Tree*
Universe/Energy: *Watch fish in an aquarium (action)*

653

Keep a clean house. Get rid of garbage, clutter, and any mess that is lying around. Disinfect your surroundings. Clear the air by replacing filters and adding fragrance. Create a happy, carefree feeling in your home to make it more warm, comfortable, and inviting.

Messengers:

Animal: *Carpenter Ant*
Nature: *Malachite (gemstone)*
Universe/Energy: *Carnival*

654

Look to the past to avoid business mistakes now. If you own a company, your decisions now could affect its longevity or put you out of business. Take responsibility for what you do. Don't place blame on others that should sit on your shoulders. Be finicky about making decisions to ensure you make the right one.

Messengers:

Animal: *Colugo (mammal/flying lemur)*
Nature: *Fiddle Leaf Fig Plant*
Universe/Energy: *Consider little things (action)*

655

You can easily hide in plain sight. You jump quickly from one project to another and do a lot of work in a short period of time. You might have to smoke out your competition because they too, like to hide what they're doing. Look to the embers for a message.

Messengers:

Animal: *Green Planthopper (insect)*
Nature: *Honeydew Melon*
Universe/Energy: *Embers (Scent)*

656

While you're perfectly capable of doing your own work, you've been riding on someone else's coattails. It's time to stand on your own. Taking credit for something you didn't do or making yourself an unwanted guest in someone else's home means it's really time to re-evaluate exactly how you're living your life.

Messengers:

Animal: *Dew-drop Spider*
Nature: *Shallot (vegetable)*
Universe/Energy: *Swimming Pool (Scent)*

657

Think about your habits for a moment. To create a new, good habit, repeat the action over and over until it is second nature, and you don't even think about it anymore. This is also a great time to replace bad habits with good ones. Music plays a part in this as does spending some time listening to the sounds of the night.

Messengers:

Animal: *West Mexican Chachalaca (bird)*
Nature: *Reed*
Universe/Energy: *Hot Summer Night (Scent)*

658

Let go of any irritating things in your life and instead, embrace laughter. Find the happiness, the fun, the silliness in all things. You need an emotional break from stress and laughter is just the thing to fill the space. Find your joy.

Messengers:

Animal: *Hobo Spider*
Nature: *Laughing Bumblebee Orchid*
Universe/Energy: *Transparency*

659

Mornings are a wonderful time to take a few moments to enjoy being with yourself before you start your day. You are peaceful, resilient, and pure. You trust your own judgement and find goodness in situations. You're the first to lend a hand to your neighbors. Think about these wonderful qualities as you await the sunrise.

Messengers:

Animal: *Platy (fish)*
Nature: *Arum Lilies*
Universe/Energy: *Coffee (Scent)*

660

Be aware of your options, especially if you're losing confidence in a situation. It's always good to have a backup plan in your back pocket. There is danger in letting someone else make your choices for you. Decide for yourself, don't let others decide for you.

Messengers:

Animal: *Sailfish*
Nature: *Evening Primrose (plant)*
Universe/Energy: *Crepuscular Rays (phenomenon)*

661

Your brain needs your attention. This is a time of stimulation, learning, and focusing on the future. It's not time to sail away to some different shore just to get away from it all. That will come later but for now you need to buckle down and study.

Messengers:

Animal: *Brain Coral*
Nature: *Sea Holly (plant)*
Universe/Energy: *Fire Opal (color)*

662

The situation you're in has been decorated and presented in a way to make it look like perfection. While you may think the person involved would never do anything wrong, they are only human. Don't expect them to be perfect. Do expect news from far away that will bring great joy.

Messengers:

Animal: *Shoebill Stork (bird)*
Nature: *Burro's Tail (succulent plant)*
Universe/Energy: *Decorations*

663

You are not defined by the situation you are in. You can rise above any events you no longer desire in your life. You are being guided toward people who can help you, who will inspire you, and who will assistance you in learning about your spirituality. It is time to awaken to your greatness.

Messengers:

Animal: *Asian Elephant*
Nature: *Red Delicious Apple*
Universe/Energy: *Circumzenithal Arc (phenomenon)*

664

Are you listening to someone just so you can answer them or are you truly trying to understand the depth of what they're saying? Give people the same undivided attention you give to your prayers. They deserve to interact with all of you, not just a part of you.

Messengers:

Animal: *Flightless Cormorant (bird)*
Nature: *Dead Leaves*
Universe/Energy: *Prayer*

665

To awaken to the truth of your soul, all you have to do is remember who you are. Create a divine connection to the time prior to your birth to remember what you planned and how you planned it. You are energy, you are light, and you are love. Once remembered, you will never forget the truth of your soul.

Messengers:

Animal: *Elk*
Nature: *Cherry*
Universe/Energy: *Change a habit (action)*

666

Stealth is necessary now. Hide in the shadows, listen carefully, and you'll discover the truth of situations around you. Go within, discover your higher self, your soul purpose, and embrace your own light. For light eliminates any darkness in those around you.

Messengers:

Animal: *Cobra*
Nature: *Flowering Talipot Palm*
Universe/Energy: *Eagerness*

667

This is a time of neutrality, of learning, and understanding how to focus and enhance your energy. Of moving forward while knowing where you've been. From learning from the past to moving into the future. Of letting go of the things that are no longer beneficial to you so you're free to embrace new things that will help you grow at all levels.

Messengers:

Animal: *Nyala (mammal/antelope)*
Nature: *Rice*
Universe/Energy: *Quiet your mind (action)*

668

Doldrums are on their way out the door. You're filled with vibrancy, high energy, and are singing your song to the entire world. You are bursting with joy and clarity of understanding. Today, something that was a mystery became clear to you, and it's made you very happy.

Messengers:

Animal: *Finch (bird)*
Nature: *Apple Tree*
Universe/Energy: *Bumblebee buzzing (sound)*

669

You're currently at the top of the food chain. You are a hunter but are rarely hunted. It is essential in your business to always be at the top of your game. That doesn't mean you never show mercy, you do. But you aim to stand tall and strong and you play to win.

Messengers:

Animal: *Eagle Owl*
Nature: *Sycamore Tree*
Universe/Energy: *Mercy*

670

Someone is protecting you and will send you a loud warning. If you ignore it, expect the next one to be a physical jab, a poke in the arm. Watch yourself closely so you do not have an accident, get in trouble at work, or lose your possessions.

Messengers:

Animal: *Sandhill Crane (bird)*
Nature: *Metamorphic (rock)*
Universe/Energy: *Lemongrass (scent)*

671

If you're being too rigid in your beliefs and unwilling to try new ways of doing things simply because they haven't been done that way before, then change is necessary. The new ideas will give a fresh start to the situation, which draws more attention. If you're running a business, this could improve your profit margins.

Messengers:

Animal: *Buffalo Fish*
Nature: *Carbon Dioxide*
Universe/Energy: *Wind Chimes (sound)*

672

Do not divide your attention at this time. You might need a kickstart to get into high gear with your plans. Focus on one thing at a time to turn any weak points into strengths. Be compassionate and caring to those around you. Someone is feeling emotional pain but isn't showing it. Your kindness will go a long way.

Messengers:

Animal: *Hammerhead Shark*
Nature: *Iolite (gemstone)*
Universe/Energy: *Compassion*

673

Release what is decaying around you. Dead weight is just pulling you down. It's draining your energy and causing mood swings. Stabilize yourself, so you don't feel exhausted and unable to complete the task at hand.

Messengers:

Animal: *Buzzard*
Nature: *Myosotis (plant)*
Universe/Energy: *Release something that no longer serves you (action)*

674

Living with family, or roommates, is appropriate now instead of living alone. Lately, you've been driven by deadlines and may have unconsciously neglected other things that need to be done. Try to find a balance so that you're able to give your attention to everything that needs it without ignoring one thing for another.

Messengers:

Animal: *Dwarf Hamster*
Nature: *Bergamot (fruit)*
Universe/Energy: *Bleating (Sound)*

675

When your path is winding, confusing, and never ending, it can become frustrating. This is the time to slow down and enjoy life more. Take some of the pressure off yourself by finishing the tasks you have and not taking on anything new for a while.

Messengers:

Animal: *Eastern Quoll (marsupial)*
Nature: *Pyroxene (mineral)*
Universe/Energy: *Ivory (color)*

676

Do you have unfulfilled ambitions? Are you in over your head when it comes to debt? Be quick to spot opportunities that will help you pay off your bills. Dream your dream but also take steps to achieve it. Surround yourself with the spirit of giving, of receiving, and of excelling.

Messengers:

Animal: *Northern Goshawk (bird)*
Nature: *Oxalis (plant)*
Universe/Energy: *Rain on a tin roof (sound)*

677

When you're prepared there's no place for nervousness. Instead, you'll reap the rewards of a job well done. Once the situation is completed, it will no longer require your attention which frees you up for new opportunities.

Messengers:

Animal: *Bufflehead (duck)*
Nature: *Cucumber*
Universe/Energy: *Fluttery (sensation)*

678

Your current situation calls for you to be cool, calm, and collected. Acting bullheaded, stubborn, and uncooperative isn't going to help you achieve your goals. Maybe you need to sleep on your decision or course of action before doing something. In the end, you'll be praised for how you handled yourself.

Messengers:

Animal: *Bullhead (fish)*
Nature: *Catnip*
Universe/Energy: *Clapping (sound)*

679

Are your emotions so out of whack? Do you feel like everything is going wrong? Are you just sitting around eating everything in sight because of it? Give yourself an olive branch and make peace with whatever core issue is causing the problem. Then pull yourself up out of your funk and get back to living a joyful life.

Messengers:

Animal: *Blobfish*
Nature: *Olive*
Universe/Energy: *Whirr of a fan (sound)*

680

You're feeling the pressure to get your house in order and to tie up loose ends. The things that you've put off now need to be done. Approach the task in a balanced way instead of going too fast and burning out before you've finished.

Messengers:

Animal: *Ball Python (snake)*
Nature: *Dolomite Flint (rock)*
Universe/Energy: *Campfire (scent)*

681

While you are drawn to the light you prefer for your waking hours to be during the nighttime. This is an excellent time to work on awakening the connection you have to your inner self and the Divine. You're surrounded by high frequencies that will help you on all levels.

Messengers:

Animal: *Owl Moth*
Nature: *Apatite (mineral)*
Universe/Energy: *Listen*

682

It's your time to shine! Your personality sparkles, your smile is infectious, and you spread joy everywhere you go. Standing out in a crowd is natural for you. Your voice inspires action, helps others understand topics, and your messages are helpful and on point.

Messengers:

Animal: *Parrot*
Nature: *Mound*
Universe/Energy: *Attractive (feeling)*

683

Be very aware of the sounds around you. They will lead to a discovery that will prevent a disaster. You are outgoing, confident, and adaptable. You're able to handle anything that is thrown at you, even if you're blindsided by it.

Messengers:

Animal: *Kiwi (bird)*
Nature: *Altostratus Clouds*
Universe/Energy: *Buzzing (Sound)*

684

Keep a smile on your face today and don't allow a negative attitude to surface. You'll be tested by someone who is trying to get under your skin, trying to take over your projects, and are basically just trying to get a rise out of you because they feel like fighting with someone today. Know that this is on them, not you, hold your ground.

Messengers:

Animal: *Deer Tick*
Nature: *Pinecones*
Universe/Energy: *Pull up weeds (action)*

685

You're an exceptional leader who also sees the strengths in people. You may have the opportunity to advance into a management position at work. Listen to your heart instead of seeking the opinion of others.

Messengers:

Animal: *Jaguarundi (feline)*
Nature: *Blue Topaz (gemstone)*
Universe/Energy: *Curious*

686

Proud, impressive, and bigger than life is how you're often perceived by others. But there are times when your emotions run so deep that you need time away just to come to terms with how you're feeling. When you love, it's unconditional, and with that sometimes comes getting hurt by others.

Messengers:

Animal: *Red Deer*
Nature: *Bleeding Heart (plant)*
Universe/Energy: *Growth*

687

Trying to come up with a plan that will result in more financial gains? Well, keep at it because you'll come up with a great idea! Keep your energy levels high to protect yourself from people with negative intentions. And keep your ideas secret.

Messengers:

Animal: *Blue Footed Booby (bird)*
Nature: *Cat's-Eye Opal (gemstone)*
Universe/Energy: *Peace of Mind*

688

You make the best of any situation and are often able to turn negative events into positive ones. You're open with your feelings. What people see is what they get. If you've been feeling like your memory isn't what it used to be, you could be overwhelmed with too much work and not enough down time.

Messengers:

Animal: *Cory Catfish*
Nature: *Longan (plant)*
Universe/Energy: *Banana (scent)*

689

Some days can just feel dismal and gray. Today is one of those days. Your get up and go got up and went and left you behind. This is a good day to just hang out around the house and let your body and mind recharge.

Messengers:

Animal: *Lone Star Tick*
Nature: *Muggy Weather*
Universe/Energy: *Give back (action)*

690

Think about something that you feel you absolutely could not live without. Now consider how your life would be without that thing. What changes would you make, how would you feel? Is this something you could let go for the betterment of your health, spirituality, or family life? You might be a little sad about it but maybe it's time to let it go.

Messengers:

Animal: *Muscovy Duck*
Nature: *Primrose (plant)*
Universe/Energy: *Write an abundance check (action)*

691

There may be a storm brewing around you but you're steadfast in your stance. Pay attention to details and look all around you before making decisions or taking action. You can function without much sleep. You tend to take on too much and are always multi-tasking.

Messengers:

Animal: *Cow*
Nature: *Sapphire (gemstone)*
Universe/Energy: *Open mindedness*

692

It's time for you to fly on silver wings and embrace the Divine within you. You're brave in the face of danger, patient with a child, and care deeply about life. You're transforming into the you that you are meant to be.

Messengers:

Animal: *Atlantic Flying Fish*
Nature: *Snake Plant*
Universe/Energy: *Spunky (feeling)*

693

How are you really doing? Are you feeling happy and excited about life, or are you hiding behind a mask? When you can pinpoint any issues that are bugging you, that's when you can transform them from darkness to something shiny and bright.

Messengers:

Animal: *American Crow*
Nature: *Iceberg Lettuce*
Universe/Energy: *Phone Ringing (Sound)*

694

You're a skilled orator who inspires others. You give freely of your time and are generous with your money. Your energy is being amplified at this time from outside sources. The sun, moon, and frequencies in the air are all affecting you positively. As you are being lifted up, take others along with you.

Messengers:

Animal: *California Quail (bird)*
Nature: *Calcite (mineral)*
Universe/Energy: *Generosity*

695

In the in-between states of awareness lies the answers that you seek. Sit beside calm, cool waters and wait for the answer to come. You are protected on this journey by the positive energy surrounding you. Let yourself move toward enlightenment.

Messengers:

Animal: *Geoffroy's Cat*
Nature: *Kentucky Bluegrass*
Universe/Energy: *Astral Body*

696

Look for inconsistencies in what you're doing. Find them and fix them. It's important to be strong in all areas right now. Pay attention to your clairvoyant impressions as they will help you avoid pitfalls. You may feel overly sensitive at this time.

Messengers:

Animal: *Panther Chameleon (reptile)*
Nature: *Field*
Universe/Energy: *Orange (Color)*

697

It's time for a makeover. Check your appearance. Do you need a style upgrade? New clothes or a new hairstyle? Upgrade your thoughts too. Are you looking at life in an outdated way? Are there new avenues that you can travel to discover more about the world you live in?

Messengers:

Animal: *Opossum*
Nature: *Evaporation*
Universe/Energy: *Self-respect*

698

Sometimes you must meander and wander about to gain clarity of sight and vision of purpose. It is important to save some things for addressing at a later date. When your plate is full, don't overfill it, otherwise you'll have waste.

Messengers:

Animal: *Musky Rat Kangaroo*
Nature: *Coastal Panic Grass*
Universe/Energy: *Triumphant*

699

Do not fear change and believe it will be something bad. Most changes happen for your well-being. Travel is important at this time. Don't ghost others and disappear from their lives with no contact or explanation. Bravely face them and end the relationship or friendship as an adult instead of running away from it as a coward.

Messengers:

Animal: *Kagu (bird)*
Nature: *Moisture*
Universe/Energy: *Uniqueness*

700

Careful... people may not be what they seem. Look deeper to find truth. Hunker down and don't waste time on unnecessary tasks. Avoid the drama and negativity of others. Don't follow others blindly but be secure in your abilities and path. When you do, you'll reach great heights in both your daily life and your spiritual growth. Everything will work out as it should.

Messengers:

Animal: *Catfish*
Nature: *Sunrise*
Universe/Energy: *Willingness*

701

Wisdom and intuition often go hand-in-hand. When you ignore one it affects the other. To be both wise and in sync with your abilities, you must listen to the messages you're being given and share those messages selflessly with others.

Messengers:

Animal: *Owl*
Nature: *Pecan Tree*
Universe/Energy: *Selfless*

702

Negativity is like poison for the soul. It can strike hard and fast, and its effects can be deadly unless you take quick action. There is power within you that enables you to reverse negativity into positivity within minutes. It's important to recognize the energy flow so you can alter it fast.

Messengers:
Animal: *Gaboon Viper (snake)*
Nature: *Delta (land formation)*
Universe/Energy: *Notice buildings (action)*

703

You're being influenced by someone . Look closely because they may be hiding something from you which could cause the relationship to sour. Pay attention to the upcoming full moon. Use its energy to invigorate your own life essence.

Messengers:

Animal: *Horseshoe Crab*
Nature: *Tamarind (tree)*
Universe/Energy: *Just sit (action)*

704

Don't look back or regret the path you've taken. Stay grounded and move on. You'll be able to leap over obstacles easily. Believe in yourself, support those closest to you, and stay on the path. Pick your battles. Now is the time to recreate yourself from the inside out. Transform. Embrace the surge in your spirituality.

Messengers:

Animal: *Kangaroo*
Nature: *Montezuma Cypress (tree)*
Universe/Energy: *Vivacious (feeling)*

705

You're in a period of growth when it comes to your ability to understand the intuitive messages you receive. Your accuracy is amazing right now. Do not be embarrassed by what you see and hear, instead share the messages with those they are meant for. Avoid boastfulness because then your accuracy will drop.

Messengers:

Animal: *Parrotfish*
Nature: *Shameplant*
Universe/Energy: *Precognition*

706

This is a time for the culmination of events. You have been standing ready for everything to finally fall into place. When it does, don't fear making decisions you've been putting off, or starting a new part of your life.

Messengers:

Animal: *Hellbender (amphibian)*
Nature: *Blood Moon*
Universe/Energy: *Duty*

707

Fan the flames of your passion. You are electric right now and rolling in the thunder of your success. Don't choke up, instead, be free with your communications, have a carefree attitude, and remain versatile in all that you do.

Messengers:

Animal: *Sea Fans (coral)*
Nature: *Artichoke (vegetable)*
Universe/Energy: *Fata Morgana (mirage phenomenon)*

708

This is a time of opening to your creative forces, connecting to higher consciousness, and making an extreme spiritual transformation within yourself. The energy of the Universe surrounds you, moves through you, and strengthens you. Intuition is on the rise, knowledge just comes to you, and dreams become prophetic.

Messengers:

Animal: *Snake*
Nature: *Wind Chill Factor*
Universe/Energy: *Lighten up (action)*

709

There is so much more to you than what people can see. Your character is very deep, solid, and infused with color. You're charismatic, interesting, and are often hard to contain. Being difficult to get in contact with only makes you more fascinating.

Messengers:

Animal: *Moccasin (snake)*
Nature: *Moonlight*
Universe/Energy: *Striped Iceberg (phenomenon)*

710

When you're connected to the Divine, reflecting what is hidden beyond comes quite naturally to you. Even though it can't be seen, doesn't mean it's not there. Your empathic nature makes you compatible with even the most annoying people because you understand them.

Messengers:

Animal: *Mayfly (insect)*
Nature: *Cocoon Plant*
Universe/Energy: *Empathic Ability*

711

Master your mind to master your words. Speak from a source of strength, power, and gratitude. Goodness can speak volumes. Think of life as a mountain. When you stand on the top you can see for miles and lose yourself in the beauty all around you. Life is as beautiful and fulfilling as you make it.

Messengers:

Animal: *Pollock (fish)*
Nature: *Ridge*
Universe/Energy: *Ice Blink (phenomenon)*

712

You're not paranoid, just on guard, and are very aware of what is happening around you at all times, so you're never caught unaware. Something or someone is stretching your patience very thin. This is an incredibly good time to practice raising your frequency though internal focus and creative visualization.

Messengers:

Animal: *Garden Snail*
Nature: *Trough (weather)*
Universe/Energy: *Coincidence*

713

Always, always, trust in your gut feelings. That is your intuition guiding you away from danger and into the light. You are living in peacefulness. There have been some hurtful events in the recent past, but you've reconciled with the situation, know it's out of your hands now, and have let it go.

Messengers:

Animal: *Agamid lizards (reptile)*
Nature: *Cattail (plant)*
Universe/Energy: *Gut Instinct*

714

You may be taking care of a child for a while. They may be shy so understanding and patience is necessary. You can move obstacles aside whenever necessary to accomplish a task. Plan ahead so you aren't late for an upcoming event. And if you are late, own it. Don't blame it on something that had nothing to do with your tardiness.

Messengers:

Animal: *Spoonbill (bird)*
Nature: *Warm Front*
Universe/Energy: *Hug (action)*

715

Do you feel like time is just passing by and you're not accomplishing what you wanted in life? Feelings of anger, regret, and sorrow may be overwhelming right now. Feel the emotions, then release them. Negativity will only hold you back and keep you from flying high.

Messengers:

Animal: *Mallard Duck*
Nature: *Sand*
Universe/Energy: *Reach out to someone (action)*

716

Go with the flow. Stop trying to force things to happen or feel responsible for the actions of other people. It is out of your hands. Adapt. Go back to the basics and find balance through trusting your inner self. Drink plenty of water and spend some time near or in water to replenish and revive yourself.

Messengers:

Animal: *Jellyfish*
Nature: *Green Diamond (gemstone)*
Universe/Energy: *Wake up early (action)*

717

Taste the sweet nectar of life. Gather those you care about the most to you. Spend time together creating memories. Laughter and happiness prevail. Feel the love surrounding you and cherish the wonderful circle of people in your life.

Messengers:

Animal: *Fjord Horse*
Nature: *Honeysuckle (plant)*
Universe/Energy: *Go camping (action)*

718

If you're given the opportunity to change, take it. When you don't, you will end up with feelings of resentment because your life isn't going the way you planned. This is a time to rise up against the negativity because it is draining you. Make changes, have fun times, look to the future with ambition and happiness.

Messengers:

Animal: *Croaker (fish)*
Nature: *Parsnip (vegetable)*
Universe/Energy: *Power of Thought*

719

This is a time for togetherness and spending time with family. It's being engaged with one another even if you're doing something as mundane as cleaning the house. It is stability and warmth. You may have difficulties within your family unit but for the moment, try to get along and spend quality time with each other.

Messengers:

Animal: *Hamster*
Nature: *Cumin (spice)*
Universe/Energy: *Energized (sensation)*

720

Complete one task at a time. Think of them as small steps to attain a larger goal. If you overlook them, then part of your foundation will be missing. The holes in the pattern will cause you to slip through, back to the beginning. Start fresh and don't skip steps or jump ahead.

Messengers:

Animal: *Toad*
Nature: *Cherimoya (fruit)*
Universe/Energy: *Light periwinkle (color)*

721

You are filled with a deep tranquility. Harmony, abundance, courage, and satisfaction are prevalent now. Be aware of how you carry yourself, so others do not get the wrong impression. You will face a stubborn individual who is disorganized and enjoys conflict. Be prepared to use finesse when interacting with them.

Messengers:

Animal: *Wild Boar*
Nature: *Magnesite (mineral)*
Universe/Energy: *Wholeness*

722

You are drawn to the water as if by an invisible thread. It doesn't matter if it's an ocean, lake, stream, or puddle. There is just something about water that resonates with your spiritual self. To satisfy the need to be around bodies of water, plan trips to various places and enjoy nature in an aquatic way.

Messengers:

Animal: *Yapok (marsupial)*
Nature: *Ice Cave*
Universe/Energy: *Self-reflection (action)*

723

You may feel like life is spinning out of control right now. Stop everything and just be for a moment. Think hard about what is happening to you right now. Someone may have tried to take over the control you had in your life by involving themselves where they didn't belong. Now is the time to take that control back.

Messengers:

Animal: *Orangutan*
Nature: *Squash*
Universe/Energy: *Root Chakra*

724

Do not feel sorry for yourself. This is a time to be strong. At work you are about to face a betrayal that is deliberate and calculated. Protect your ideas, make backups of your emails and texts so if it should come to it, you will be able to prove your side of the story.

Messengers:

Animal: *Spectacled Owl (bird)*
Nature: *Tarragon (herb)*
Universe/Energy: *Consistency*

725

Honor, leadership, and respect are required. You command attention and have the ability to get the job done. Take your responsibilities seriously and with decisive confidence. Stay watchful and listen to your intuition. You never know when someone else might be looking at you as their role model for how they should conduct themselves in life.

Messengers:

Animal: *Gorilla*
Nature: *Tangerine*
Universe/Energy: *Resolve*

726

Be vibrant, active, and engaging in all you do to achieve all you want. This may mean putting yourself outside of your comfort zone but sometimes that is needed to achieve the results you want to obtain. Try to think of unique ways to accomplish goals.

Messengers:

Animal: *Bird of Paradise*
Nature: *Mulberry*
Universe/Energy: *Compose a Song*

727

Today is a day for optimism, ambition, and good fortune. Be charitable to others. Help them on their own path so they may enjoy the riches they deserve. Unselfish abundance is prevalent for you and yours. Bask in your good fortune.

Messengers:

Animal: *Shovelnose Guitarfish*
Nature: *Bear's Breeches (plant)*
Universe/Energy: *Gladness (feeling)*

728

Use your inner light to illuminate the way for others and for yourself. You are wealthy in spirit and share your knowledge freely with others. However, there are those who will abuse your kindness. Use shrewdness when dealing with them. You already know who they are.

Messengers:

Animal: *Doodlebug*
Nature: *Gooseberry*
Universe/Energy: *Breathtaken (feeling)*

729

The road to wealth is not paved in gold. It requires hard work, persistence, and determination to achieve your financial dreams. It may mean sacrificing to pay off bills and not creating new ones. Others may taunt and tease but stay the path. You are headed toward greatness.

Messengers:

Animal: *Tern (bird)*
Nature: *Cattleya (plant)*
Universe/Energy: *After It Rains (Scent)*

730

Be cautious, practical, and take one step at a time. You tend to move forward quickly, jumping from one thing to another until you reach great heights. Now is not the time for that. Instead take it easy, move forward with caution, and don't give up. This journey is just beginning, and it will be a long path that leads to success.

Messengers:

Animal: *Goat*
Nature: *Azalea (plant)*
Universe/Energy: *Nurture a plant (action)*

731

Keeping secrets is on the top of your list. There are things you're working on and doing that you don't want anyone to know about in case they don't work out. When you stay silent about something you're doing, it gives it power. The more power you give to a project or idea, the stronger it grows.

Messengers:

Animal: *Corncrake (bird)*
Nature: *Sea Oats*
Universe/Energy: *Ethics*

732

Loud noises at night will be disruptive in the near future. You will only experience them for a short while so don't get upset. Roll over and go back to sleep. In the light of day, you'll remember a dream that was prophetic. Heed what you saw and heard for it is important.

Messengers:

Animal: *Guava Moth*
Nature: *Brown Mustard*
Universe/Energy: *Conversation*

733

Don't let the storms of life flatten your dreams. Instead, use the emotional and spiritual energy within you to lift you to new heights. You are a leader who is responsible and dependable. This is just a setback and you'll be back on your feet in no time.

Messengers:

Animal: *Mountain Lion*
Nature: *Derecho (weather)*
Universe/Energy: *Misty Rose (color)*

734

Creative expression is at the forefront. It takes courage and an instinctive nature to know when the time is right to present your work to the public. You may feel a bit vulnerable displaying your work for others to see but it is an essential step in your growth, both personal and spiritual.

Messengers:

Animal: *Ocelot (feline)*
Nature: *Snap Peas*
Universe/Energy: *Tackle a goal (action)*

735

You have the gift of perfect timing, of knowing when to wait, to use stealth to discover secret information, to sneak up on the competition and when to pounce. Use what you have in creative ways. Take your time and do things right the first time so they don't have to be redone later.

Messengers:

Animal: *Tarantula (spider)*
Nature: *Fig*
Universe/Energy: *White (Color)*

736

You may be a little freaked out because an opportunity has presented itself to you, but it seems veiled with some uncertainty. Ask questions to get to the root of the matter to be entirely sure how you feel about it before committing. It is a great prospect and can be beneficial to you. Just make sure you'll be able to work with the people involved.

Messengers:

Animal: *Przewalski's Wild Horse*
Nature: *Palm Wood*
Universe/Energy: *Nurture a good habit*

737

A balancing act is needed in your current situation. Strategy, intelligence, and stealth are important too. There are fragile and dominant personalities involved and each needs to be handled differently. You're a leader who is used to managing others but this time it's a fine line. Be careful in your actions and always have good intentions.

Messengers:

Animal: *Bobcat*
Nature: *Loquat (plant)*
Universe/Energy: *Destiny*

738

You've been caught up in a situation that seems to have a life of its own and you're not sure how to get uninvolved. People are being nosy and quite ridiculous in their actions. It may be hard to step away. You might just have to pull a disappearing act and separate yourself from the people involved to get out of it.

Messengers:

Animal: *Gharial Crocodile (reptile)*
Nature: *Jet Stream (weather)*
Universe/Energy: *Nickel (color)*

739

Cut loose and purify any negative energies that are connected to you so you can get back in the swing of things. These energies have been pulling you away from the good things in your life. It's time to examine which is more important to you. Goodness is always a better choice.

Messengers:

Animal: *Nuthatch (bird)*
Nature: *Peridotite Pumice (rock)*
Universe/Energy: *Forest ambience (sound)*

740

Timing is of utmost importance. Consider all possibilities as you wait for just the right moment to take action. Flexibility, predictability, and being solidly grounded will serve you best now. Maintain harmony in your relationships. Explore the unknown. Delve deeper into a topic that interests you.

Messengers:

Animal: *Cat*
Nature: *Spinel (gemstone)*
Universe/Energy: *Wisdom*

741

You have thick skin. Endurance and durability help keep you going in tough times. You can withstand just about anything as long as you stay balanced and are secure in your own worth, spirituality, and ability to draw from all sources when needed.

Messengers:

Animal: *Palmetto Bug*
Nature: *Sheanut (nut)*
Universe/Energy: *Wading in Water*

742

When a new opportunity presents itself, this time, don't take it. Instead, do your investigative research because there is deception behind it. If something looks too good to be true, it probably is. Avoid costly mistakes by being picky about what you do.

Messengers:

Animal: *Pleco (fish)*
Nature: *Acorn*
Universe/Energy: *Proactive*

743

Are you old-fashioned in how you think? Time passes every day and will never end. But if you let yourself, you could feel as if time is running out, as if you're being hunted and can't get ahead in life. Look to the future with a modern approach. Make the best use of the time you have and instead of feeling hunted, become the hunter.

Messengers:

Animal: *Great Horned Owl*
Nature: *Boulder Opal (gemstone)*
Universe/Energy: *Hawk calls (sound)*

744

You're an enlightened, mystical, sensitive person who follows your instincts. You created your own path, followed your dreams, and stayed grounded, which keeps you successful. You're not easily intimidated and have a plethora of patience. All these characteristics will be beneficial in the coming weeks as new opportunities present themselves.

Messengers:

Animal: *Snapping Turtle*
Nature: *Chayote (fruit/vegetable)*
Universe/Energy: *Friendliness*

745

These are exciting times. Travel, visitation, and new opportunities await. Keep your heart full of love for those dearest to you. When you meet new people let them see the real you, not the person you want them to believe you to be. Honesty is of utmost importance right now.

Messengers:

Animal: *Barock Pinto (equine)*
Nature: *Desert*
Universe/Energy: *Adventure*

746

Don't show signs of weakness regardless of the situation you find yourself in. There is a primal power within you that is just waiting to burst forth. Dig deep, be patient, and decisive. Remember that strength is an inner virtue, not something to be used over others to get what you want.

Messengers:

Animal: *Blackbird*
Nature: *Gorge*
Universe/Energy: *Saddle brown (color)*

747

Pay attention to your body, mind, and spirit. These comprise you as a spiritual whole and caring for one without the other will lead to feelings of being off center. This is a good time to absorb new knowledge and to learn to put your ego aside to be successful in a variety of endeavors.

Messengers:

Animal: *Demosponge (sea animal)*
Nature: *Lemon Verbena (plant)*
Universe/Energy: *Skip stones on water (action)*

748

It's a busy time and you're moving about from place to place with your work. You may feel like everything around you is moving at double time and you're keeping up but aren't getting the rest you need. Try to make time for yourself and get enough rest.

Messengers:

Animal: *Spotted Linsang (mammal)*
Nature: *Basin*
Universe/Energy: *Tibetan Singing Bowl (sound)*

749

Open your third eye and look. In this case you don't need permission to look at someone intuitively because they have you in their sights, for good or bad, and you need to know the truth of what's going on to protect yourself. Give every situation your full attention. Simply *be* in the stillness of the moment.

Messengers:

Animal: *Iguana*
Nature: *Euclase (gemstone)*
Universe/Energy: *Synchronicity*

750

You're a solitary creature by nature but have been craving more companionship lately. There is a truth that you are seeking. Do not let others influence you to stray from the path or corrupt the goodness in your heart. It's time to claim a new destiny.

Messengers:

Animal: *Angel Shark*
Nature: *Gas*
Universe/Energy: *Chestnut (Color)*

751

Your mind is stimulated, and you're prepared for any type of tests, presentations, or negotiations. You enjoy interpreting challenging subjects. You are driven to obtain results. Keep at it, you're doing a great job.

Messengers:

Animal: *Bonobo (primate)*
Nature: *Azurite (gemstone)*
Universe/Energy: *Gentleness*

752

You are willing to stand out from the crowd. To be the center of attention. You represent harmony, unity, and peace. Family is important and you'll do anything necessary to keep the family stable and united. Together you are stronger than you are individually.

Messengers:

Animal: *Koi (fish)*
Nature: *Nacreous Clouds*
Universe/Energy: *Isolate Briefly for Clarity (action)*

753

You're committed to developing your intuitive abilities, understanding your spirituality, and taking care of your higher self through connections with the Divine. This is a time of exploration and discovery in the spiritual realm. To understand your soul truth. Seek guidance from those who are already walking the same path, whose knowledge will advance your growth.

Messengers:

Animal: *Sheep*
Nature: *Rye Grass*
Universe/Energy: *Moonbow (phenomenon)*

754

You tend to look at situations deeper than most people. If you're going through a dry spell, you can withstand it because you've prepared ahead. It would be easy for you to imitate others, but you choose instead to follow your own soul song and do things in your own unique way.

Messengers:

Animal: *Mockingbird*
Nature: *Bulrush (plant)*
Universe/Energy: *Fresh cut pine (scent)*

755

Your connection to ancient and divine knowledge has enabled you to become a spiritual warrior, a guardian to protect those who are still learning and to guide them along their path. You believe that everything and everyone has a unique purpose, which leaves nothing to chance. Instead, it was meant to be for a reason.

Messengers:

Animal: *Crocodile*
Nature: *Pegmatite Peridotite (rock)*
Universe/Energy: *Chance Encounter*

756

Do not let power corrupt you. Remain honest to overcome negative intent that is pretending to be goodness. If you succumb, then your luck may turn and negativity can take hold. Avoid this if possible. Picture your future in positivity and light.

Messengers:

Animal: *Red-winged Blackbird*
Nature: *Coco de Mer (tree)*
Universe/Energy: *Straw (color)*

757

Protect yourself from injury by avoiding sharp objects. You may feel pressure that you've placed on yourself or that others are putting on you. Take time for yourself in order to regain your balance and eliminate stress. While you typically do not like to avoid issues, this is a good time to do so for a short time.

Messengers:

Animal: *Brown Pelican*
Nature: *Cay / Key (landform)*
Universe/Energy: *Exhilaration (emotion)*

758

Don't ignore messages from the Universe just because you don't like what you hear. Sometimes the thing you need most is what you least desire. Life is not a competition or a game to be played. It is a path to walk towards enlightenment.

Messengers:

Animal: *Paca (rodent)*
Nature: *Riverbank*
Universe/Energy: *Sonar (sound)*

759

This is a time of new growth, of being larger than life. It's time to climb the highest mountains, to see a clear way to your higher purpose. Let go of anything that is holding you back. You're starting a new chapter of your life, sing loudly and celebrate the changes happening around you.

Messengers:

Animal: *American Robin (bird)*
Nature: *Mountain*
Universe/Energy: *Reverence*

760

You may feel like you're on an emotional rollercoaster. Things are changing and some of it isn't good. But you are adept at turning bad situations into good ones so keep the faith. Don't listen to the murmurings of others. Gossip isn't going to help you deal with this situation.

Messengers:

Animal: *Rainbow Snake*
Nature: *Beech Tree*
Universe/Energy: *Release Drama*

761

You're on a quest for knowledge. It feels as if something you should know is just out of your reach. Connect to your intuition to bring clarity. If something seems not quite right in your world, now may be the time to let go of extra baggage. Take additional precautions to prevent injuries.

Messengers:

Animal: *Partridge*
Nature: *Cauliflower*
Universe/Energy: *Sleigh bells (sound)*

762

Sometimes you need to move slowly even though you're on fire. Protect your home and health. Remember, you cannot lose what you did not have to begin with. Experience teaches the truth of all matters; you simply need to pay attention to the lessons.

Messengers:

Animal: *Green Turtle*
Nature: *Lava*
Universe/Energy: *Splendid (sensation)*

763

Look for the signs of success all around you. When you need confirmation that you're on the right track, it will come in a manner you least expect. Be watchful so you don't miss what the Universe is trying to tell you.

Messengers:

Animal: *Cod (fish)*
Nature: *Sassafras (plant)*
Universe/Energy: *New Car Smell (Scent)*

764

Are you misinterpreting the information you're receiving? Changing it around to fit your own purposes instead of taking it as it is meant to be? Scrutinize yourself and determine if you really are acting in your best interest for spiritual growth or if you're being manipulative to get what you want.

Messengers:

Animal: *Molly (fish)*
Nature: *Sprite (weather)*
Universe/Energy: *Sparks (phenomenon)*

765

Look out for pranks, practical jokes, and hoaxes. Someone else might think they're funny but hijinks will only make you mad. Everything comes in cycles, and you must climb high at different times in your life to attain the growth you seek.

Messengers:

Animal: *Island Fox*
Nature: *Giant Sequoias (tree)*
Universe/Energy: *Nourish*

766

You're going on a spiritual quest. Plan with both direction, movement, determination, and foresight. Leaving everything to the last minute or venturing out without preparation will cause undue stress and problems during what should be a happy occasion. Embrace the difficulties while knowing things will get better soon.

Messengers:

Animal: *Argus (bird)*
Nature: *Devil's Claw (plant)*
Universe/Energy: *Camera shutter (sound)*

767

Missed deadlines, change of plans, failed deliveries. It's enough to make you mad at the world. But that's not who you are. You take a higher road and handle everything going wrong in stride. Instead of sitting on the fence you make a decision and jump to the side you prefer.

Messengers:

Animal: *Stonefish*
Nature: *Iris (plant)*
Universe/Energy: *Smoke (color)*

768

Now is the time to become more respectful of nature and the natural laws of the Universe. Get outside to experience the natural world firsthand. Appreciate what you have been given. You may not always get what you want, but you'll always receive what you need.

Messengers:

Animal: *Buffalo*
Nature: *Meteorite Remnants*
Universe/Energy: *Underwater (sound)*

769

If you feel weary of fighting to get ahead, of taking one step forward and two steps back just remember that the difficult tasks are the ones that make you stronger. Have an emotional meltdown by yourself if you need too, and then get right back in the saddle.

Messengers:

Animal: *Hanoverian (equine)*
Nature: *Spathiphyllum (plant)*
Universe/Energy: *Attentive*

770

Be authentic with yourself. Denying parts of your being will only cause you to deceive yourself. Yes, there is a need for self-preservation, but you can do that with honesty from within. No one else needs to know everything about you. Boundaries are necessary to keep your authentic self safe.

Messengers:

Animal: *Oystercatcher (bird)*
Nature: *Lotus (plant)*
Universe/Energy: *Fun (feeling)*

771

Your brain may be telling you one thing when your heart is telling you something completely different. This is a time of weighing pros and cons, of deciding what path you will take, and stepping forward to make any changes needed.

Messengers:

Animal: *Dutch Warmblood (equine)*
Nature: *Anyolite (rock)*
Universe/Energy: *Ride a Horse (action)*

772

Be pure of spirit, innocent by nature, and seek clarity in all things. Open the doorways that lead from darkness into light so that all may see the Divine. Replenish your energy frequently for you are light, love, what comes before, and what comes after.

Messengers:

Animal: *Indigo Bunting (bird)*
Nature: *Gardenia*
Universe/Energy: *Be modest (action)*

773

Your home is your sanctuary. Brighten it up with color, laughter, and love. This is a time of forgiveness. Be compassionate so you can understand the reasons for another's actions. All isn't what it seems, and you need clarity to realize the truth. You can either accept it or reject it.

Messengers:

Animal: *House Finch*
Nature: *Lima Bean*
Universe/Energy: *Blue (Color)*

774

There should be balance between pecking away at something or building it up. The decision is yours to make but will affect others. You might start off strong and then give up prematurely. Don't cast doubt on your ambitions. See them through.

Messengers:

Animal: *Pileated Woodpecker*
Nature: *Steam*
Universe/Energy: *Jolly (emotion)*

775

Your normal schedule may be topsy-turvy now. You may be hiding out during the day and being more active at night or vice versa. There are energies moving around you making things happen that could be beneficial to you in the long run. This is a temporary situation. Soon things will slow down and go back to normal.

Messengers:

Animal: *KodKod (feline)*
Nature: *Mold*
Universe/Energy: *Rooster Crowing (Sound)*

776

Electrifying! Exciting! That's what people think when they meet you even if they keep their distance. Some people are shy and may not come up and talk to you, but you never know who you may be influencing with your words and actions. Your positive nature attracts others yet slipping away unnoticed is a natural talent for you.

Messengers:

Animal: *Eel*
Nature: *Fluvial Island (topography)*
Universe/Energy: *Green Flash (phenomenon)*

777

It's time to have fun! Add color, lightness, and brightness to your life. Become more carefree, embrace change, and let go of the old to embrace the new. Break out of your cocoon to welcome the exciting adventures waiting for you with joy and vitality.

Messengers:

Animal: *Butterfly*
Nature: *Broadleaf Arrowhead*
Universe/Energy: *Fairy Ring*

778

Being in complete harmony with your life can start from the smallest of songs. Live with lightness of being, encasing everything around you with your spiritual light. Base your actions on truth and honesty to have lasting happiness.

Messengers:

Animal: *Towhee (bird)*
Nature: *Pampas Grass*
Universe/Energy: *Gong (sound)*

779

Do not believe everything you read. Half-truths are still lies and if you let them overtake your life you'll never know what to believe. Weed them out. Stay away from people who are greedy or who try to wield their power over you. Let your eyes open to the truth.

Messengers:

Animal: *Sage Grouse (bird)*
Nature: *Sea Lettuce (seaweed)*
Universe/Energy: *Inquisitive (feeling)*

780

New relationships may be started at this time. It's time to shed your old skin and revel in the new. Shield your heart from the hurts of the past to embrace a new love and new joy. Negativity cannot take root when overwhelmed by goodness. Take your time, there's no need to rush things.

Messengers:

Animal: *Water Monitor (reptile)*
Nature: *Ruby (gemstone)*
Universe/Energy: *Patience*

781

You're self-reliant but make sure you reserve your energy. You're about to take a journey, either a physical one to a new location or a spiritual journey. Look inside for clarity and empowerment. You carry your own burdens, are your own cheerleader, and have everything you need to survive. It's your time to be of service to others.

Messengers:

Animal: *Camel*
Nature: *Rainbow*
Universe/Energy: *Heart-warming (feeling)*

782

Keep some plans on the back burner for now because you'll have the opportunity to work with those in the future. You're hungry for success and will go the extra miles needed to achieve it. This is the time to hunker down and get things done instead of putting things off. You can rest later.

Messengers:

Animal: *Ghost Bat*
Nature: *Cannonball Tree*
Universe/Energy: *Blue Violet (Color)*

783

You're hungry for the things that success will bring into your life. You're working endlessly to manifest the material. Don't forget about the spiritual. You could hide inside the coolness of a cavern and still feel the heat of the sun if your heart isn't in the right place.

Messengers:

Animal: *Ptarmigan (bird)*
Nature: *Cave*
Universe/Energy: *Cymbals (Sound)*

784

Dreams can become reality and you can make it happen. New beginnings surround you. Innovative ideas you can implement and develop seem to bombard you at every turn. Which one do you pick? Stop, listen intuitively, and then go with the one you feel most drawn too. Now is the time to build. Start your own business.

Messengers:

Animal: *Wasp*
Nature: *Black Pepper*
Universe/Energy: *Noble (feeling)*

785

Expect interruptions or delays in your plans. Things will not completely change directions but will instead take a pitstop. Once a situation is sorted out, you'll once again be moving in forward motion. You'll gain more from dealing with this situation now than you will by avoiding it. Ignoring it will end up costing you a lot of money later.

Messengers:

Animal: *Yellowtail (fish)*
Nature: *Galena (mineral)*
Universe/Energy: *Radio waves (phenomenon)*

786

To protect against damage from the storms of life, be responsible, stable, and reliable. Make sure all your paperwork is in order to give you the security you need. This could lead to new opportunities, jobs, or growth. Keeping family close is important now to enjoy their company and acquire their help within your family unit as needed.

Messengers:

Animal: *Wombat (marsupial)*
Nature: *Prevailing Wind*
Universe/Energy: *Cadet Blue (Color)*

787

Watch for hidden dangers that occur when you're participating in events held outside. Be careful where you step so you don't fall on your face. Things aren't always what they seem so be careful with your words to avoid the open mouth, insert foot syndrome.

Messengers:

Animal: *Tokay Gecko (reptile)*
Nature: *Red Hot Lips Flower*
Universe/Energy: *Turning a page (sound)*

788

Forward navigation and steadiness under pressure is at the forefront. You hide in plain sight and often go unnoticed if you're making the effort. Otherwise, you're a force of nature and demand people's attention. Blending in will allow you to uncover vital information required at this time.

Messengers:

Animal: *Stingray*
Nature: *Ethiopian Opal (gemstone)*
Universe/Energy: *Flexibility*

789

Pay attention to a third person who is going to try to mess things up for you. This could be someone who wants to take your significant other away from you or just cause trouble in your relationships. Meet this situation head on to put it out immediately. This troublemaker isn't someone you want in your life.

Messengers:

Animal: *Spotted Quoll (marsupial)*
Nature: *Jicama (vegetable)*
Universe/Energy: *Mindfulness*

790

Avoid being encased in a destructive situation that completely clouds your vision. Instead, get away. Open your wings to fly toward Universal clarity of purpose. No one can hold you down if you don't want them to. It is your decision to be held down by another or to fly free on your own wings.

Messengers:

Animal: *Monarch Butterfly*
Nature: *Pyroclastic Flow*
Universe/Energy: *Fawn (color)*

791

Sensibility is your nature. If something seems dangerous, you'll balk at doing it. If you're asked to carry too much of a load, you'll refuse. You rely on your own wit and intelligence to get your points across. You're entirely capable of handling what you take on, and you don't mind helping others, but you can see right through someone taking advantage of you.

Messengers:

Animal: *Mule*
Nature: *Boysenberry*
Universe/Energy: *Electromagnetic energy (phenomenon)*

792

Your guides are seeking you out. They're patiently waiting for you to answer their call, to pay attention to their presence, and to listen to what they have to say. It's time to uncover the wisdom hidden inside of you, to defrost it, and set it free. You will be praised by your guides for purposefully following your path of spiritual discovery.

Messengers:

Animal: *Maned Sloth (mammal)*
Nature: *Frost*
Universe/Energy: *Applause (Sound)*

793

It is more important to believe in what you feel than what you're seeing right now. You may find yourself in an unusual situation where there are many demands on your time, energy, and kindness. Remain faithful in your beliefs. There is a conflict brewing that isn't going to be obvious at first. Pay close attention so you can nip it in the bud.

Messengers:

Animal: *Mole*
Nature: *Diabase Quartz Diorite (rock)*
Universe/Energy: *Socialize (action)*

794

Do not stray from your path. Maintain forward motion, look for what is hidden underneath. Analyze situations to find balance, pay attention to your ultimate goals, and act on your intuitive impressions. Abundance surrounds you so avoid distractions. If some knowledge doesn't feel right to you, or feels impossible to grasp, come back to it in the future.

Messengers:

Animal: *Hippopotamus*
Nature: *Halite (mineral)*
Universe/Energy: *Music*

795

You took a risk, and it paid off. You're independent and follow your instincts, especially when it comes to business. Success is the result of your high drive and determination to make things work to your advantage. Even with everything going great you remain respectful and approachable to others.

Messengers:

Animal: *Rainbow Fish*
Nature: *Passion Fruit*
Universe/Energy: *Humble*

796

For someone else, you are their rock, their foundation, their strength. They rely on you to feel the loving and nurturing comforts of home when their world feels topsy-turvy. You are their safe harbor. This is a time of cleansing. Of making wrongs right.

Messengers:

Animal: *Mushroom Coral*
Nature: *Rain Shower*
Universe/Energy: *Cookies Fresh from the Oven (Scent)*

797

Reserve your inner strength, control your emotions, and above all else, give yourself time to heal. Pain can be relieved through various techniques, but it is important to not reinjure yourself. Be wary of the desires you're hiding from others. They may not turn out as you plan if you achieve them.

Messengers:

Animal: *Boomslang (snake)*
Nature: *Rosemary (herb)*
Universe/Energy: *Copper Penny (color)*

798

Nighttime activities need your attention. Keep a journal beside your bed so you can write down your dreams. Also make note of the time when you wake up during the night and any intuitive or paranormal events happening at that time. You're in a trifecta of events. Anything you note may be important over the next few days so write it all down.

Messengers:

Animal: *June Bug*
Nature: *Angelica (plant)*
Universe/Energy: *Comfortable (feeling)*

799

It's time to rebuild what has fallen apart. Things happen in life that you don't like or expect. When everything falls apart, that's when you realize just how strong you are and how much of a burden you can carry. There is magick, hope, and the purest energy from the Universe helping you succeed.

Messengers:

Animal: *Crested Gecko (reptile)*
Nature: *Dale (topography)*
Universe/Energy: *Light waves (phenomenon)*

800

When you need to save money, creativity is called for to help you through until you can earn more. Being thrifty can also lead to the discovery of a creative talent you have for making something that others will want to buy. You could start a new business which will improve your financial situation.

Messengers:

Animal: *Shrew (mammal)*
Nature: *Fenugreek (plant)*
Universe/Energy: *Brainstorming (action)*

801

Be alert to false promises and impersonations. The situation isn't what it appears. It looks like a diamond, shines like a diamond but isn't a real diamond. You may feel restless and out of sorts. Take a walk, get out in nature, or do something to move your body. Patience and wisdom of judgement is called for now.

Messengers:

Animal: *Tanager (bird)*
Nature: *Beehives*
Universe/Energy: *Nonverbal communication*

802

Do not try to force things to move. When you push too hard you can end up locked up and frozen in place instead of moving forward. There are times when waiting is the best course of action to take. Prepare, think things through, and when the time is right, then you make your move.

Messengers:

Animal: *Sloth Bear*
Nature: *Gorse (plant)*
Universe/Energy: *Problem solving (action)*

803

You always see someone's true colors, their unique abilities, strength, and inner beauty. It is because you possess all these qualities yourself that enables you to see them in others. You're perceptive, a strong leader, and excel in business. You are a flirt and make others feel good about themselves. You are courageous and usually stay on the path you've chosen.

Messengers:

Animal: *Tiger*
Nature: *Red Diamond (gemstone)*
Universe/Energy: *Giddy*

804

Getting out and about and meeting new people is helpful now. Engage in the arts, enjoy culture, and the beautiful joy they'll bring. Show your feelings, speak your truth. In all that you do, blessings will follow if you take a chance on yourself.

Messengers:

Animal: *Tundra Swan*
Nature: *Marsh Blazingstar (plant)*
Universe/Energy: *Shyness (feeling)*

805

Expect your current projects to pick up steam and move forward quicker than you expected. You'll be rewarded for the effort you've put into getting this off the ground. Be inventive as you progress. There are a few changes you can make to improve upon what you're doing. Take time to consider the intentions of the people around you so you can make appropriate decisions .

Messengers:

Animal: *Corn Snake*
Nature: *Saturation Point*
Universe/Energy: *Hunter Green (color)*

806

You're mysterious and intriguing to others. They want to know your secrets, but you keep them to yourself no matter how much prodding they do. You have a curious nature that can often spice up your life due to situations you get involved in. If you need to escape from the world for a while, go for a drive and let yourself settle.

Messengers:

Animal: *Squid (cephalopod)*
Nature: *Lovage (plant)*
Universe/Energy: *Wind Gusts (sound)*

807

Working together for the greater good is important now. Don't get discouraged if there are a few setbacks. You'll be able to bounce back. Opportunities are bountiful now so grab onto them and get to work. This is a time of joy. Celebrate the life you're living.

Messengers:

Animal: *Purple Martin (bird)*
Nature: *Bamboo Shoots*
Universe/Energy: *Decision making (action)*

808

There are latent abilities within you that are just waiting to be discovered. A catalyst is needed to spark their emergence. Read about topics that interest you to get started. Don't let the things others say make you disillusioned about yourself or create an inflated ego. Stay grounded.

Messengers:

Animal: *Northern Pike (fish)*
Nature: *Blackberry*
Universe/Energy: *Witty (feeling)*

809

You are a unique individual who makes great strides in life if you set your mind to accomplishing your goals. Don't get lazy. Leap at opportunities. Trust your natural rhythm and first instincts instead of second guessing yourself. Find uniqueness in unconventionality. Don't doubt yourself now.

Messengers:

Animal: *Grasshopper*
Nature: *Paradise Nut*
Universe/Energy: *Pink (Color)*

810

You may be on a slippery path that could turn dangerous at this time. Be careful of how you're treating others because they may have negative feelings toward you due to your actions. Don't fall through into icy waters just because you're unable to act appropriately in difficult situations.

Messengers:

Animal: *Elephant Shrew (mammal)*
Nature: *Frozen Lake*
Universe/Energy: *Jungle Ambience (sound)*

811

You do not have to do anything you don't want to do just because someone else wants you to do it. Stand your ground. You may experience a feeling of becoming emotionally distant from someone that you thought was a friend because of their recent actions. Is it forgivable? If not, take the path you need to take.

Messengers:

Animal: *Aye Aye (primate)*
Nature: *Fjord (topography)*
Universe/Energy: *Bonding (feeling)*

812

You're resistant to change. You like the way things are and don't see any reason to do things differently. If it's not broken don't fix it. Use your wisdom when facing a challenge. The answer is already inside of you. You are about to face a turning point in your life which will bring powerful energy to you. Take your own advice.

Messengers:

Animal: *Coelacanth (fish)*
Nature: *Naiad (aquatic plant)*
Universe/Energy: *Advice*

813

This is not the time to be complacent. There's work to be done and you need to get busy doing it. Putting it off, procrastinating, or ignoring the situation will end up producing negative results. It's time to swim in the waters of your creation to understand fluidity of motion.

Messengers:

Animal: *Sea Lily (crinoid)*
Nature: *Summer*
Universe/Energy: *Trying*

814

Store supplies, food, and necessities but don't hoard them. Make sure to clear away all the cobwebs from both your home and mind to allow the energy to flow as it should. Consider past hurts and find ways to learn from the experience and move forward from it. Being prepared is a multi-level task encompassing the physical, mental, and emotional.

Messengers:

Animal: *Brown Recluse (spider)*
Nature: *Pitcher Plant*
Universe/Energy: *Air Conditioner Turning on/off (sound)*

815

Little things are getting on your nerves. Don't let them build up until you feel like you're living in a horror movie. Everything doesn't have to be pitch perfect to run well. Make adjustments and find a way to get centered and calm so every little thing doesn't get blown out of proportion.

Messengers:

Animal: *Fire Ant*
Nature: *Nitrogen*
Universe/Energy: *Shouts of Joy (Sound)*

816

There's a song in your heart that you can happily sing as you go about your work. Enjoy living quietly for a while and let the rush of a busy schedule sit by the wayside. Prosperity in all things is waiting for you. Overall, your wellbeing is positive and full of joy.

Messengers:

Animal: *Jersey Cow*
Nature: *Pelican Flower*
Universe/Energy: *Person Whistling (Sound)*

817

You're happy when you succeed but you're even happier when those you care about succeed. Take a break from work to play. This will recharge your creativity and spark your imagination. This is a great time to start something new that you've been thinking about or to launch a new campaign at work.

Messengers:

Animal: *Otter*
Nature: *Joshua Tree*
Universe/Energy: *Dog Panting (Sound)*

818

Protect what is yours. You're lucky in many ways that others can't see. This is a magical time for you where you will achieve goals you never expected to achieve. You work hard and it shows. Scavenging will result in surprising rewards.

Messengers:

Animal: *Sandpiper (bird)*
Nature: *Cumulonimbus Clouds*
Universe/Energy: *Relationship building (action)*

819

Watch out for those who want to take from you what doesn't belong to them. The act will be devious, sneaky, and you may not even realize it is happening until you start to feel the drain on your lifestyle. Once the situation is known to you, eliminate the pest immediately. Don't let your emotions play havoc with your decision.

Messengers:

Animal: *Mahi-mahi (fish)*
Nature: *Pansy (plant)*
Universe/Energy: *Sentimentality*

820

Love, affection, and gratitude are important emotions to share with others now. Plan an event for family and close friends to let them know how much you feel for them and appreciate their part in your life. This is a time of sharing deep emotions, of clearing murky waters, and moving past old grievances.

Messengers:

Animal: *Reef Shark*
Nature: *Bellflower*
Universe/Energy: *Grilling Outside (Scent)*

821

Are you ready for a 360-degree change? If so, make it happen. This is a time of letting go of the old and embracing everything that is new and exciting. Adventure is on the top of your list, doing things that satisfy you emotionally, spiritually, and physically. Don't listen to the critics. You follow your dreams. Game on!

Messengers:

Animal: *Mole Rat*
Nature: *Cayenne Pepper*
Universe/Energy: *Sound waves (phenomenon)*

822

Sometimes to boost your output of work you need to take a break and separate yourself from the job. When you return to it, you will have a clearer vision of how to proceed, or you will have reenergized yourself enough that you can continue with ease.

Messengers:

Animal: *Crown of Thorns (starfish)*
Nature: *Moldavite (gemstone)*
Universe/Energy: *Productivity*

823

Transformation is essential. Release any negativity that is holding you back. You may experience an inner change or a change in your physical location. Participating in group events will keep your keen sense of observation active. Just remember to let people rely on themselves instead of hanging on to you in the long run.

Messengers:

Animal: *Bat*
Nature: *Mountain Lake*
Universe/Energy: *Pipe (Scent)*

824

Find the answers you see in the repetitive things happening around you. You might slip and slide as you climb to greater heights but that's part of the lesson you're learning. Create an impenetrable barrier around yourself so you can attune to the Divine. It can be removed when you feel your frequency is elevated to where it protects you seamlessly.

Messengers:

Animal: *Rail (bird)*
Nature: *Sand Dunes*
Universe/Energy: *Frequency*

825

If you feel as if you're been here, done this before, then it is a sign you're on the right path. Continue as you were in order to reach the level of understanding of Universal Consciousness that you need. If something is hidden it will only be for a short time. Be observant as you move forward.

Messengers:

Animal: *Plover (bird)*
Nature: *Lunar Eclipse*
Universe/Energy: *Déjà vu*

826

It's important to be strong yet flexible in your current situation. There are times when you need to bend but not break so others can learn from you. Growth by example is key now. You are protected from negativity by unseen forces. Abundance and good fortune are drawn to you.

Messengers:

Animal: *Longhorn Beetle*
Nature: *Azurmalachite (gemstone)*
Universe/Energy: *Indigo (Color)*

827

Study and learning are on the agenda. Whether it's deciding to go back to school to get a degree or studying something just because you want to know about it, it's time to become a student. Find others with shared interests, become part of a group, and ask lots of questions. Multiple teachers will show up to guide you on this path.

Messengers:

Animal: *Zokor (rodent)*
Nature: *Riverbed*
Universe/Energy: *Spend time with friends (action)*

828

The odds are for you, so take a chance. Gambling and risk taking could have very good outcomes now. Don't risk or gamble too much where you could be left in dire circumstances if it doesn't go well. Just risk a little and you could gain a lot. This is not only in regards to finances but in other areas of life as well.

Messengers:

Animal: *Harlequin Duck*
Nature: *Sweet Pea*
Universe/Energy: *Sit and think on a park bench (action)*

829

Be humble, thankful, and emotionally strong. You are connected to ancient wisdom. The element of choice is on your side. People can't hurt or upset you unless you allow them to do so. If you choose to remain happy regardless of their actions, that is your choice. Choose positivity over negativity.

Messengers:

Animal: *Map Turtle*
Nature: *Bluebells (plant)*
Universe/Energy: *Opportunity*

830

It is risky to just accept what life sends your way. By doing so, you're giving other people the power to control what you're doing. By voicing a decision and sticking with it, by selecting one thing over another, you retain the power over your life.

Messengers:

Animal: *Shrike (bird)*
Nature: *Ash*
Universe/Energy: *Mint (Scent)*

831

Be careful of believing urban legends. If a story sounds too wild, crazy, or amazing then it really requires further investigation. Look up what you're being told to see if it is factual before believing it. Be enthusiastic in your approach to life to get better results.

Messengers:

Animal: *Camel Spider*
Nature: *Icicle*
Universe/Energy: *Ardent*

832

Things happen and it's your response to the events that will set you apart from others. Instead of falling apart in the face of adversity, stand tall, and look it in the eye. Instead of hiding from your responsibilities, own them and do what is right.

Messengers:

Animal: *Dung Beetle*
Nature: *Fig Tree*
Universe/Energy: *Lively*

833

Your words can cause harm right now when you don't mean for them too. Be careful with your actions because they too can give the wrong impression. Follow these rules as part of your growth. Never doubt your intuition and don't take yourself too seriously. Remember to laugh.

Messengers:

Animal: *Hyena*
Nature: *Estuary (topography)*
Universe/Energy: *New Baby Smell (Scent)*

834

There are rapid developments taking place in your life. Don't delude yourself about what the results will be in the end. Be logical and rational and expect the best outcome. Make sure you're walking on solid ground, so you don't lose your footing.

Messengers:

Animal: *Giant Grouper (fish)*
Nature: *Siltstone (rock)*
Universe/Energy: *Cocreation*

835

Transformation often consists of highs and lows as you experience the changes happening to you. Change doesn't always have to be dramatic. It can be quiet and calm. You'll find you're overflowing in many areas of your life, which means there's no room for new opportunities to come to you. Let go of the old to make way for the new.

Messengers:

Animal: *Salamander*
Nature: *Broccoflower (vegetable)*
Universe/Energy: *Red ochre (color)*

836

Negative traits are causing you to want to fight with someone. Instead, get away from the situation for a while and connect with the Divine. Ask which path you should take in the given circumstances and an answer will be delivered to you. Believe the first thing you hear instead of second guessing it if you don't like the answer.

Messengers:

Animal: *Buelingo (cattle)*
Nature: *Mangosteen (fruit)*
Universe/Energy: *School Bell (sound)*

837

Don't be afraid if you are asked to walk a difficult path. Take careful steps, go slowly, and remain alert to any possible changes in direction. Clarity of mind and vision are important now. What you put into motion now will have long term effects.

Messengers:

Animal: *Blue Tongue Skink (reptile)*
Nature: *Kale (vegetable)*
Universe/Energy: *Cleanliness (sensation)*

838

You can apply the lessons you learned in the past to situations you're encountering today. Repeat failures only happen when you don't learn from past ones. To ensure happiness, remain pure in thought, intention, and actions.

Messengers:

Animal: *House Martin (bird)*
Nature: *Snow*
Universe/Energy: *Nirvana*

839

Listen to your own truth. Don't let others push their beliefs on you. Trust yourself. You'll never lead yourself astray but someone else might make you doubt yourself. Don't. You know what you want, so go out and get it. Be strong but don't be conceited.

Messengers:

Animal: *Trout (fish)*
Nature: *Sunset*
Universe/Energy: *Congratulate someone (action)*

840

Embark on a courageous adventure. Try something you've always wanted to do but never thought the time was right to do it. There will never be a better day than today to get started. Sometimes you don't take instructions very well and will just adjust your crown and do what you want to do anyway.

Messengers:

Animal: *Mongoose (mammal)*
Nature: *Pencil Plant*
Universe/Energy: *Doldrums (phenomenon)*

841

Let awareness guide you. There isn't a need for words but instead watch the actions of others. You can determine a lot through quiet observation. Truths will be revealed. If you're trying to capture a specific outcome in your venture, sweeten the deal to entice a quick resolution.

Messengers:

Animal: *Red Wolf*
Nature: *Sweet Pepper*
Universe/Energy: *Pursuit of Dreams*

842

Everything must happen in its own time. You are in a period of transformation. Keep revelations to yourself. Release that which no longer serves you and embrace what is manifesting in your life. Look for lessons in your daily life because when the student is ready, the teacher shows up.

Messengers:

Animal: *Caterpillar*
Nature: *Goshenite (gemstone)*
Universe/Energy: *Olive (color)*

843

Examine the dark aspects of the power inside of you. They will reveal things that can be used for your greater good. Darkness doesn't always mean death and destruction. It can be that which hasn't found the light yet. When darkness is brought into the light, it can shine like the sun.

Messengers:

Animal: *Fire Fish*
Nature: *Cantaloupe*
Universe/Energy: *Answers*

844

Change your plans. There is a destructive energy at work that could pull you into its depths. It's best to avoid it if possible. This may mean a delay on your end, but it will be worth it in the long run. Remember, you're supposed to be where you're supposed to be and if you're delayed, there's a reason for it.

Messengers:

Animal: *Desert Horned Lizard*
Nature: *Maelstrom (whirlpool)*
Universe/Energy: *Willpower*

845

Holding onto emotions and never letting them out will eventually cause you to break apart. Then those emotions will flow so much that you'll feel drained and exhausted. Deal with emotions as they happen to ensure you are living as stress free as possible.

Messengers:

Animal: *Giant Panda*
Nature: *Dam*
Universe/Energy: *Feedback*

846

Stop. Look. Listen. Now move! It's time for quick thinking and fast action. Something is happening behind your back so become more aware to uncover it. Not everything hidden is bad so don't judge too quickly. Keep quiet to discover it faster. You can maneuver out of situations you don't want to be in quickly and efficiently.

Messengers:

Animal: *Weasel*
Nature: *Pyrite (gemstone)*
Universe/Energy: *Spend Quality Time (action)*

847

Expect a weight to be lifted from you as someone else takes over. You can withstand others giving you the cold shoulder because what they think simply isn't that important to you. You tend to be your own person and you don't require permission or the blessings of others to do what you want.

Messengers:

Animal: *Musk Ox*
Nature: *Horehound (plant)*
Universe/Energy: *Test Your Theory*

848

Concentration and focus are necessary now. You are being called to protect someone close to you. The battle will be won if you are honest and forthright in your dealings with people in authority. There may be a few sacrifices made but all will be as it should in the end.

Messengers:

Animal: *Ruddy Duck*
Nature: *Cedar Sedge (plant)*
Universe/Energy: *Moonflower (scent)*

849

What was lost can be recovered. There isn't a time limit for finding what was missing. One day it'll just turn up. Pay attention to your intuition so you can work on developing your strengths. Be clever and cunning when necessary to advance your growth in your job.

Messengers:

Animal: *Stag Beetle*
Nature: *Night Blooming Jessamine (plant)*
Universe/Energy: *Chorus of the Katydids (Sound)*

850

When you walk in other dimensions, you transform, cleanse, and are reborn into the truth of your spiritual essence. The rewards will be immediate and long term. What you have learned now will stay with you always. Unexpected growth is a blessing.

Messengers:

Animal: *Green Frog*
Nature: *Precipitation*
Universe/Energy: *Film projector reel (sound)*

851

This is a bad time to start something new. Wait a few weeks until the energy flow is once again moving forward instead of backwards. Everything will feel like it's at a standstill. Make effective use of this time by doing additional planning to ensure more growth. Have a glass of wine while you're at it to celebrate the success you've already achieved.

Messengers:

Animal: *Dovekie (bird)*
Nature: *Red Grapes*
Universe/Energy: *Gift*

852

Impatience will get you nowhere. Wait for the storm to pass. It's important to remember that while you can easily carry a heavy load, others around you may be overwhelmed by it. Take time to lighten the weight someone else is carrying whenever possible.

Messengers:

Animal: *Brown Skua (bird)*
Nature: *Rainstorm*
Universe/Energy: *Suspension of Disbelief (action)*

853

Speed of thought and quick decisions are important in this situation. Forward progress is contingent upon your ability to think fast and act even faster. Opportunities can slip through your fingers if you take too long. You're fascinated by possibilities.

Messengers:

Animal: *Sawflies (insect)*
Nature: *Rotting Logs*
Universe/Energy: *Infatuation*

854

Embrace your connection to the Divine. Let its positive energy flow through you, elevating your frequency even higher. Even in the hardest of times, the Divine never gives up on you and will empower your spirit. Learn from the lessons given. Never give up on yourself or those who you believe in.

Messengers:

Animal: *Cormorant (bird)*
Nature: *Stevia (plant)*
Universe/Energy: *Consider the Big Picture (action)*

855

That which is difficult to find and exceedingly rare can guide and direct you on your path. You do not have to have it in hand for it to be helpful to you. Watch out for practical jokers who will try to lead you astray. Know what you want and how you plan to get it before setting out.

Messengers:

Animal: *Snipe (bird)*
Nature: *Painite (mineral)*
Universe/Energy: *Cypress Wood (Scent)*

856

If you've been holding onto relationships from the past when you should have let them go a long time ago, now is the time to release them. You may have to camouflage yourself so you can't be seen or contacted to make the separation complete.

Messengers:

Animal: *Cuscus (marsupial)*
Nature: *Mariposite Novaculite (rock)*
Universe/Energy: *Helicopter Flying (Sound)*

857

Opening your third eye is important for you to be able to see the miraculous events unfolding before you. Messages will be more easily received from the spiritual realm. This is also a time to trust in others to lead so you can step back for a while.

Messengers:

Animal: *Green Snake*
Nature: *Double Rainbow*
Universe/Energy: *Miracles*

858

Clarity of thought and broadmindedness will enable you to consider all options in a professional manner. If there's a race to be won, you'll win it. You get out in front of the competition and that's where you stay. You're often in public view so it's imperative to be upfront and honest.

Messengers:

Animal: *Standardbred (equine)*
Nature: *Brazil Nut*
Universe/Energy: *Frivolous (feeling)*

859

Gather all the information you need, then spend some time alone to sort it out. If you realize you are on the wrong path, then turn back and start again. Touch, sound, and relying on your senses is of utmost importance.

Messengers:

Animal: *Ant*
Nature: *Molybdenite (mineral)*
Universe/Energy: *Saffron (color)*

860

Spend more time with family through activities, outings, meals, or just hanging out. Watch people's actions, and not just what they say, to gain a deeper understanding of them. Some may not have your best interest at heart, but you'll be able to tell if you pay attention.

Messengers:

Animal: *Fox*
Nature: *Horseradish (vegetable)*
Universe/Energy: *Empathy*

861

This is a time for you to be mature and have meaningful insights that you can share with others. It's important to connect with the soil of the Earth, to plant seeds that will grow to abundance, to increase the fertility of the season. Some mysteries in life will be revealed.

Messengers:

Animal: *Tree Frog*
Nature: *Cirrostratus Clouds*
Universe/Energy: *Damp Earth (Scent)*

862

You're filled with lighthearted joy. Luck is on your side at every turn. You're open minded, curious, and live with vibrance. Thrilling adventures excite you. Fear or any other negative emotions have no place in your life right now. Live large.

Messengers:

Animal: *Asian Lady Beetle*
Nature: *Naked Man Orchid*
Universe/Energy: *The Beach (scent)*

863

You are being divinely guided toward positive goals. Consider the paths you could take and expect the outcome will be in your best interest. Blindly following what you're guided to do is showing trust, faith, and strength in forces you cannot see.

Messengers:

Animal: *Canvasback (duck)*
Nature: *Filbert (nut)*
Universe/Energy: *Slurp (sound)*

864

This is a time to make something with your hands. Simplicity or complexity doesn't matter. It's the act of creation that is important. Be brave in your efforts, comfortable in your surroundings, and engaging when communicating with others. Calmness and a unique approach are important now.

Messengers:

Animal: *Takin (mammal)*
Nature: *Lavender*
Universe/Energy: *Rustling of Leaves in the Wind (sound)*

865

Problem solving is going to be taking up your time. Remember to look at the issue through the lens of a prism to see all the reflective colors and possibilities. There is more than one way to accomplish a goal. Use your intuition to guide you on this journey.

Messengers:

Animal: *Rook (bird)*
Nature: *Moonflower*
Universe/Energy: *Easy (feeling)*

866

Become more grounded, balanced, and secure within yourself. You tend to nurture others but now is a time to nurture yourself. You're growing at a rapid rate so keep working on your spirituality, especially meditation and understanding your dreams.

Messengers:

Animal: *Penguin*
Nature: *Sawgrass*
Universe/Energy: *Euphoric (emotion)*

867

Someone from your past is coming back around. Messages from the spiritual realm from loved ones who have passed over are also prevalent at this time. Your insight is immensely powerful as is your intuition. Pay close attention to the music around you so that you can see the dance clearly.

Messengers:

Animal: *Harpy Eagle*
Nature: *Dancing Lady Orchid*
Universe/Energy: *Drum Roll (sound)*

868

It feels like you've been traveling for a long time in the darkness but now you're emerging into the light. The lessons learned along the way have dramatically changed you and opened your eyes to the infinite possibilities of the Universe. Continue the path. You're not done yet.

Messengers:

Animal: *Butter Fish*
Nature: *Tunnel*
Universe/Energy: *Jet Fly By (sound)*

869

Sometimes you must wipe the slate clean and start over. Things that are ruined can be replaced. Matters of the heart can be resolved. There is no timeline needed to accomplish your reboot. Just start over and let things play out as they will.

Messengers:

Animal: *Common Whelk (snail)*
Nature: *Flash Flood*
Universe/Energy: *Infinity*

870

Are you trying to hold things together too tightly? Instead of holding on let go a bit and jump around. Move your body to energize your being. Look at the layers from above to see what is below. You may be surprised at what is revealed.

Messengers:

Animal: *Kangaroo Rat*
Nature: *Red Clay*
Universe/Energy: *Subsun (phenomenon)*

871

Putting your heart out there for all to see can be a bit intimidating but can result in a tremendous amount of understanding and guidance. There are times when it will feel like your world is being ripped apart by the storms of life, but they carry deep lessons too.

Messengers:

Animal: *Bleeding Heart Monkey*
Nature: *Supercell (weather)*
Universe/Energy: *Channeling*

872

If you're opening your mouth, have something meaningful to say. Problems can sometime appear to be enormous, but when you really dig into them, they're not big at all. You may experience turbulence, but you will be able to stay afloat.

Messengers:

Animal: *Purple Swamphen (bird)*
Nature: *Cirrus Clouds*
Universe/Energy: *Float on a Raft (action)*

873

Always speak the truth in tactful ways. Explain in a way that is easy to understand, not convoluted and confusing. People look up to you and appreciate the wisdom you share with them, even if it's not what they really want to hear.

Messengers:

Animal: *Conch (mollusk)*
Nature: *Black Bat Flower*
Universe/Energy: *Coins Jingling (Sound)*

874

If you're trying to put things together and it's just not working, step out of the rut you've put yourself in. This should be a time of hope and renewal, not repetition and failures. Snap yourself out of whatever is holding you back. Make each and every day count.

Messengers:

Animal: *Plumed Basilisk (reptile)*
Nature: *Fir Tree*
Universe/Energy: *Sewing Machine (sound)*

875

Live with your eyes wide and ears wide open. Take in everything, even the smallest detail. This will move you along your path in an energetic forward motion. See opportunities in difficult situations. Leap when necessary and sit quietly to see a variety of possibilities.

Messengers:

Animal: *Tarsier (primate)*
Nature: *Feijoa (fruit)*
Universe/Energy: *Train Moving (Sound)*

876

You may feel warm and cozy, but something also feels a bit off. Do an inspection of your energy levels to make sure an outside source isn't draining your energy. It's better to discover the source sooner than later to avoid exhausting repercussions.

Messengers:

Animal: *Vicuña (mammal/camel)*
Nature: *Plagioclase (mineral)*
Universe/Energy: *Rumble (sound)*

877

You're stable and strong during trying times. You can take a lot of brute force thrown your way as words or actions and then calmly stand your ground. Make sure you're getting enough sleep. You're working hard and need your rest. There are quick movements ahead and you'll need to be on your game.

Messengers:

Animal: *Bass (fish)*
Nature: *Mangrove (tree)*
Universe/Energy: *Tangerine yellow (color)*

878

Enjoy the noise around you. Whatever the sound, listen to it with your whole being. If you can't hear it, feel its beat move through you. Let the wholeness of divine light energize and boost the frequency within you. There is so much more to learn.

Messengers:

Animal: *Caspian (equine)*
Nature: *Jujube Fruit*
Universe/Energy: *Pots and Pans Clanging (Sound)*

879

Embrace the joy of friendship. It is different than the joy of family. Spending time with friends is an important part of every person's path. You are a social being. Don't cut yourself off from the world out of fear of being unaccepted. People will love you just for who you are.

Messengers:

Animal: *Herring Gull (bird)*
Nature: *Typhoon*
Universe/Energy: *Sandalwood (Scent)*

880

It's time to get tuned up and balanced in your spiritual life. If you've been dressing up and hopping from one event to another until you feel like you're at your wits end, then it's time to take a break, reenergize, and recharge.

Messengers:

Animal: *Tree Hopper (insect)*
Nature: *Clasping-Leaf Pondweed*
Universe/Energy: *Frogs croaking (sound)*

881

Can you see what is going on all around you? Some ideas need to be left behind while others need to be lifted to higher levels. Both require grit and determination to make the result happen. It's important to remain calm and not get upset in stressful situations. It will help you see and understand the situation clearly so that you can take the appropriate action.

Messengers:

Animal: *Triggerfish*
Nature: *Supernumerary Rainbow*
Universe/Energy: *Vibration*

882

Pinpoint the positive aspects in your life that have made you successful. What have you accomplished? What do you still want to do? Obstacles may appear in your path, but you easily move them aside. You can move in waves to fulfill whatever need you have. Keen observation is needed to hunt down what you want.

Messengers:

Animal: *Siberian Tiger*
Nature: *Kelvin-Helmholtz Wave Cloud*
Universe/Energy: *Gaze at the night sky (action)*

883

You have the stamina to carry yourself great distances. If you find that your passion for something has diminished, then maybe it's time to let it go and make room for something else that holds your interest. Keep your word, especially to yourself. Don't give up too soon.

Messengers:

Animal: *Black Snake Millipede*
Nature: *Ember*
Universe/Energy: *Promises*

884

Calm down and pay attention to details. It's fun to party but now is the time to focus on work and moving forward in life instead of living carefree. Responsibilities should come first, fun later. Don't waste your energy on others but focus on yourself.

Messengers:

Animal: *Mouse*
Nature: *Grains of Paradise (spice)*
Universe/Energy: *Antique White (color)*

885

Are you being overly irritated and defensive? Are you taking your emotions out on those who are just trying to help you? If so, it's time to take a good, hard look at your behavior. People have your best interest at heart. They're not attacking you or berating you. They're only trying to be there for you during a challenging time.

Messengers:

Animal: *Turkey Vulture*
Nature: *Allspice*
Universe/Energy: *Boiling water (sound)*

886

Make yourself slow down before you hurt yourself. When you push yourself to the limit, you get tired and make unnecessary mistakes. This is a time to heal, restore, and renew yourself on all levels. Let the opinions of others just roll off your back. Their words should not sway you one way or the other. Your opinion is the one that matters now.

Messengers:

Animal: *Gadwall (bird)*
Nature: *Cistus (shrub)*
Universe/Energy: *Regeneration*

887

This is a time of building and destruction. You're able to see intricate designs, can see the end result on a blank canvas. When something is no longer needed, you have no problem eliminating it to make way for something better. Working in groups and cooperation takes the forefront.

Messengers:

Animal: *Termite (insect)*
Nature: *Matrix Opal (gemstone)*
Universe/Energy: *Foghorn (Sound)*

888

Others want your attention now. It's a time of learning, teaching, and engaging in interesting conversations. Roles may be reversed in an upcoming situation. While you may expect to be doing one thing, you'll be assigned the opposite. After this project take some time off for family.

Messengers:

Animal: *Rhea (bird)*
Nature: *Broccoli*
Universe/Energy: *Chanting (sound)*

889

Anchor yourself to Earth through an in-depth energy alignment. Focus on allowing Earth's frequency to radiate into your body, and then aligning that frequency with your own. You will be able to heal yourself by using bands of color. Honesty and optimism are needed now.

Messengers:

Animal: *Anhinga (bird)*
Nature: *Iris Agate (gemstone)*
Universe/Energy: *Call to Action*

890

Uncertainty allows you to challenge yourself and to create your own path. Follow where your heart leads you, where you are living in each moment and where you don't have to try so hard to get ahead. When the path becomes easier, walking it becomes a joy. Not everything in life must be difficult. It's all in your perception.

Messengers:

Animal: *Savannah Monitor (reptile)*
Nature: *Scallion (vegetable)*
Universe/Energy: *Introspection (action)*

891

Search for the cause to find the solution. There is always a reason behind reactions. Some unknown fact (or gossip) has others looking at you in a different way. This should tell you they aren't on the same frequency level as you if they stoop to hiding things or talking about you behind your back.

Messengers:

Animal: *Tusk Shells (mollusk)*
Nature: *Escarpment (topography)*
Universe/Energy: *Improvisation*

892

Pay attention to everything around you. Awareness is important right now. You can see the truth behind the disguise, the unexplained within reality, and the intention behind the actions. Lies will be revealed, and wisdom reigns supreme. Observe, read, and be open to all possibilities.

Messengers:

Animal: *Blue Catfish*
Nature: *Rainforest*
Universe/Energy: *Look for Symbols (action)*

893

Stretch yourself to go beyond what you think you're capable of doing. Look to the horizon and try to meet it. There is always more to you than you think you can give. Sometimes you will need to follow the rules and do things exactly as expected but other times bending the rules just a little bit will allow you to obtain even greater results.

Messengers:

Animal: *Cat Snake*
Nature: *Horizon*
Universe/Energy: *Awakened Interest*

894

Numbers matter. It's time to look over the books of your company, balance your checkbook, or maybe play the lottery. Patience is necessary to find any oddities. Security, stability, and protection from outside sources is at an all-time high. Count your blessings as you look for discrepancies.

Messengers:

Animal: *Desert Tortoise*
Nature: *Ginger (spice)*
Universe/Energy: *Cherry blossom (color)*

895

Point yourself to your next goal and move toward it with all the passion and vigor you possess. This is the opportunity of a lifetime if you recognize it. Don't get stalled out in your efforts but keep moving forward. It might be difficult but achieving the goal will be that much sweeter because of it.

Messengers:

Animal: *Coho Salmon (fish)*
Nature: *Dracaena Plant*
Universe/Energy: *See beyond the veil*

896

Did you know that when you're almost to your goal you'll encounter the most resistance? This is when you'll be ready to throw in the towel and give up. Don't. Hang in there longer and keep trying. Just when you think you'll never make it, you will.

Messengers:

Animal: *Monitor Lizard*
Nature: *Curly-Leaf Pondweed*
Universe/Energy: *Pronoia*

897

Embracing your inner spirituality is like coming home. It's acknowledging your Divine spirit living within your physical body. It is knowing all yet knowing nothing. You have more to give than you will ever realize, both to yourself and to those around you. Infinity lives within you.

Messengers:

Animal: *Hawk Moth*
Nature: *Marjoram (spice)*
Universe/Energy: *Spiritual Self*

898

You can fly if you only try. You're clever and creative. When attempting new things, you have unique ideas about what will work. Sometimes they do and sometimes they don't. You don't get discouraged, you just look at the situation from a different angle and then move forward.

Messengers:

Animal: *Reindeer*
Nature: *Snow Pea*
Universe/Energy: *Typing (Sound)*

899

To become one with the Divine, you must first open doors to the various levels of existence. Embrace them tightly and once you are in harmony with one level, continue to the next. Do not let yourself get soured by attempting and failing to harmonize with a level. It takes time. Don't give up.

Messengers:

Animal: *Burmese Python (snake)*
Nature: *Green Grapes*
Universe/Energy: *Astral Plane*

900

Conceit isn't an emotion that is ever worn well. Do not think of yourself as better than another. Every spirit incarnated on the earthly plane is here for the reason of spiritual growth. To learn from one another and to reconnect with the Divine. Practice patience, love, and humility with everyone you meet because some have lost the memory of the reason they're here.

Messengers:

Animal: *Giant Salamander*
Nature: *Breccia Caliche (rock)*
Universe/Energy: *Modesty*

901

You have created an inviting and comforting ambience in your life that others want to be a part of. An opportunity is coming your way with a small window of time for you to take advantage of it. Don't wait. If taken, it will allow you to start something that will grow into a great business.

Messengers:

Animal: *Bighorn Sheep*
Nature: *Purslane (plant)*
Universe/Energy: *Vanilla (Scent)*

902

People you haven't seen in a while will contact you out of the blue. Don't just talk about ideas, mold them into something substantial. Before you start judging or having strong opinions about someone or some topic, look at yourself first. Be in touch with your spiritual self before saying something you'll regret.

Messengers:

Animal: *King Salmon (fish)*
Nature: *Clay*
Universe/Energy: *Gurgle of a coffee machine (sound)*

903

You need protection from your own emotions. To gain clarity you must release all the negativity within you. This includes any behavior patterns you do that you know are bad for you. They will only eat away at you. Leave them behind and move towards the Divine.

Messengers:

Animal: *Greater Siren (amphibian)*
Nature: *Anhydrite (mineral)*
Universe/Energy: *Adaptability*

904

A sweet first impression may hide an infestation within. Use caution in your dealings with people. While some are exactly who they seem, others are wearing a theater mask and playing a part. Be a little wary of people you've recently met until you've determined that they are truly as they seem. Investigate to make sure you can really trust them before telling them secrets.

Messengers:

Animal: *Amberjack (fish)*
Nature: *Trillium Plant*
Universe/Energy: *Cake (Scent)*

905

Do you know why you do what you do every day? Or are you just going through the motions? To make sure your life is purpose driven, post images of your goals or the dreams you're trying to achieve where you can see it frequently. Don't get squeezed to death by your surroundings because you lose sight of your goals. Keep moving forward.

Messengers:

Animal: *Python (snake)*
Nature: *Clear Ice*
Universe/Energy: *Preparations (action)*

906

Don't let yourself become radioactive. When negativity affects you consistently over an extended period it can break you down until eventually you start to release negativity too. If the situation you're in is consistently keeping you on edge and bringing you down, then create a plan for what you'll do afterwards and then change or leave the current situation.

Messengers:

Animal: *Brown Snake*
Nature: *Monazite (mineral)*
Universe/Energy: *Genuine (feeling)*

907

You do not need to be ruthless and cruel to survive. Instead, you can move lightly, freely, with joyfulness and still obtain the same goals. It's all in the approach. As the saying goes: you can catch more flies with honey than with vinegar. Try a sweeter, gentler approach to achieve what you want in life but don't let people walk all over you either.

Messengers:

Animal: *Butcherbird*
Nature: *Napa Cabbage (vegetable)*
Universe/Energy: *Dance*

908

You have the ultimate self-control. But when it breaks, it breaks hard, which can leave you feeling embarrassed or powerless depending on what you did when your self-control broke. Everyone has a breaking point. It's important to know yours so you don't ever reach it.

Messengers:

Animal: *Mandrill (primate)*
Nature: *Lead (metal)*
Universe/Energy: *Helpfulness*

909

Confusing circumstances keep happening which are keeping you on your toes. Don't worry, it will be over soon, and you'll be led to greener pastures. Continue to shed your light to those around you because they may be as confused as you are by the current circumstances.

Messengers:

Animal: *Baltimore Oriole (bird)*
Nature: *Papaya*
Universe/Energy: *Ecru (color)*

910

Love is all around you. This is a time to be with family, friends, or your significant other to celebrate love. It's also a great time to connect with your spirituality. Love yourself as much as you love those around you. Don't allow yourself to sink into negative feelings if you're not with someone right now. Sometimes you need to walk your path by yourself.

Messengers:

Animal: *Lovebird*
Nature: *Sink Hole*
Universe/Energy: *Humming (Sound)*

911

You may feel overwhelmed by your current circumstances, but you have the ability to move on from them to create a new reality for yourself. Releasing negative feelings are an important part of raising your frequency and moving forward in life. Do not be discouraged. Never forget.

Messengers:

Animal: *Muskrat*
Nature: *Precious Opal (gemstone)*
Universe/Energy: *Overjoyed (feeling)*

912

Awaken to the power within you. You are protected from negativity as you explore your intuitive abilities. Now is the time for testing, fine tuning, and exploring abilities you hadn't realized you had. Expect to reach great heights of accuracy. You know more than you think, see more than you expect, and will grow into the truth of yourself.

Messengers:

Animal: *Galapagos Hawk*
Nature: *Granite Obsidian (gemstone)*
Universe/Energy: *Honeydew (color)*

913

There are times when you need just a few minutes to get your emotions under control due to the things happening in life. If you're carrying a heavy weight, cast it off for just a moment so you can breathe freely. Then pick it back up and carry on. Eventually, the burden will no longer be yours to bear. You'll get through this.

Messengers:

Animal: *House Mouse*
Nature: *Backwater*
Universe/Energy: *Cold (feeling)*

914

Paint your world with color to let go of negativity. You can sail over the highest mountains when you allow your frequency to lift you up. Don't be too proud or think that you must do everything by yourself. Accept the help of others to avoid hurt feelings.

Messengers:

Animal: *Blue Marlin (fish)*
Nature: *Danxia Landforms*
Universe/Energy: *Drip (sound)*

915

Talking is essential now. If you don't say what's on your mind, or how you feel about something, then you'll begin to fester with negative emotions. Talk it out to find balance in the situation. What is beautiful and sweet to some could be deadly for others.

Messengers:

Animal: *Starling (bird)*
Nature: *Red Maple (tree)*
Universe/Energy: *Wellness*

916

Mockery and contempt are knocking. You don't have to let them in. Those who participate in these negative behaviors will try to drag you along with them. They aren't what they seem so beware of participating in the hopes of acceptance.

Messengers:

Animal: *Tanuki (canine)*
Nature: *Grove*
Universe/Energy: *Important (feeling)*

917

Push yourself backwards to move forwards. Look to the past for guidance. You'll have the opportunity to take on a sudden responsibility you weren't expecting. Responsibility, communication, and being fully aware of how your actions are affecting others are key right now.

Messengers:

Animal: *Shrimp (crustacean)*
Nature: *Kidney Bean*
Universe/Energy: *Roses (Scent)*

918

Pay attention because you're being contacted by the Divine. There are messages that require awareness, enlightenment, and connecting to higher consciousness to be received. Intense focus may be needed until the seasons change. At that time, understanding will be complete, and the lesson learned.

Messengers:

Animal: *Harrier Hawk*
Nature: *Dragon's Blood Tree*
Universe/Energy: *Amicable (feeling)*

919

Look at your layers. How complicated are you? Do you create drama for yourself without reason? Instead of letting yourself get trapped in dullness, repetition, and the blahs, get up, get outside, and move. Physical work will help what ails you. Grow a garden, mow the grass, play sports.

Messengers:

Animal: *Crocodile Skink (reptile)*
Nature: *Mud puddles*
Universe/Energy: *Hair Ice (phenomenon)*

920

Practice using your intuitive abilities to get better levels of accuracy. The more you try, the better you will become in anything in life. Don't scurry around from thing to thing but be focused and make a grand effort to bloom into the best you can be.

Messengers:

Animal: *Ground Squirrel*
Nature: *Marigold (plant)*
Universe/Energy: *Sneezing (Sound)*

921

Sometimes things can be cute but deadly. This is a time to be wary of things that are strange to you. Animals, people, or circumstances. Be very aware because danger is nearby. Shallow waters can overwhelm you in minutes if you're not paying attention. Listen, watch, and move quickly when necessary.

Messengers:

Animal: *Blue-ringed Octopus*
Nature: *Tsunami*
Universe/Energy: *Train Whistle (sound)*

922

You're very aware of how others perceive you. Remember you're not living for them but for yourself. Don't let your desire to fit in make you give up on your own dreams. Strive for perfection within yourself, not for others.

Messengers:

Animal: *Sloth (mammal)*
Nature: *Dragonfruit*
Universe/Energy: *Key Lime (color)*

923

You've got your own rhythm going on. You're dancing to your own beat and taking great steps toward happiness. You've let go of the secrets you've kept and moved on. You are adaptable and tend to flourish in any situation.

Messengers:

Animal: *Downy Woodpecker*
Nature: *Lupine (bean)*
Universe/Energy: *Confession*

924

Upbeat and positive, you're a joy to be around. You are proficient in adding spice to your life, to livening things up when the situation gets boring. While you might be loud and obnoxious at times in your exuberance, your heart and intentions are always pure.

Messengers:

Animal: *Canada Goose*
Nature: *Beach Saltbush (plant)*
Universe/Energy: *Nutmeg (Scent)*

925

This is a time of transition. You may have been in a fiery or toxic situation but have left that behind for a calmer, more grounded life. You've faced and overcome great challenges. You gained insight from those who stayed in the background but who guided you along the way. Appreciation, respect, and loyalty abound.

Messengers:

Animal: *Fire Salamander*
Nature: *Canyon*
Universe/Energy: *Shadow People*

926

Never apologize for being yourself. If you've done something wrong, then make amends. You're grounded, sincere, and often compromise for others. Don't compromise yourself though. Stay true to your spiritual essence, your higher self, and the moral fabrication of your soul.

Messengers:

Animal: *Atlantic Cod (fish)*
Nature: *Hornblende (mineral)*
Universe/Energy: *Dry Woods (Scent)*

927

Optimism, clarity, and an increase of frequency are abundant now. It's time to take your intuition up a few notches. The clearer you are in your intention, the more accurate you are in your predictions. Take some time to just lie around and practice grounding and centering yourself. You can rest and can practice soul work at the same time.

Messengers:

Animal: *Sea Lion*
Nature: *Maw Sit Sit (gemstone)*
Universe/Energy: *Satisfaction*

928

If you can choose one thing today, choose to be as real as you can be. Don't put on fake airs, pretend to be someone you're not, or blame others for your mistakes. Own yourself and your actions. You're intelligent, colorful, and vibrant. People trust you and are loyal to you. Don't give them a reason to be otherwise.

Messengers:

Animal: *Parakeet*
Nature: *Jungle*
Universe/Energy: *Grounding*

929

It's time to clean and get rid of things. Out with the old to make room for the new. Thinking of moving? Pack up and go if you can. Change is upon you, and you embrace it with ease. Remember to take time for yourself to rejuvenate during the hectic, but fun, times ahead. Reinforce any areas of your life that need it.

Messengers:

Animal: *Cockroach*
Nature: *Dust Devil*
Universe/Energy: *Delight in the Happiness of Others*

930

There are tasks you want to undertake that will require agility and stamina to complete. You're up for the job so don't put it off. Make sure you're paying attention to your emotions. Avoid getting upset about things that aren't within your control.

Messengers:

Animal: *Albacore (fish)*
Nature: *Feldspar (mineral)*
Universe/Energy: *Rapturous (feeling)*

931

You are different than you appear. Now is the time for speed which will lead to abundance, fertility, and good fortune. Be independent and survive by your own hard work. Take quick action and make deliberate decisions. Look at the big picture, not immediate gratification. .

Messengers:

Animal: *Hare*
Nature: *Brussel Sprouts*
Universe/Energy: *Faith*

932

Being distinct only makes you more unique. You go out of your way to be just a little bit weird because that's who you are, and you enjoy the shock effect you can have on others. You like trying new things just to prove you can do them. Smile, people will wonder what you're up to.

Messengers:

Animal: *Beach-hopper (crustacean)*
Nature: *Brown Diamond (gemstone)*
Universe/Energy: *Affection*

933

Feelings of unease are prevalent now. You feel as if you need to be moving, accomplishing something, but you feel stagnate and lost. To get back on track in all aspects of your life, create a strategy you can implement and follow. Once you have a guideline, it will be easier to settle down emotionally and stay true to your plan.

Messengers:

Animal: *Striped Possum*
Nature: *Plantain (fruit)*
Universe/Energy: *Tap dancing (sound)*

934

Don't become numb to your environment. This is a good time to clean both the inside and outside of your home. Rotting vegetation, overgrown plants, and broken tree limbs can make your yard look uncared for and abandoned. Inside clutter can make your house look a mess. Once cleaned the energy flow will increase dramatically and your overall feelings of well-being will elevate.

Messengers:

Animal: *Banana Slug (invertebrate)*
Nature: *Fleabane (plant)*
Universe/Energy: *Baby blue (color)*

935

You can do a lot of good in the world, but you must give yourself permission to do it. You tend to hold yourself back because you worry about what other people think. What they think doesn't matter. If you're following your path, are happy with what you're doing and the results you're achieving, then that's what matters.

Messengers:

Animal: *Guppy*
Nature: *Plum*
Universe/Energy: *Empowerment*

936

Set your worry aside for a while. This is a time of understanding the frequencies of peacefulness, lightness of being, and the dynamic energies of Universal consciousness. This gives you the ability to overcome obstacles, to know when to speak and when to remain silent.

Messengers:

Animal: *Roseate Spoonbill (bird)*
Nature: *Royal Poinciana (tree)*
Universe/Energy: *Zippy (sensation)*

937

While you may hang out with lots of people and acquaintances, you only have a few close friends. These people are essential to your life. Just as you would do anything for them, they would do anything for you. Respect is everything.

Messengers:

Animal: *Rainbow Trout (fish)*
Nature: *Buttonbush (plant)*
Universe/Energy: *Color (action)*

938

Everything has its place but don't get upset if something is out of place. Plans can be changed without problems. Look for the positive instead of expecting the negative. Lose yourself in music to loosen up and connect with your own rhythm.

Messengers:

Animal: *Grouse (bird)*
Nature: *Morado Opal (gemstone)*
Universe/Energy: *Let go (action)*

939

A deadline is approaching for an important goal. Now is the time to hunker down and really get to work to finish on time. Don't let distractions pull you away from what you need to do. The project demands your attention.

Messengers:

Animal: *Gibbon (primate)*
Nature: *Purple Loosestrife (plant)*
Universe/Energy: *Balsam Fir (scent)*

940

It's time to become an overachiever. Take a deep breath and jump into the water. Changes are happening quickly and the work you're doing has taken off with a life of its own. Keep a fast pace to stay on top of it. This could be a new product you've invented or a project at work that just got the green light.

Messengers:

Animal: *Coley (fish)*
Nature: *Scapolite (gemstone)*
Universe/Energy: *Breathing*

941

The more sunlight and exercise you get the better you'll feel. Being in nature is needed now to elevate your mood and frequency. If you're waiting for an apology, don't hold your breath. It may never come. Don't fear change.

Messengers:

Animal: *Mountain Goat*
Nature: *Sun*
Universe/Energy: *Carrot Orange (color)*

942

You are made of many interesting parts when put together create the uniqueness of your soul. No one is exactly the same as another. While you may share similar features, ideals, and abilities, your spark only belongs to you. Raise your voice in song to celebrate all that you are.

Messengers:

Animal: *Echidna (mammal)*
Nature: *Bok Choy (plant)*
Universe/Energy: *Approachable (feeling)*

943

Speech is a way to smoothly navigate through the process of change. The more you can discuss it, the more comfortable you feel with the decisions being made. Take time to embrace your reality while creating new dreams you want to reach.

Messengers:

Animal: *Inland Bearded Dragon*
Nature: *Soapstone*
Universe/Energy: *Baby Chicks (sound)*

944

Repetition is necessary now. Yes, it's boring, no you can't stop. It's a requirement to reach the end result. Sing a song or hum a melody while you work to eliminate some of the monotony. Unfortunately, some things require you to just deal with them until they're finished. Then you will feel a sense of achievement once it's completed.

Messengers:

Animal: *Snow Goose*
Nature: *Lychee (tree/fruit)*
Universe/Energy: *Windshield Wipers (Sound)*

945

Sometimes other people's expectations of you are too high which can cause you stress. Be attentive to the vibrations and ripples around you. Attune to the frequencies even if they feel small or insignificant. The greatest change can be brought about by the smallest burst of energy.

Messengers:

Animal: *Pond Skater (insect)*
Nature: *Navy Bean*
Universe/Energy: *Heroism*

946

Are you tired of wandering? Of lacking purpose? Have you run out of energy? This is a good time to dig deep and think about what you can do to create a change in your life. It could be something very simple or something complex. It just has to be something you will follow through and actually do. Take action now.

Messengers:

Animal: *Wandering Albatross (bird)*
Nature: *Clear Sky*
Universe/Energy: *Motivated Reasoning*

947

There are times when self-protection must be your number one focus. That time is now. If it means seeking guidance from someone more knowledgeable about the kind of situation you're in then take that route. It doesn't hurt to ask for help sometimes. This is a time of change but don't fear the changes happening.

Messengers:

Animal: *Stink Bug*
Nature: *Black-eyed Pea*
Universe/Energy: *Inner Peace*

948

There are times when you are a problem solver and other times when you just need to listen. This is a difficult thing if you're used to taking action right away. Ease a problematic situation with joy. It's hard to be mad if you can find a reason to laugh.

Messengers:

Animal: *Knifefish*
Nature: *Horned Melon (fruit)*
Universe/Energy: *Laughter (Sound)*

949

If you could look at yourself frozen in a moment in time, what would you see? Would you be proud of yourself, embarrassed, or wish you were doing something differently? Once examined, you can take a new path or change something you've been doing so you'll be happy with how you're living if you look back at yourself at some point in the future.

Messengers:

Animal: *Sulphur Butterfly*
Nature: *Mistletoe (plant)*
Universe/Energy: *Cicadas at Night (sound)*

950

While your memory may be long, you can choose to hold onto the positive and not the negative. Let go of grudges, resentments, and old hurts. This will enable you to feel as light as the breeze, and peaceful in spirit. Forgive and forget the bad but always remember the good.

Messengers:

Animal: *African Elephant*
Nature: *Breeze*
Universe/Energy: *Spirit*

951

When you help someone, you often receive help in return. Just don't expect it though. Give without conditions. Watch what you're saying, or you could say too much and regret it later. Pay attention to your body so you can get in better shape physically.

Messengers:

Animal: *Remora (fish)*
Nature: *Dried Plums*
Universe/Energy: *Follow your gut instincts*

952

You show people only what you want them to see. You're a very private person who wards off negativity at every turn. What you do outside of your job is no one's business but your own. You feel secure within yourself and confident in your abilities.

Messengers:

Animal: *Umbrellabird*
Nature: *Garlic*
Universe/Energy: *Swimming (action)*

953

A situation is evolving that will require you to take a stand or to choose a side. You have high ideals so make sure you follow in what you believe instead of letting peer pressure lead you into a situation you don't want to be in.

Messengers:

Animal: *Wolverine*
Nature: *Irisation Clouds*
Universe/Energy: *Peaceful*

954

This is a good time to cleanse away toxins. When they build up, you could feel sluggish and slow in your thinking. Pay attention to the nonverbal sounds around you for subtle, helpful messages. Scents and symbols will also bring messages of growth.

Messengers:

Animal: *Hibiscus Beetle*
Nature: *Prasiolite (gemstone)*
Universe/Energy: *Snoring (Sound)*

955

You'll be able to let go of any fears that are holding you back from making changes needed. You may be afraid but do it anyway. It's a good time to right past wrongs and move forward in life. Don't lose your temper but instead keep yourself out of trouble by walking away.

Messengers:

Animal: *Viper (snake)*
Nature: *Anthurium Plant*
Universe/Energy: *Receptivity*

956

Sweet feelings of joy and happiness surround you. You understand even the smallest things in life have abundant power which can be celebrated. The little things you do to help others can change their lives for the better. You may never know the true impact you've had on someone so always act in kindness.

Messengers:

Animal: *Black-capped Chickadee (bird)*
Nature: *Maple Syrup*
Universe/Energy: *Confetti*

957

You have many interests in life but only one true passion. Once you discover what that passion is, let all your other interests be affected by it. As your passion grows so will your other interests. The more you learn, the stronger you stand. You can accomplish anything.

Messengers:

Animal: *Australian Golden Whistler (bird)*
Nature: *Cedar Tree*
Universe/Energy: *Read a Book (action)*

958

Don't touch that which can kill you. You are brave in the face of danger but you're not stupid. Don't go out on a limb for someone who is exerting pressure to make you do what they want. Do things for others because you *want* to, not because someone else is trying to make you do them.

Messengers:

Animal: *Coral Snake*
Nature: *Peonies (plant)*
Universe/Energy: *Bravery*

959

Sometimes rules that weren't meant to be broken can be bent just a little if there is a specific need or reason. Someone needs your help, and they need you to listen to what they have to say. Don't discount their words. Truth is being told.

Messengers:

Animal: *Wolf Snake*
Nature: *Stinkhorn Mushroom*
Universe/Energy: *Repetition (action)*

960

Don't lose faith in what you believe in. Times can be troubling but will turn around. Survival and emotional strength are needed. Don't let darkness overtake you because the light is stronger. Face fears and repair relationships to move forward.

Messengers:

Animal: *Bilby (marsupial)*
Nature: *Elephant's Foot Plant*
Universe/Energy: *Relax in a Sauna (action)*

961

Open your mind and pay attention to what is going on. Don't be unaware of the world you live in. Be tolerant of others. Listen to their point of view even if you don't agree with it. Sometimes you must agree to disagree. Everyone's truth is different.

Messengers:

Animal: *Cassowary (bird)*
Nature: *Pebble*
Universe/Energy: *Awareness of the Obvious*

962

You have cleared a trail to make it easier for others to walk their paths. You've made plans and put things in place so that others will not have to face the same struggles you've faced. Remain aware and keep up the honorable deeds.

Messengers:

Animal: *Redback Spider*
Nature: *Anise (plant)*
Universe/Energy: *Goodwill*

963

Being bitter about the circumstances you find yourself involved in can cause dire results for your spiritual self. Harboring negativity allows it to fester and eventually explode. You're highly intelligent and understand what's happening but emotionally you're letting someone get the best of you. You're sensible and down to earth. Let go of the bitterness.

Messengers:

Animal: *Virginia Opossum*
Nature: *Escarole (vegetable)*
Universe/Energy: *Reward Others (action)*

964

Expect a sacred message from the Divine regarding your spiritual growth. You have made a lot of progress, but something has stopped you, causing you to question what you believe. Now is when the Universe is stepping in to bring confirmation that you are on the right path.

Messengers:

Animal: *White Hawk*
Nature: *Cactus Pear*
Universe/Energy: *Don't hesitate (action)*

965

There is a situation coming up that will be emotional for you. This could be a very positive thing, or it could be negative. Your reaction to the situation and the way you choose to handle it will determine how long it lasts.

Messengers:

Animal: *Tennessee Walking Horse*
Nature: *Overcast Sky*
Universe/Energy: *Remember someone (action)*

966

This is a good time to put out feelers. If you're looking for a new job, or want to take classes to further your education, start investigating the possibilities. The more you discover, the easier it will be to decide the right path to take. There are career opportunities available now.

Messengers:

Animal: *Star-nosed Mole*
Nature: *Lemongrass*
Universe/Energy: *Lavender (Scent)*

967

Overconfidence can get you into trouble. You may find that you've gotten in too deep and are under pressure in your current situation. Set yourself apart so you can drift away, create a plan, and get yourself back on solid ground.

Messengers:

Animal: *Pomfret (fish)*
Nature: *Drift Ice*
Universe/Energy: *Affirmation*

968

Sit back and relax. Take time to regenerate, rejuvenate, and transform yourself. You can't do this if you're going at 100 miles per hour, so slow down and take a moment for yourself. You will feel more protected and stronger, which will allow you to reach goals with ease.

Messengers:

Animal: *Crab*
Nature: *Skarn (rock)*
Universe/Energy: *Prophecy*

969

You may often wonder why you're here on the earthly plane, what's your purpose, your reason for being? There isn't one answer to this question. Your purpose can be a thousand-fold and it can change over your lifetime. Embrace all that you are in the past, present, and future.

Messengers:

Animal: *Anglerfish*
Nature: *Celery*
Universe/Energy: *Reason for Being*

970

It's time to travel! Look for an upcoming trip to suddenly appear in relation to a joyous occasion. It may be a wedding, the birth of a new baby, or a house-warming party. Watch your mouth. You can be too blunt at times and inadvertently offend someone.

Messengers:

Animal: *Mosquito*
Nature: *Guava (fruit)*
Universe/Energy: *Take control of your life (action)*

971

Let go of any baggage holding you down. You work hard to help others achieve what they want in life, and you are happy when they succeed. You are also able to take care of yourself and don't rely on others to help you get by. You figure it out and then do what you need to do.

Messengers:

Animal: *Sea Otter*
Nature: *Spearmint (herb)*
Universe/Energy: *Turkey gobble (sound)*

972

Are you fiercely competitive? Can you unravel mysteries? Can you see in the dark? Your many unique abilities make a massive impact on who you are spiritually. You have control over your emotions, are innovative and adaptable. You excel at many things so do what you enjoy the most.

Messengers:

Animal: *Cat Shark*
Nature: *Sweet Potato*
Universe/Energy: *Sit in Darkness (action)*

973

Burrow down deep to feel safe within yourself and then come up to face any fears that may be preventing you from experiencing the joy of being you. Learn as much as you can and make decisions from the heart and soul.

Messengers:

Animal: *Striped Faced Unicorn Fish*
Nature: *Turmeric (spice)*
Universe/Energy: *Play with a Yoyo (action)*

974

You may encounter pests in life, but they will not be an obstacle in meeting your goals. There is luck around you which will bring about positive transformations and opportunities you never imagined. Make time for fun and entertainment to keep yourself balanced.

Messengers:

Animal: *Black Snake*
Nature: *Olivine (mineral)*
Universe/Energy: *Toasted Marshmallow (Scent)*

975

Wholeness is at your core being and is reflected through your eyes. Your energy is a gift to others. You are balanced and the Universe has your back in everything you want to do. When all elements align within, you will know which direction to take.

Messengers:

Animal: *Taipan (reptile)*
Nature: *Clementine (fruit)*
Universe/Energy: *Viewpoint*

976

Be persistent to be successful. Keep things hidden from others until your goal is met. Silence is important so others don't spoil your plans, undermine your achievements, or steal your ideas. Avoid getting stuck in a rut by making sure there is variety in your day.

Messengers:

Animal: *Tick*
Nature: *Spodumene (gemstone)*
Universe/Energy: *Soul Energy*

977

Move instead of standing in one place. The energy contained within you needs an outlet. Let it out to set yourself free. Facing your own truths, even difficult ones, can be easier with a grounded sense of realism. Learning is lifelong and you absorb information with gusto.

Messengers:

Animal: *Jewel Wasp (insect)*
Nature: *Cape (topography)*
Universe/Energy: *Car Horn (sound)*

978

Let go of any stress that is holding you back from achieving what you've set out to do. The world might be going crazy around you but it's not the time to take action. You are important too. Work hard to ensure success.

Messengers:

Animal: *Rat*
Nature: *Prairie*
Universe/Energy: *Clary Sage (scent)*

979

Expect sudden changes to occur in the way you think. You've been bolted awake; your energy had been activated. Things you once enjoyed may now disgust you. Foods you once craved may now be a thing of the past. Look to the future with hope and joy.

Messengers:

Animal: *Blue Crab*
Nature: *Lightning Storm*
Universe/Energy: *Telephone ringing (sound)*

980

Surround yourself with nature and allow information to fill you completely. You are being guided from above. Write down messages received so you don't forget them. You may come up with great new ideas or find resolutions to issues you've been concerned about.

Messengers:

Animal: *Sturgeon (fish)*
Nature: *Red Oak (tree)*
Universe/Energy: *Crisp Spring Morning (Scent)*

981

You can withstand the harshest weather, the coldest temperatures, and still move forward in fluidity. Swaddle yourself deep within the covers of your bed and snuggle with yourself. Now is a good time to meet new people and create deeper relationships with the people already in your life.

Messengers:

Animal: *Burrowing Owl*
Nature: *Drizzle (weather)*
Universe/Energy: *Tranquility*

982

Feel secure in yourself and your ability to take care of yourself. Have a discussion with others to prevent emotions from surging over. Success is yours through hard work and perseverance. What you need is within you, look inward to find it. You are wonderful.

Messengers:

Animal: *Tamarin (primate)*
Nature: *Mace (spice)*
Universe/Energy: *Oranges (Scent)*

983

Be humble and modest. While you can be feisty, outgoing, and assertive, now is the time to pull back and watch, even possibly mimic the actions of another, before soaring to achieve new heights. Enthusiasm is the spark that lights your fire.

Messengers:

Animal: *Blue Jay*
Nature: *Tuff (rock)*
Universe/Energy: *Juniper Berry (scent)*

984

Now is not the time to trust what others are doing or saying. This will pass quickly. Be wary in the meantime. Connect with family to find harmony in mind, body, and spirit. Your energy is a rare high frequency that elevates you to new heights daily.

Messengers:

Animal: *Wattlebirds*
Nature: *Hydnellum Peckii (fungus)*
Universe/Energy: *Take a positive action*

985

You may feel like you're getting the cold shoulder from someone, but it is an issue within them, not a reflection upon you. Let them believe what they want for now because in the end you'll receive the success you deserve.

Messengers:

Animal: *Brown Trout (fish)*
Nature: *Asian Pear*
Universe/Energy: *Character*

986

You're a bright light for others but you must take care of yourself to take care of them too. What you put out into the Universe will come back to you. Make sure your deeds, words, and thoughts carry positivity and light.

Messengers:

Animal: *Wood Wasp*
Nature: *Lapis Lazuli (gemstone)*
Universe/Energy: *Law of Attraction*

987

Social events are on the horizon! Get ready to socialize, to have fun, and to relax. Live your life filled with passion and vitality. Don't waste time with people who don't see the bigger picture or who are stuck in negativity.

Messengers:

Animal: *Society Finch (bird)*
Nature: *Talc (mineral)*
Universe/Energy: *Humor*

988

Meet new people, you just might find a new long-term friend. Listen to other points of view to gain a broader understanding. Now is a time to learn more and to really connect with the impressions you receive from the spiritual realm.

Messengers:

Animal: *Dottyback (fish)*
Nature: *Water Canna (plant)*
Universe/Energy: *Lend a Sympathetic ear (action)*

989

You often don't see what a positive impact you have on the lives of others simply by being you. If you've been putting off starting something out of fear, now is a good time to try. You have your own unique way of doing things so stick to it.

Messengers:

Animal: *Sunbird*
Nature: *Waterspout*
Universe/Energy: *Iris (color)*

990

Believe in yourself as you believe in those you love. Lift your head high and feel the wind in your face. If you need any kind of healing, be it physical or emotional, you will achieve great results now. Relax and let go of any stress that is pulling you down.

Messengers:

Animal: *Sawfish*
Nature: *Virginia Bluebells (plant)*
Universe/Energy: *Antarctica's Blood Falls (phenomenon)*

991

Optimism shines brightly. You are a bright light in the darkness. Influential people are drawn to you and your ideas. Keep quiet about any inventions, plans, or business ideas at this time so they're not taken from you. Not everyone is as trustworthy as you are.

Messengers:

Animal: *Goldfish*
Nature: *Tanzanite (gemstone)*
Universe/Energy: *Inner Guide*

992

Be comfortable at home and eliminate stress. If you're feeling overwhelmed, let go of some of the causes of your anxiety. Don't burn yourself out by taking on too much. Find a way to discover your own unique path as you use your abilities to help people.

Messengers:

Animal: *Sulcata Tortoise*
Nature: *Wildfire*
Universe/Energy: *Peach (Color)*

993

Important discoveries are waiting for you, but you must look where you don't expect them to be. Shine your light because hope is eternal and can bounce from one person to another seamlessly. When a door is stuck try to pry it open.

Messengers:

Animal: *Coot (bird)*
Nature: *Rubber Plant*
Universe/Energy: *Myrrh (scent)*

994

You're affectionate and gentle, a kind soul. Fear can hold you back if you let it. So don't let it. You'll move forward in leaps and bounds once you trust that the Universe has your back. Reconnect to the Earth. Go barefoot to feel the pulse of the planet.

Messengers:

Animal: *Tomato Clownfish*
Nature: *Nectarine (fruit)*
Universe/Energy: *Coziness*

995

Your inner voice will guide you and show you the way to enlightenment. You can do whatever you want to in life, there is nothing holding you back except yourself. Embrace your inspiration. Take everything in stride as you move in a new direction.

Messengers:

Animal: *Veiled Chameleon (reptile)*
Nature: *White Ash Tree*
Universe/Energy: *Dream Interpretation*

996

To get unstuck, write down your goals and the steps to achieving them. Don't put all your eggs in one basket, instead, toss everything out in front of you and then decipher the meaning. It's time to let sweetness overcome sourness in your life.

Messengers:

Animal: *Box Turtle*
Nature: *Sweetgum Tree*
Universe/Energy: *Giggle (sound)*

997

Socialization is important to you and helps you connect to others on many levels. Quiet your mind and gain clear focus. Rest, rejuvenate, and then move forward. To keep your frequency high, push off the bad mood and adjust to the change.

Messengers:

Animal: *Ulysses Butterfly*
Nature: *Spring*
Universe/Energy: *Astral Projection*

998

There are times when all great things must end. This is a time of new beginnings, of transformation, and self-discovery. Take control of your life and start something new. The only thing that will hold you back from achieving success on this new path is yourself.

Messengers:

Animal: *Sunbittern (bird)*
Nature: *Tulip (plant)*
Universe/Energy: *Midnight (color)*

999

Slow down and find a quiet place. You're extremely sensitive and can get emotionally stressed in noisy or chaotic environments. In a group event, sit slightly apart from the rest. Imagine a bubble around you that can reflect energy away from you instead of your absorbing it. It's important to take time to enjoy yourself. You've been working hard and pushing yourself to the limit.

Messengers:

Animal: *Panda*
Nature: *Sugar-Apple Tree*
Universe/Energy: *Tobacco (Scent)*

1000

You are a powerful guardian, protective, and courageous but you need to listen more. Be fearless but empathic. You are connected to the astral realm and can find peace and renewal of power in the darkness. Open to your intuitive abilities, heal wounds, and move stealthily into your future. Take some time for yourself and do whatever you want to do.

Messengers:

Animal: *Black Panther*
Nature: *Cliff*
Universe/Energy: *Rocking Chair (sound)*

1001

You intuitively understand the people you work with and help them use their skills to excel in their own jobs. You pay attention, which benefits you in all areas of your life. Your instincts are clear, your energy flows strong and sure.

Messengers:

Animal: *Sunfish*
Nature: *Kelp (sea vegetable)*
Universe/Energy: *Puppies (Scent)*

1002

Expect an increase in visions, prophetic dreams, and your ability to just *know* things. Your frequency is elevating as your experiences increase. Accept love and support from others in difficult times. Acceptance and trust in yourself to do the right thing to correct mistakes is of importance.

Messengers:

Animal: *Tenrec (mammal)*
Nature: *Granny Smith Apple*
Universe/Energy: *Make things happen (action)*

1003

Instead of regretting paths not followed, walk them now. It's not too late. Explore new ideals, concepts, and thoughts. Lessons will appear when the student is ready to learn them. Sharing your joy endears you to others. You're a pleasure to be around. Never doubt that others care deeply for you.

Messengers:

Animal: *Collared Lizard*
Nature: *Fennel (vegetable)*
Universe/Energy: *Use Time Wisely (action)*

1004

Do not leave things behind that need your attention. Instead, gather them up and hold them close. This is a time to get things done, to complete tasks and to finish what you've started before moving on to something new.

Messengers:

Animal: *Chinese Water Dragon (reptile)*
Nature: *Scoria Welded Tuff (rock)*
Universe/Energy: *Find Treasure at a yard sale (action)*

1005

Love, romance, and fidelity are at the forefront. This may be a current relationship that is growing deeper, or you may meet someone new that will be the love of your life. You have an intuitive and empathic ability to understand the needs and desires of others which will enable you to have a successful relationship.

Messengers:

Animal: *Swan*
Nature: *Sweet Chestnut Tree*
Universe/Energy: *Cool (sensation)*

1006

Don't say one thing and do the opposite. That is hypocrisy at its best. Remember that getting to the truth of a matter can be simple or difficult, it's all in the approach you take in discovery. Finding a place that is comforting and where you can relax is important now.

Messengers:

Animal: *Red Angus (cattle)*
Nature: *Swamp*
Universe/Energy: *Make something out of beads (action)*

1007

Renewal and transformation are happening to you, but you need to do your part to move the process along. Enjoy the fruits of life along the way and avoid feelings of superiority. Listen to the impressions you're receiving and the guidance from the Divine. New intuitive abilities may start developing now.

Messengers:

Animal: *Plumed Whistling Duck*
Nature: *Cabbage*
Universe/Energy: *Footsteps (Sound)*

1008

You'll be involved in a high-stakes event in the near future and will need to act quickly (don't second guess yourself) to succeed. Your strength of character empowers you, so trust in yourself that the decisions you're making are the right ones.

Messengers:

Animal: *Bush Dog (canine)*
Nature: *Clinozoisite (mineral)*
Universe/Energy: *Align with your goals (action)*

1009

You're strong, silent, and can see right through people if you really look. It's time to open up mentally and emotionally to allow blessings and opportunities to present themselves to you. People look up to you and admire all you have achieved in life. Don't forget those in your past.

Messengers:

Animal: *Kob (mammal/antelope)*
Nature: *Juniper Tree*
Universe/Energy: *Learn a new skill (action)*

1010

While you tend to be more solitary, you also need to interact with friends. Don't lock yourself away for too long. You have access to ancient knowledge so start delving deeper into the topics that interest you. Breathe and clear your energy. Smile and know that everything is all right in your world.

Messengers:

Animal: *Swallow (bird)*
Nature: *Bristlecone Pine Tree*
Universe/Energy: *Confidence*

1011

You do not have to be in a romantic relationship to be committed to someone. Once you commit to someone in any kind of relationship, you tend to commit for life, even if you no longer see the person daily, you'll always be there for the other person if they need you. You are extremely loyal and caring and will always do what you can for others.

Messengers:

Animal: *Bottlenose Dolphin*
Nature: *Pepper (spice)*
Universe/Energy: *Prophetic Dreams*

1012

Challenges can wear you down, even if you meet them all, and you need time to recharge. It's time to let go of the stress that is causing you to push yourself to the extreme. When you have a clear breakthrough of understanding it will cascade over you like music, cleansing and healing your soul.

Messengers:

Animal: *Texas Longhorn (cattle)*
Nature: *Potato*
Universe/Energy: *Bagpipes (sound)*

1013

Find your inner magic again. It's been lost along the way. You can intuitively pick up information about the past of people, places, and things. You will be able to steam ahead in your search for new ideals. Your mind is open, the page is blank. Write your story.

Messengers:

Animal: *Ruff (bird)*
Nature: *Marcasite (gemstone)*
Universe/Energy: *Splashing (Sound)*

1014

There is a confusing situation that will arise. Gain clarity before getting involved. Don't look for ulterior motives in those around you. This is a situation where you need to look with elevated frequency, whether you want to or not. Everything is okay.

Messengers:

Animal: *Tuco Tuco (rodent)*
Nature: *Slot Canyon*
Universe/Energy: *Cold Mountain Air (Scent)*

1015

Look to those younger than yourself for answers to a problem you're facing. If you're not feeling secure in your home, add a security system. If you're not content, look for the reason you're feeling that way. You're directly connected to the Divine and the answers will be provided to you. You tend to stay put until you're ready to move on.

Messengers:

Animal: *Pigeon*
Nature: *Garnet (gemstone)*
Universe/Energy: *Desire*

1016

Look at yourself through the eyes of another. Do you like what you see or is there room for change? This is a wonderful time to make new plans because they should work out well. Someone may show up without notice. It will be a good time so welcome them with open arms.

Messengers:

Animal: *Drill (primate)*
Nature: *Cenote (topography)*
Universe/Energy: *Ylang Ylang (scent)*

1017

Listen to the heartbeat, the pulse, of what is happening around you for clearer direction. Your inventiveness is at an all-time high and any inventions you come up with now could be very successful. When you fight yourself, you set yourself back. Other people might not understand you, but that's okay.

Messengers:

Animal: *Vampire Squid*
Nature: *Drought*
Universe/Energy: *Familiars*

1018

You hold power in your attitude. You can accept your situation, resent it, or change it. Make sure you're listening to your own advice. You know yourself better than anyone else. Make time to slow down and enjoy life instead of going through it too fast.

Messengers:

Animal: *Water Buffalo*
Nature: *Flint Hematite Iron Ore (rock)*
Universe/Energy: *Plan your time (action)*

1019

Stability, flexibility, patience, and persistence will benefit you the most as you take on new tasks. Look at your soul's purpose. Are you on the right path? There will be times when you'll hop around and other times when you'll walk or run. Do everything in moderation.

Messengers:

Animal: *Surinam Horned Frog*
Nature: *Nighttime*
Universe/Energy: *Wind Blowing Outside (Sound)*

1020

Embrace the calm wildness inside of you. You are independent, courageous, and loyal. Trust in yourself and maintain a high sense of integrity. Make time for fun and social activities instead of always assuming the role of the responsible one.

Messengers:

Animal: *Wolf*
Nature: *Macadamia Nut*
Universe/Energy: *See opportunities everywhere*

1021

You can see situations clearly from above, below, and from the side, a gift that most people don't have. Use it to your advantage. There is a metamorphosis in everything you do, and growth is exponential. You may need to trust someone even though trust is difficult for you to give.

Messengers:
Animal: *Sweat Bee*
Nature: *Carambola (fruit)*
Universe/Energy: *Become more organized (action)*

1022

Watch out for those who want to prey off you. There are things happening behind the scenes that you may not see. Look closely in the background before agreeing to anything, signing contracts, or making major decisions. Avoid selfish behavior or taking advantage of someone else. Be responsible for your own actions.

Messengers:

Animal: *Leech (parasite)*
Nature: *Almond (nut)*
Universe/Energy: *Bathe*

1023

You've accomplished more than you realize. Think back for a while and look at what you've done. You'll always land on your feet, but others nearby may need your help to get back on track. Life is an education that offers valuable lessons.

Messengers:

Animal: *Tortoise Beetle*
Nature: *Mountain Stream*
Universe/Energy: *Follow through*

1024

Draw attention away from what is most important to you, keep your secrets safe from interfering people or curiosity seekers. Let your emotions breathe and connect to those you hold the deepest. You are a teacher, your intuition is very on point, and your frequency is high.

Messengers:

Animal: *Wedge-tailed Eagle*
Nature: *Sweet Alyssum (plant)*
Universe/Energy: *Unblock Energy*

1025

Consider what you feel, the ideas and images that appear to you. There is an elegant beauty surrounding your work, which not only helps you but others as well. Let go of things holding you back so you can embrace the new.

Messengers:

Animal: *Blacktip Shark*
Nature: *Sunstone (gemstone)*
Universe/Energy: *Whinny (Sound)*

1026

Understand yourself to see the world around you in a new perspective. Be careful of negativity that is trying to grow out of control. You do too much so rest is important. Look for new opportunities to present themselves after dark.

Messengers:

Animal: *Bandicoot (marsupial)*
Nature: *Centaurea (plant)*
Universe/Energy: *Conceptualization*

1027

Remember that good times do not have to last long to become a long-held memory. You're very empathic and have the ability of psychometry so use these abilities to glean even more information. Things are moving along as they should. Stay brave and forge ahead.

Messengers:

Animal: *American Woodcock (bird)*
Nature: *Eve's Pin Cactus*
Universe/Energy: *Terra Cotta (color)*

1028

This is a time of exploration, healing, and laughter. If you have an itch, scratch it within reason. Make sure you're genuinely understanding what others are really saying to you instead of just hearing the words they use. Help others along the way. Be flexible, not stubborn. Good things are coming to you.

Messengers:

Animal: *Swallow-tail Kite (bird)*
Nature: *Maple Tree*
Universe/Energy: *Inspired action*

1029

This is a time of great enlightenment for you. Challenging work and being a team player are required and will result in great accomplishments. Remain stable and grounded. Slow down, you're moving too fast. Take small steps. Patience is needed now; with it you can accomplish anything.

Messengers:

Animal: *Elephant Seal*
Nature: *Bismuth (metal)*
Universe/Energy: *Energetic self-starter*

1030

Hidden knowledge will be shown to you. Negative situations are temporary and will return to normal soon. Don't give up hope. Be graceful, balanced, and pure within your soul as you share your messages with others. To be in harmony, you must bring all parts of yourself to a place of equilibrium.

Messengers:

Animal: *Tawny Frogmouth (bird)*
Nature: *Irish Eyebright (plant)*
Universe/Energy: *Cheerfulness*

1031

Plan for a rainy day by saving money instead of blowing it on things you really don't need. Make sure you take time to rest because you tend to overdo it without taking breaks. Something big is on the horizon for you. Be prepared and ready to reap the rewards you deserve.

Messengers:

Animal: *Cuckoo Bird*
Nature: *Pearls*
Universe/Energy: *Whooshing (sound)*

1032

Take steps to change what's happening so you don't lose control. Avoid judgmental actions. Make sure you are practical in your approach and alert to all facets of the situation. You have better things waiting for you. Just be patient. When the time is right, when you have grown in spirit, they will come.

Messengers:

Animal: *Fisher (mammal)*
Nature: *Sea*
Universe/Energy: *Enchanted*

1033

Ancient knowledge is within you, tap into it for great spiritual rewards. You have the innate ability to know what's going to happen before it does and are ready to roll with whatever comes your way. You're very capable of taking care of yourself, regardless of what other people might think.

Messengers:

Animal: *Groundhog*
Nature: *Red Rose*
Universe/Energy: *Self-reliance*

1034

People have to make their own mistakes, even if you'd like to spare them from the disaster you see coming. You may have to protect someone younger than yourself at this time. Hang on to the friends from the past even while making new friends in the future.

Messengers:

Animal: *Egyptian Cobra (snake)*
Nature: *Rubber Tree*
Universe/Energy: *Move your body (action)*

1035

Go with the flow through intention to increase the flow of energy to you. This is also a time of being humble, thankful, and hopeful for the future. You have thick skin and a high tolerance for pain. Choose to pick your battles.

Messengers:

Animal: *Rudd (fish)*
Nature: *Bermuda Grass*
Universe/Energy: *Hiccup (sound)*

1036

Stay firm in your beliefs, even if others disagree with them. When you commit to something it's for the long haul. Be sure before committing. Don't get bogged down by the little things. Be assertive but don't be a pest.

*** Messengers: ***

Animal: *Waxwing (bird)*
Nature: *Blueberry*
Universe/Energy: *Purple (Color)*

1037

Procrastination and complaining aren't part of your path. Move past negative people to find those that sing with delight and soar in happiness. Look for ways to find enjoyment every day. Embrace what makes you smile. Don't take yourself too seriously.

*** Messengers: ***

Animal: *African Grey Parrot*
Nature: *Bauxite (rock)*
Universe/Energy: *Hold someone's hand (action)*

1038

Avoid confrontations but if unavoidable, be strong and sure. Let go of past grievances, clear up misunderstandings, and repair differences to achieve peace with others. Don't let yourself fall into suspicious obsessions over what others are doing. Walk your own path in the light of love.

Messengers:

Animal: *Binturong (mammal)*
Nature: *Grape Hyacinth (plant)*
Universe/Energy: *Ultramarine (color)*

1039

Now is the time to help others understand their own intuitive nature and develop their gifts. You are filled with light and joy and share it in abundance with those around you. Sometimes you may have to listen closely because the message seems to come from far away, yet it will be clear.

Messengers:
Animal: *Bushbaby (primate)*
Nature: *Cloud Iridescence*
Universe/Energy: *Hunch*

1040

This is a good time to turn up the heat on situations that have been idling. It's time for completion so you can put them in the past. Try a new haircut or buy some new clothes. Changes do not have to be big to be beneficial.

Messengers:

Animal: *Rat Snake*
Nature: *Passion Fruit Flower*
Universe/Energy: *Muscle car (sound)*

1041

Take your time in peeling back the layers of the situation you're in. If you go too fast, it will cause feelings of sadness. You can get through to someone that others are having a difficult time understanding. Patience is key.

Messengers:

Animal: *Swift (bird)*
Nature: *Onion*
Universe/Energy: *Charisma*

1042

It's time for new beginnings. Of moving with the flow of life to experience new places and meet new people. You have an eye for seeing potential in old things. Restoring them to look new and unique will help relax you and could generate additional income.

Messengers:

Animal: *Whitefish*
Nature: *Current (water flow)*
Universe/Energy: *Solstice*

1043

Love is in the air. This is a happy time filled with excitement and joy. There is no need to hide your true self, but instead you can be you. You may meet someone you knew in a past life and even remember that lifetime. The bond between you will be strong from the start.

Messengers:

Animal: *American Black Bear*
Nature: *Lilac (plant/flower)*
Universe/Energy: *Ocean current (phenomenon)*

1044

You've got some dirty work ahead of you. This may include working outside in the rain and mud or any other job where you're going to get dirty. There's a lot of cleaning, sorting, and throwing things away that needs to be done.

Messengers:

Animal: *Swamp Rat (rodent)*
Nature: *Dry Lake*
Universe/Energy: *Unselfish*

1045

Sometimes you just need to take risks and see what happens. The result might be fantastic, or it may flop. But you'll never know until you try. There may be a time of separation from your family and friends coming up for you because of your job.

Messengers:

Animal: *Curlew (bird)*
Nature: *Ginger Lily (plant)*
Universe/Energy: *Take A Chance*

1046

You're not afraid to disagree with someone. You may understand their point of view and even sympathize with them, but it doesn't change your thoughts on the matter. You enjoy staying in your comfort zone but if pushed will move outside of it.

Messengers:

Animal: *Eider (bird)*
Nature: *Bloodroot (plant)*
Universe/Energy: *Magnetic field (phenomenon)*

1047

Someone is going to try to start something with you today. End it quickly by not engaging with them. Just leave it alone. Staying focused and calm in the face of adversity is your strong suit. Listen to your heart in all matters to stay true to yourself.

Messengers:

Animal: *Portuguese Man o' war (marine hydrozoan)*
Nature: *Chalcopyrite (mineral)*
Universe/Energy: *Squeaky toy (sound)*

1048

Be aware of outside forces that can affect what you're trying to accomplish. There are some that will push you forward towards success while others will pull you backwards, delaying your progress. Roll with it and use tactics to counteract their impact.

Messengers:

Animal: *Blue Runner (fish)*
Nature: *Sea Breeze*
Universe/Energy: *Blue Moon (phenomenon)*

1049

You feel comfortable in your surroundings and with the work that you're doing. You may be recognized for your honorable deeds. Remain modest and humble. Avoid bragging or excessively talking about how great you are. Face your fears, whatever they may be.

Messengers:

Animal: *Assassin Bug*
Nature: *Reef*
Universe/Energy: *Flaming torch (sound)*

1050

You have the power of song, speech, and creative expression in abundance. If you've ever wanted to write a song, try it now. You are a born leader and people will respond well to what you have to say. You can guide and assist someone with your words.

Messengers:

Animal: *Canary (bird)*
Nature: *Neptune Grass*
Universe/Energy: *Innocent*

1051

You're the kind of person who will go out of their way to help others. Nice, engaging, enjoyable, and simply great company. However, there's a negative situation you're going through that you're hiding from people. This needs to be dealt with so you can release it.

Messengers:

Animal: *Budgie (bird)*
Nature: *Paprika (spice)*
Universe/Energy: *Blueberries (scent)*

1052

There are times when you come across too strong and demanding, which creates fear in others. Back off and take a good look at yourself. What can you do to change? You can approach with power without being rough and antagonist.

Messengers:

Animal: *Tasmanian Tiger*
Nature: *Sprouts*
Universe/Energy: *Sunflower Yellow (color)*

1053

Everything is improving at this time. You're finishing projects and making headway in all areas of your life. There's pep to your step and a song in your heart. Decisions are easy as you plan and go after your dream.

Messengers:

Animal: *Water Deer*
Nature: *Peppermint*
Universe/Energy: *Be Decisive*

1054

An idea is going to feel like it just dropped out of the sky and into your lap. Go with it! When things are meant to be they happen in the most amazing, and unbelievable ways. There's someone looking out for you. Make the best of all gifts received. Be appreciative for the blessing.

Messengers:

Animal: *Sea Snake*
Nature: *Sphalerite (gemstone)*
Universe/Energy: *Spontaneous (feeling)*

1055

Focus on one thing and do it well. Now isn't the time to be unfocused or to jump from one thing to another. Relationships can be restored, opportunities are there for the taking, and new beginnings can be created. It's time to hide in plain sight, to keep secrets, and to protect those closest to you.

Messengers:

Animal: *Frog*
Nature: *Banana*
Universe/Energy: *Secrets*

1056

Are you taking yourself so seriously that you've lost your joy? Do you feel as if you're not measuring up to what others expect of you? What do you expect of yourself? Consider what changes you could make so you're filled with happiness again and then make them.

Messengers:

Animal: *Vireo (bird)*
Nature: *Red Sand Verbena (plant)*
Universe/Energy: *Be exceptional (action)*

1057

Look for the potential within yourself. You quickly absorb knowledge and use it to increase your inner strength. Business matters are on the rise and any inspiration you receive will only enhance your work. Messages will be sent to you so make sure you're open to receiving them.

Messengers:

Animal: *Sponge (sea animal)*
Nature: *Moonstone (gemstone)*
Universe/Energy: *After Death Communication*

1058

You're feeling the pressure right now. It's time to open up to what has you so tense, to understand and resolve the situation. Frustration is at an all-time high. Release is needed to bring your energy back to a calm state. It's time to let go of what is holding you down.

Messengers:

Animal: *Reticulated Python (snake)*
Nature: *Broad Bean*
Universe/Energy: *Zipper (Sound)*

1059

You're blessed with so many things, however, money is evading you at the moment. A situation where you thought you'd bring in the dough just fell through. Don't give up though because there's something else better waiting for you. Avoid negative feelings because those will set you back.

Messengers:

Animal: *Sea Angel (sea slug)*
Nature: *Pear*
Universe/Energy: *Cherish*

1060

Feeling confident and calm is essential for you to move forward at this point. Watch out for those who will swim away at the first chance they get. It's time to put in the work to reap the reward. Don't be surprised if the person who bailed shows back up when its reward time.

Messengers:

Animal: *Bowfin (fish)*
Nature: *Nephrite (gemstone)*
Universe/Energy: *Leaves in the forest (Scent)*

1061

At first you may experience fear but when you look closely, you'll see that what you were afraid of will not harm you. Do things for yourself instead of asking others to do it for you. Not only does this heighten your frequency but it shows that there is no limitation to what you can accomplish.

Messengers:

Animal: *Skate (fish/ray)*
Nature: *Anthracite Gneiss (rock)*
Universe/Energy: *Ocean Breeze (Scent)*

1062

Everything is moving along smoothly right now. There are many little lucky things happening to you. Appreciate them. Avoid becoming bored with your life by always doing something every day that brings you joy. Share some of your abundance with those closest to you.

Messengers:

Animal: *Rat Squirrel*
Nature: *Pumpkin Seed*
Universe/Energy: *Yawning (Sound)*

1063

Appreciate everything and forget nothing. Turn on the light within yourself to illuminate your world even more. Small steps taken consistently will get you to your end goal and it will feel effortless. Should you help someone else, or let them try on their own? Whatever you decide, stick with it, and then examine the results.

Messengers:

Animal: *Tetra (fish)*
Nature: *Hydnora Africana (fruit)*
Universe/Energy: *Share Knowledge*

1064

Enjoyment, pleasure, and fun times abound. Clear out the old to make room for the new. Once you do, you'll be surprised at the opportunities that will come your way. Take appropriate steps so that you can function at your very best every single day. Stay strong and thrive.

Messengers:

Animal: *Whooping Crane (bird)*
Nature: *Parachute Flower*
Universe/Energy: *Agreement*

1065

Look closely, listen to your intuition, and choose wisely when you're making important decisions. Keep changing to reap the benefits of life. Do not betray the confidence of others by telling their secrets. Live each day to the fullest and with appreciation.

Messengers:

Animal: *Manta Ray*
Nature: *Curry (spice)*
Universe/Energy: *Prosperity*

1066

Make sure you know which feelings are actually yours and when your empathic abilities are connecting you with someone else's emotions. Trust in yourself and your abilities. Look for the lesson and maintain a bright outlook.

Messengers:

Animal: *Thoroughbred (equine)*
Nature: *Rainclouds*
Universe/Energy: *Searching*

1067

Keep confidential information a secret or it will be shared by others when you don't want it to be known. There are nosy people who want to gossip about you close by. Look for the unexpected, be regal and quiet.

Messengers:

Animal: *Tube Sponge (sea animal)*
Nature: *Cacao (tree)*
Universe/Energy: *Secret Codes*

1068

You are connected to the natural world, your own spirituality, and Universal knowledge. You can see clearly even in darkness. The path you choose is the right one. Someone will come to you for advice soon.

Messengers:

Animal: *Poison Dart Frog*
Nature: *Benitoite (gemstone)*
Universe/Energy: *Zeal*

1069

Pay extra attention to your appearance and avoid getting chilled or overheated. Moderation is important. Any problems that arise are not with you, but with another person's expectations and their own perception. Hold your head high.

Messengers:

Animal: *White Marlin (fish)*
Nature: *Stinking Corpse Lily (plant)*
Universe/Energy: *Lawn Mower (sound)*

1070

Make sure you don't lose sight of the lessons you need to learn on this plane of existence because you're too connected to the spiritual realm. Feed yourself well and take care of both your physical body and spiritual self. It's time for rejuvenation.

Messengers:

Animal: *Angora Goat*
Nature: *Cloudburst*
Universe/Energy: *Solutions*

1071

Don't dampen experience, get out there and live! You can fly on wings of positivity and abundance, so keep moving forward. Look to the beauty of the mornings for inspiration. Only you can choose how your day will go. Choose wisely.

Messengers:

Animal: *Tomato Fruitworm*
Nature: *Frost Flowers*
Universe/Energy: *Study something new (action)*

1072

Let yourself see what others see in you and appreciate yourself as they do. The heaviness you've created by seeing yourself differently is holding you back from the joy you deserve. Release it. You need time by yourself to focus and decide on a sense of direction as you figure out the situation.

Messengers:

Animal: *Gila Monster (reptile)*
Nature: *Knoll (topography)*
Universe/Energy: *Solve a Puzzle (action)*

1073

Avoid spending just for the sake of spending. Only get what you need. Quiet positivity goes a long way in achieving your goals. Everyone needs help at some point, it is your turn to give assistance to those around you who have helped you in the past.

Messengers:

Animal: *Kodiak Bear*
Nature: *King's Holly Plant*
Universe/Energy: *Yellow (Color)*

1074

Let go of all negative emotions and live in the moment with joy and positivity. Your outlook, personality, and the way you live life is unique. Take time for self-discovery while you're waiting for something new to enter your life.

Messengers:

Animal: *Thresher Shark*
Nature: *Orthoclase (gemstone)*
Universe/Energy: *Sensitive*

1075

The time is at hand to create and the approach you take will guarantee success or failure. Someone from your past will be able to help you with this new venture. Take a chance to make something great through hard work and sacrifice.

Messengers:

Animal: *White Rhino*
Nature: *Gypsum (mineral)*
Universe/Energy: *Craving*

1076

Be cautious of what you are hearing from others. Go to the source to obtain the correct information. Your loyalty and deep sense of what is right and wrong will see you though. Be persistent in your endeavors.

Messengers:

Animal: *Glass Sponge (sea animal)*
Nature: *Charoite (gemstone)*
Universe/Energy: *Visit a loved one (action)*

1077

Don't look back with regret, just look forward with anticipation. Don't sit back and observe, instead dig in and take action. Be strong as the stone of the earth, be brave, and decide what is right for you in this moment.

Messengers:

Animal: *Tiger Beetle*
Nature: *Plunge pool (topography)*
Universe/Energy: *Higher Self*

1078

Learn from the experiences of others through reading or speaking with them in person. Growth surrounds your spirit. Ground yourself, stay balanced, and deliver the messages. You can handle anything that crosses your path. You will experience what you allow yourself to learn lessons.

Messengers:

Animal: *Cooper's Hawk*
Nature: *Peridot (gemstone)*
Universe/Energy: *Anthelion Halo (phenomenon)*

1079

Start each day with a fresh outlook. You'll reach your goal. Honor yourself and the gifts you've received. Keep your secrets to yourself and be careful of your interactions with others until you know for sure who will be loyal and who might betray you.

Messengers:

Animal: *Trumpeter Swan*
Nature: *Clove (spice)*
Universe/Energy: *Forest (Scent)*

1080

You flow in the Universal Consciousness of all that is because you are intimately connected to that energy. Breathe deeply, move quickly but know when to be still and absorb everything around you. Your heart is large, and you often take others under your wings to care for them.

Messengers:

Animal: *Dromedary (mammal/camel)*
Nature: *Poppy Seed*
Universe/Energy: *Glee*

1081

You are primed for success. Start a new project as soon as you're ready. You can strike out when pushed too hard and the results can be devastating. Watch your words so you don't have regrets for saying things in the heat of the moment that you might not really believe or mean.

Messengers:

Animal: *Highland Cattle*
Nature: *Spicebush (plant)*
Universe/Energy: *Express your empathy (action)*

1082

Find the reasons behind your feelings to face them and grow from them. Time spent near water is important at this time and will produce beautiful results. Follow your muse often and soon you will see an increase in prosperity in your life.

Messengers:

Animal: *Whiting (fish)*
Nature: *Peanut Wood*
Universe/Energy: *Go for a run (action)*

1083

If you need to begin something again because it wasn't working out, an innovative approach and new beginning are just what you need. It can be as straightforward or as complicated as needed. Do a good deed today, hold open a door or help someone with a task. Little things matter.

Messengers:

Animal: *Tur (mammal)*
Nature: *Nimbostratus Clouds*
Universe/Energy: *Dream Travels*

1084

You will know when someone is secretly preying on your energy with theirs and be able to intuitively block any type of psychic attack on your spirit. Be like a vine and let your true self spread out into the sun so you can grow and flourish.

Messengers:

Animal: *Red-fan Parrot*
Nature: *Flood*
Universe/Energy: *Make a craft (action)*

1085

Take charge but remember that a little bit of sweetness goes a long way in attaining results. You'll always be there as a loyal friend while honoring your own beliefs. You're not going to disappear or hide away. Create happiness, joy, and memories with every day you're given.

Messengers:

Animal: *Thrush (bird)*
Nature: *Chalk Chert (rock)*
Universe/Energy: *Anticipation*

1086

Take time to enjoy the warmth of the day. Get outside and do something fun. For the areas of your life that you're not happy about, make an uplifting change instead of letting negativity spread. You can maneuver over or around obstacles to obtain what you want.

Messengers:

Animal: *Bushmaster (snake)*
Nature: *Hail*
Universe/Energy: *Beauty*

1087

There are responsibilities that are pulling you down like weights. Can you let someone else carry part of that load? Once you have settled into the peacefulness of your soul self, then your power will grow strong and lead to a centered, balanced approach to life.

Messengers:

Animal: *Tiger Centipede (arthropod)*
Nature: *Patchouli (plant)*
Universe/Energy: *Auburn (color)*

1088

Pay attention to what the world is saying to you, so you become more flexible, balanced, and grounded. Don't repeat the same thing over and over, expecting to get a different result. If it doesn't work on the first try, then try a different way.

Messengers:

Animal: *Sea Urchin*
Nature: *Lenticular Clouds*
Universe/Energy: *Read poetry (action)*

1089

New people will come into your life that are at your frequency or higher levels and you'll find a deep connection with them. Make sure you don't come across as a know-it-all though by spitting out spiritual information when someone just wants to have a nice conversation about the weather.

Messengers:

Animal: *Tuna (fish)*
Nature: *Bean Sprouts*
Universe/Energy: *Cherry (Scent)*

1090

Look deeply and you'll discover a place of peace and quiet where you can turn negatives into positives and plan for your future. Soaking in warm water, whether it's a bath, a jacuzzi, or the ocean is what you need.

Messengers:

Animal: *Tiger Swallow Tail Moth*
Nature: *Stars*
Universe/Energy: *Seek*

1091

Don't muddy the water or stir up trouble. Now is the time to hunker down and get to work. You are in a time of reproduction and growth and whatever you pursue will expand to massive proportions. Thinking about starting your own business? Now is a suitable time. You may need to travel to accomplish your goals.

Messengers:

Animal: *Carp (fish)*
Nature: *Marble Mariposite (gemstone)*
Universe/Energy: *Purring (Sound)*

1092

Pick up a book, open it, and the first thing you read will guide you. You often see (or know) what is invisible to others. It is one of your great strengths. Use this information to help others along their own path.

Messengers:

Animal: *Yellow-spotted Hyrax*
Nature: *Banana Tree*
Universe/Energy: *Be resilient (action)*

1093

Set your priorities in life and never let them fall by the wayside because of work or other things you feel you must do. Strive for more and you'll achieve it. Leave pettiness behind. This will help take away the sting that the clearing of any hurts may have caused.

Messengers:

Animal: *Dugong (marine mammal)*
Nature: *Altocumulus Clouds*
Universe/Energy: *Never Forget*

1094

Read as much as you can about ideals that interest you. If something doesn't seem to fit, leave it until later. If you've ever wanted to write a book, learn to paint, grow a garden, or any other things you've wanted to try, this is a great time to start.. You are a teacher and now is the time to share your knowledge with those around you.

Messengers:

Animal: *Timber Rattlesnake*
Nature: *Caraway (spice)*
Universe/Energy: *Sun Dog (phenomenon)*

1095

Find a way to take the lead, bring organization and clarity to the situation. Now is the time to take a risk or make a move to take back control. Your drive and determination are unmatched, yet you have the ability to not let it take over your life.

Messengers:

Animal: *Conger (eel)*
Nature: *Grapefruit*
Universe/Energy: *Snappy (sensation)*

1096

You can create a private get-away to faraway lands from the comfort of your own home. Pick a place, sit back in a comfy chair and watch videos online to enhance your experience. This is a happy time filled with good things that are happening to you and those around you. Enjoy it.

Messengers:

Animal: *Eland (mammal/antelope)*
Nature: *Custard-Apple (fruit)*
Universe/Energy: *Tractor (sound)*

1097

You're a great person and your virtuous deeds should be acknowledged. Allow it to happen because it brings the person acknowledging you joy. When you turn down a compliment, you're disrupting the energy flow. Following your own path is a part of the uniqueness of your soul.

Messengers:

Animal: *Gray Owl*
Nature: *Kadupul Flower*
Universe/Energy: *Engine cranking (sound)*

1098

Don't become obsessive about control. Look at the beauty in the sky today and colorful messages. To forgive, you'll have to view the situation from a different perspective. Good news is coming your way which will lead to a celebration.

Messengers:

Animal: *Guan (bird)*
Nature: *Bitter Melon*
Universe/Energy: *Jovial (feeling)*

1099

There are colors all around you that will guide you on your path. Just go with the flow and appreciate your intuitive abilities and the fact that you can help others with them. Spend some time in or near water as it will play a big part in your progress.

Messengers:

Animal: *Treecreeper (bird)*
Nature: *Aloe Plant*
Universe/Energy: *Peach Nectar (Scent)*

1100

Family is at the heart of the matter. You're an excellent communicator, which will be important in the near future. Make sure you don't get so involved in the problems of others that you forget what is important to you. Stay on your own path and you will be guided to situations which will increase your own frequency as you help others.

Messengers:

Animal: *Goose*
Nature: *Opal (gemstone)*
Universe/Energy: *Energy Balancing*

1101

You are as bright as the sun, as fragile as a flower, and can navigate turbulent waters with ease. You protect yourself from the elements by being wise and planning ahead. You're loyal, steady, and dependable year after year. You enjoy finding the fun in everyday living.

Messengers:

Animal: *Blue Shark*
Nature: *Black-eyed Susan (plant)*
Universe/Energy: *Dance in the Rain*

1102

When clearing energetic attachments from you, imagine the roots dissolving completely instead of pulling or cutting them off. This way, you're sure to completely rid yourself of the energy drain. It's time to get organized and prepare for the job ahead. You'll move slowly at first but pick up speed. Recognize those around you who are doing a great job.

Messengers:

Animal: *Russian Tortoise*
Nature: *Horse Tails (plant)*
Universe/Energy: *Be punctual (action)*

1103

The people around you at this time are sincere and have your best interests at heart. Their advice is meant with the greatest kindness. While it may seem like you're waiting forever, the time for change is not quite right yet. Be patient a little longer.

Messengers:

Animal: *Tungara Frog*
Nature: *Iron Ore Limestone*
Universe/Energy: *Wait (action)*

1104

Be mindful of both the image you present to the world and how you see yourself. These two can be in complete contradiction if you're not balanced at a spiritual level. Find a compromise so you are both living and presenting to the world the truth of your spiritual being.

Messengers:

Animal: *Sable (mammal)*
Nature: *Bird Nests*
Universe/Energy: *Self-image*

1105

Not carrying your weight and waiting for someone else to do your job or other acts of laziness will cause disagreements and distress in your immediate circle. Do more than is expected of your own accord instead of waiting for someone to do it for you. Look out for others who are there for you instead of pushing them away.

Messengers:

Animal: *Tree Kangaroo (marsupial)*
Nature: *Pecan*
Universe/Energy: *Laugh at yourself*

1106

There is trouble on the horizon. With the help of those closest to you in the situation, you'll be able to avoid catastrophe and turn the turbulence into a solution. Control your temper during this tense time. It will be over quickly and with minimal disturbances.

Messengers:

Animal: *Colorado Potato Beetle*
Nature: *Fire*
Universe/Energy: *Balance*

1107

You're being pestered by something that is out of your control. To ward away the energy of this situation, put up an energy block as a deterrent. You will have moments of frustration during this time but in the end, you will emerge rejuvenated and on a different path.

Messengers:

Animal: *Abalone (sea snail)*
Nature: *Bay Leaf*
Universe/Energy: *Encourage others*

1108

Do not let yourself get stuck in a situation where you will be injured or have your heart broken. The sting of betray will feel like a death. Learn from it and move on. Make sure to eat properly and not go hungry because of your emotions.

Messengers:

Animal: *Box Jellyfish*
Nature: *Asparagus*
Universe/Energy: *Love yourself*

1109

How much energy are you putting into what you don't want? Is it causing you to be on edge, upset, and with a feeling of panic? Take a break, go fishing, or do some other leisurely and mundane activity that will allow your mind to wander and your soul to reorganize. Put your energy into the things you *do* want, not those you don't.

Messengers:

Animal: *Fishing Cat*
Nature: *Hydrangea (plant)*
Universe/Energy: *Be fully present in life*

1110

You are a spiritual healer filled with joy, love, and laughter. You have a deep appreciation of the physical and spiritual world, and you work diligently to help others understand their place in both. You guide others along their spiritual path and are an inspiration to all you encounter. Keep up the magnificent work.

Messengers:

Animal: *Quokka (marsupial)*
Nature: *Equinox*
Universe/Energy: *Alive (feeling)*

1111

Creativity, intuition, and manifestation serve you now. You are in a great time of spiritual awakening, of growth and Divine influence. Moon cycles are important, and the knowledge of the moon's power should be applied to all areas of your life. Listen to the night, it has messages that will bring about tremendous growth and you do your best work then. What you have sought will now be given.

Messengers:

Animal: *Whip-poor-will (bird)*
Nature: *Moon*
Universe/Energy: *Raising Consciousness*

CONCLUSION

Intuition is a large part of being receptive to the messages the Divine wants to deliver to you through repetitive numbers and messengers from the animal, natural, and universal realms. When you think about it, it is utterly amazing that you could be contacted by something greater than yourself, by Divine energy which guides all that is, and given messages that will guide you through all kinds of situations you may be going through. Yet it happens multiple times a day. It's up to you to be receptive to the energy around you and your own unique frequency. When the two connect, the messages will be delivered, and you'll have an aha moment.

It is my hope that you enjoy using this book on a daily basis for guidance from the spiritual realm. It's eye-opening, especially when numbers just keep popping up. It seems like the more you notice them, the more they appear. Pay close attention if that happens because you'll be in a period of transformation and need lots of information to complete it. The Divine is helping out as much as possible. When you open your spiritual self to the wonderfully inspiring messages that are sent to you, which will help you progress on your spiritual path, then you're receptive to becoming one with the Divine. Walk in wonder, live in love, and appreciate all that you are and can be.

BIBLIOGRAPHY

Alderton, David. *The Encyclopedia of Animals*. New York: Chartwell Books, 2013.

Alexander, Skye. *The Secret Power of Spirit Animals*. Avon, MA: Adams Media, 2013.

Allaway, Zia. *Encyclopedia of Garden Plants for Every Location*. New York: Dorling Kindersley, 2014.

Alvarez, Melissa. *365 Ways to Raise Your Frequency*. Woodbury, MN: Llewellyn Worldwide, 2012.

Alvarez, Melissa. *Animal Frequency*. Woodbury, MN: Llewellyn Worldwide, 2017.

Andrews, Ted. *Animal-Speak: The Spiritual & Magical Powers of Creatures Great & Small*. Woodbury, MN: Llewellyn Publications, 2004.

Angell, Madeline. *America's Best Loved Wild Animals*. New York: Bobbs-Merrill Company, 1975.

Austin, Elizabeth, and Oliver Austin. *Random House Book of Birds*. New York: Random House, 1990.

Dorling Kindersley. *Trees, Leaves, Flowers, and Seeds: A Visual Encyclopedia of the Plant Kingdom*. New York: Dorling Kindersley, 2019.

Brickell, Christopher. *Encyclopedia of Plants and Flowers*. New York: Dorling Kindersley, 2019.

Burnie, David, and Don E. Wilson. *Animal: The Definitive Visual Guide to the World's Wildlife*. New York: Dorling Kindersley, 2001.

Cheung, Theresa. *The Element Encyclopedia of 20,000 Dreams*. New York: Barnes and Noble, by arrangement with HarperElement, 2006.

Chevalier, Jean, and Alain Gheerbrant. *A Dictionary of Symbols*. London: Penguin Books, 1996.

Conant, Roger, and Joseph T. Collins. *A Field Guide to Reptiles and Amphibians: Eastern and Central North America*. New York: Houghton Mifflin Company, 1998.

Farmer, Steven D. *Animal Spirit Guides*. Carlsbad, CA: Hay House, 2006.

Gilpin, Daniel. *The Complete Illustrated World Guide to Freshwater Fish & River Creatures*. London: Lorenz Books, 2014.

Goldworthy, Brigit. *Totem Animal Messages: Channelled Messages from the Animal Kingdom*. Bloomington, IN: Balboa Press, 2013.

Hall, Derek. *The Ultimate Illustrated Guide to Marine & Freshwater Fish of the World*. London: Lorenz Books, 2012.

Jackson, Tom. *Animals of the World*. London: Anness Publishing, 2014.

———. *The Illustrated Encyclopedia of Animals, Birds & Fish of North America*. London: Lorenz Books, 2012.

Johnson, Sylvia A. *The Wildlife Atlas*. Minneapolis, MN: Lerner Publishing, 1977.

Kays, Roland W., and Don E. Wilson. *Mammals of North America*. Princeton, NJ: Princeton University Press, 2002.

King, Scott Alexander. *Animal Dreaming Book: The Symbolic and Spiritual Language of the Australian Animals*. Woodbury, MN: Llewellyn Worldwide, 2014.

Meyer, Regula. *Animal Messengers: An A-Z Guide to Signs and Omens in the Natural World*. Rochester, VT: Bear & Company, 2015.

Murphy-Hiscock, Arin. *Birds: A Spiritual Field Guide: Explore the Symbology and Significance of These Divine Winged Messengers*. Avon, MA: Adams Media, 2012.

O'Connell, Mark, Raje Airey, and Richard Craze. *The Illustrated Encyclopedia of Symbols, Signs & Dream Interpretation*. New York: Anness Publishing, 2009.

Walters, Martin. *The Illustrated World Encyclopedia of Insects*. London: Lorenz Books, 2011.

WEBSITE RESOURCES

www.crystalwind.ca/animal-totems
http://www.dreammoods.com/dreamthemes/animals.htm
https://www.nationalgeographic.com/animals
https://www.bbc.co.uk/search?q=animals
https://davesgarden.com/guides
https://www.desertusa.com/animals.html
https://www.dictionary.com
http://www.dreambible.com
https://geology.com
https://www.audubon.org/bird-guide
https://www.crystalvaults.com/guides-crystals
http://www.merriam-webster.com
https://psychiclibrary.com/animal-spirit-guides
http://seaworld.org
https://www.spiritanimal.info
https://www.universeofsymbolism.com/animal-totems.html
https://www.spirit-animals.com
https://www.spiritwalkministry.com/spirit_guides
https://www.birds.cornell.edu/home
https://garden.org/plants
https://www.nwf.org/educational-resources/wildlife-guide
https://plants.sc.egov.usda.gov/home
www.visualdictionaryonline.com/animal-kingdom/insects-arachnids.php
http://www.starstuffs.com/animal_totems
https://www.wildscreen.org/
http://www.wildspeak.com/animaldictionary.html

MESSENGER LIST AND INDEX

In this index I have separated each main messenger category (animal, nature, Universe/Energy) into separate lists with sub-categories that are bolded so that it will be easier for you to find each messenger. Each item has been put into the closest category to what it is. However, some may fit into multiple categories, so I chose the most prevalent one. For example, some fish live in saltwater, others in freshwater, still others in brackish water. Some live in all three. So, I chose the place the fish likes to spend most of its time in as the main category. This index is set up a little differently than most indexes, but hopefully it will help you find what you're looking for quickly when you want to search by messenger.

ANIMAL MESSENGERS

Amphibians
Alpine Newt, 187
Axolotl, 336
Greater Siren, 466
Hellbender, 368
Mudpuppy, 217
Newt, 80

Birds

Auks, Murres, Puffins
Auk, 83
Dovekie, 440
Puffin, 19
Blackbirds and Orioles
Baltimore Oriole, 469
Blackbird, 388
Grackle, 269
Meadowlark, 339
Oriole, 140
Red-winged
 Blackbird, 393

Boobies and Gannets
Blue Footed Booby, 358
Gannet, 49
Cardinals, Grosbeaks and Buntings
Cardinal, 279
Indigo Bunting, 401
Northern Cardinal, 131
Painted Bunting, 176
Tanager, 415
Chachalaca, Guan, and Curassows
Guan, 564
Plain Chachalaca, 203
West Mexican
 Chachalaca, 343
Chickadees and Titmice
Black-capped
 Chickadee, 493
Boreal Chickadee, 337
Titmouse, 96
Cormorants
Cormorant, 442

Cranes
crane, 286
Gray Crowned
 Crane, 276
Sandhill Crane, 350
Whooping Crane, 547
Crows, Magpies, Jays
American Crow, 361
Black-billed
 Magpie, 311
Blue Jay, 506
Brown Jay, 331
Green Jay, 230
Magpie, 79
Raven, 320
Rook, 447
Cuckoos, Roadrunners, Anis
Cuckoo Bird, 530
Roadrunner, 44
Dippers
Dipper, 158

Raise Your Frequency Through Number Messages

Ducks, Geese, and Water Birds
American Wigeon, 232
Anhinga, 459
Black Swan, 191
Blue Duck, 231
Brant, 236
Bufflehead, 353
Canada Goose, 477
Canvasback, 446
Cinnamon Teal, 113
Common Goldeneye, 243
Coot, 511
duck, 141
Eider, 538
Gadwall, 458
goose, 565
Harlequin Duck, 429
King Eider, 61
Mallard Duck, 372
Mandarin Duck, 340
Merganser, 250
Muscovy Duck, 360
Nene, 136
Pintail, 288
Plumed Whistling Duck, 518
Ruddy Duck, 439
Snow Goose, 487
swan, 517
Trumpeter Swan, 554
Tundra Swan, 417
Wood Duck, 37
Falcons
American Kestrel, 224
Barred Forest Falcon, 81
Crested Caracara, 322
Falcon, 142
Merlin, 263
Peregrine Falcon, 44
Finches
American Goldfinch, 281
finch, 349
House Finch, 401
Society Finch, 508
Flamingos
Flamingo, 223
Flightless Birds
Cassowary, 495
Emu, 249
Flightless Cormorant, 347

Flightless Birds *(continued)*
Kagu, 364
Kiwi, 356
Ostrich, 161
Rhea, 459
Flycatchers
Alder Flycatcher, 211
Forest Birds
Bird of Paradise, 378
Game Birds
Golden Pheasant, 149
Kori Bustard, 277
turkey, 104
Wild Turkey, 24
Grebes
Grebe, 168
Ground Foraging/Dwelling Birds
Hoopoe, 69
Mallee Fowl, 226
Gulls and Terns
Arctic Tern, 277
Herring Gull, 454
Kelp Gull, 254
Pacific Gull, 333
Skimmer, 300
Sooty Tern, 49
tern, 379
Hawaiian Honeycreepers
Palila, 54
Hawks and Eagles
Bald Eagle, 18
Cooper's Hawk, 554
eagle, 15
Galapagos Hawk, 471
Golden Eagle, 68
Goshawk, 133
Harpy Eagle, 448
Harrier Hawk, 474
hawk, 196
Hen Harrier, 232
kite, 32
Northern Goshawk, 353
Red Tailed Hawk, 326
Sea Eagle, 289
Swallow-tail Kite, 529
Wedge-tailed Eagle, 527
White Hawk, 497
Herons, Egrets, and Bitterns
Great Blue Heron, 105
Great Egret, 227
heron, 74

Herons, Egrets, and Bitterns *(continued)*
Night Heron, 102
Sunbittern, 514
Honeyeaters, Wattlebirds, 507
Hummingbirds
hummingbird, 275
Ibises and Spoonbills
ibis, 21
Roseate Spoonbill, 483
Scarlet Ibis, 205
Junglefowl
chicken, 321
Red Jungle Fowl, 126
Kingfishers
Kingfisher, 279
Kookaburra, 323
Loons
loon, 214
Mockingbirds
mockingbird, 392
New World Quail
California Quail, 362
Northern Bobwhite Quail, 271
Quail, 22
New World Vultures
Buzzard, 351
California Condor, 315
Turkey Vulture, 457
Vulture, 227
Nuthatches
Nuthatch, 384
Oilbirds
Oilbird, 73
Old World Sparrows
House Sparrow, 136
Ospreys
Osprey, 298
Owlet-Nightjars
New Caledonian Owlet-Nightjar, 39
Nighthawk, 124
Tawny Frogmouth, 530
Whip-poor-will, 570
Owls
Barn Owl, 70
Barred Owl, 303
Burrowing Owl, 505
Eagle Owl, 349
Gray Owl, 563
Great Horned Owl, 386
owl, 365

576 Raise Your Frequency Through Number Messages

Owls *(continued)*
  Screech Owl, 42
  Snowy Owl, 23
  Spectacled Owl, 377
Oystercatcher
  Oystercatcher, 400
Parrots and Parakeets
  African Grey Parrot, 533
  Amazon Parrot, 333
  Budgie, 540
  Cockatiel, 170
  Cockatoo, 335
  Kaka, 297
  Kakapo, 263
  Kea, 273
  Lorikeet, 237
  Lovebird, 470
  Macaw, 43
  Parakeet, 479
  Parrot, 356
  Rainbow Lory, 113
  Red-fan Parrot, 557
Pelicans
  Brown Pelican, 393
  pelican, 21
Penguins
  Emperor Penguin, 341
  penguin, 448
Perching Birds
  Cacique, 328
  Canary, 540
  Cebu Flowerpecker, 130
  European Starling, 167
  Gray Catbird, 55
  House Martin, 434
  Lyrebird, 180
  Pitta, 192
  Shrike, 430
  Sunbird, 509
  Treecreeper, 564
  Umbrellabird, 491
  Vireo, 543
  Weaver, 302
Pheasants, Peafowl, Guinea Fowl, and Grouse
  Argus, 398
  Chukar, 234
  Grouse, 484
  Guinea Fowl, 281
  partridge, 395
  Peacock, 103
  pheasant, 176
  Prairie Chicken, 146
  Ptarmigan, 406

Pheasants, Peafowl, Guinea Fowl, and Grouse *(continued)*
  Ring-necked Pheasant, 150
  Sage Grouse, 404
  Willow Ptarmigan, 95
Pigeons and Doves
  dove, 15
  Mourning Dove, 33
  pigeon, 522
  Pink Pigeon, 127
  Rock Dove, 283
  Turtle Dove, 178
Plains Wanderers
  Plains Wanderer, 251
Plovers
  Killdeer, 178
  plover, 427
Rails, Gallinules, and Coots
  Black Rail, 164
  Corncrake, 380
  Moorhen, 92
  Purple Swamphen, 451
  rail, 427
  Sora, 68
Sagittariidae Family
  Secretary Bird, 75
Sandpipers
  American Woodcock, 528
  Curlew, 537
  Ruff, 521
  Sanderling, 270
  sandpiper, 424
  Snipe, 442
  Willet, 48
Seabirds
  Albatross, 262
  Brown Skua, 441
  Frigate Bird, 219
  Shearwater, 195
  Wandering Albatross, 488
Sheathbills
  Snowy Sheathbill, 275
Skuas and Jaegers
  jaeger, 265
Songbirds
  Australian Golden Whistler, 493
  Butcherbird, 468

Sparrows
  Towhee, 404
Starlings and Mynas
  starling, 472
Storks
  stork, 195
Swallows
  Barn Swallow, 213
  Purple Martin, 418
  swallow, 520
Swifts
  Black Swift, 114
  swift, 535
Thrushes
  American Robin, 394
  Eastern Bluebird, 260
  Mountain Bluebird, 160
  thrush, 557
Toucans
  toucan, 204
Trogons
  Quetzal, 268
Vultures
  Andean Condor, 77
Wading Bird
  African Spoonbill, 228
  Limpkin, 139
  Shoebill Stork, 346
  Spoonbill, 372
Waterfowl
  Screamer, 88
Waxwings
  Waxwing, 533
Woodpeckers
  Downy Woodpecker, 476
  Pileated Woodpecker, 402
  Woodpecker, 304
  Yellow-bellied Sapsucker, 27
Wrens
  House Wren, 88

Crustaceans
  Barnacle, 321
  Beach-hopper, 481
  Blue Crab, 504
  Crab, 499
  Crayfish, 299
  Hermit Crab, 109
  Horseshoe Crab, 366
  Krill, 306
  Lobster, 185

Crustaceans *(continued)*
  Shrimp, 473
  Tadpole Shrimp, 181

Fish

Anadromous Fish
  Atlantic Salmon, 128
  Coho Salmon, 462
  Dog Salmon, 95
  King Salmon, 466
  Lake Sturgeon, 156
  Pink Salmon, 67
  salmon, 301
  Sea Lamprey, 211
  Shad, 143
  Smelt, 292
  Sockeye Salmon, 53
  Sturgeon, 505
Freshwater Fish
  Alligator Gar, 152
  Angelfish, 53
  Arapaima, 165
  Arctic Char, 78
  Arowana, 266
  bass, 453
  Bichir, 69
  Black Molly, 144
  Blue Catfish, 461
  Bluegill Sunfish, 169
  Bowfin, 545
  bream, 200
  Brook Trout, 225
  Brown Trout, 507
  Buffalo Fish, 350
  Bullhead, 354
  carp, 560
  catfish, 365
  Channel Catfish, 282
  Cory Catfish, 359
  Dace, 207
  Danio, 135
  Discus, 129
  Dogfish, 230
  Gar, 46
  Goby, 148
  Goldfish, 510
  Gourami, 208
  Grayling, 121
  Guppy, 482
  Jack Dempsey, 229
  Knifefish, 489
  Koi, 391
  Lake Trout, 102

Freshwater Fish *(continued)*
  Lake Whitefish, 207
  Loach, 57
  Minnow, 271
  Moon Fish, 175
  Neon Tetra, 52
  Northern Pike, 419
  Oscar Fish, 175
  Parrotfish, 367
  Perch, 48
  Pike, 320
  Piranha, 216
  Platy, 344
  Pleco, 386
  Pomfret, 498
  Rainbow Fish, 412
  Rainbow Trout, 483
  Rudd, 532
  Siamese Fighting
    Fish, 190
  Snakehead, 294
  Sunfish, 515
  Tench, 198
  Tetra, 546
  Trout, 434
  Whitefish, 536
  Zebrafish, 82
Saltwater Fish
  Albacore, 480
  Amberjack, 467
  Anchovy, 40
  Anglerfish, 499
  Atlantic Cod, 478
  Atlantic Flying Fish, 361
  Bar Jack, 209
  Barracuda, 145
  Black Dragonfish, 338
  Black Sole, 311
  Blobfish, 354
  Blue Marlin, 472
  Blue Runner, 539
  Bluefin Tuna, 111
  Bonefish, 201
  Bonito, 240
  Butter Fish, 449
  Cobia, 278
  Cod, 396
  Coelacanth, 421
  Coley, 342
  Croaker, 374
  Cuttlefish, 248
  Dory, 272
  Dottyback, 509

Saltwater Fish *(continued)*
  Escolar, 202
  Fire Fish, 436
  Florida Pompano, 307
  Flounder, 222
  Giant Grouper, 432
  Green Jack, 119
  Haddock, 170
  Hagfish, 104
  Hake, 296
  Halibut, 330
  Herring, 60
  Jack Fish, 122
  Lionfish, 267
  Mackerel, 35
  Mahi-mahi, 424
  Marlin, 156
  Milk Fish, 247
  Molly, 397
  Monkfish, 278
  Oarfish, 40
  Oil Fish, 115
  Permit Fish, 188
  Pollock, 370
  Pompano, 143
  Red Mullet, 77
  Red-lipped Batfish, 58
  Remora, 490
  Ribbon Fish, 329
  Rockfish, 305
  Sailfish, 345
  Sawfish, 510
  Sea Bass, 153
  Sea Dragon, 196
  Shark Sucker, 177
  Shovelnose
    Guitarfish, 378
  Skate, 545
  Skipjack, 106
  Sole, 65
  Spanish Mackerel, 76
  Spiny Pufferfish, 151
  Sprat, 204
  Stonefish, 398
  Striped Faced Unicorn
    Fish, 501
  Swordfish, 325
  Tarpon, 149
  Tomato Clownfish, 512
  Triggerfish, 455
  Tuna, 559
  Turbot Fish, 74
  Unicorn Crestfish, 31
  Wahoo, 72

Saltwater Fish *(continued)*
White Marlin, 549
Whiting, 556
Yellow Tang, 38
Yellowfin Tuna, 291
Yellowtail, 407

Insects

Ants
ant, 444
Carpenter Ant, 341
Fire Ant, 422
Leaf Cutter Ant, 130
Arachnids
Black Widow
 Spider, 223
Brown Recluse, 422
Camel Spider, 430
Cobweb Spider, 303
Daddy Longlegs, 166
Deer Tick, 357
Dew-drop Spider, 343
Dog Tick, 186
Funnel Web Spider, 322
Garden Spider, 85
Goliath Birdeater, 82
Hobo Spider, 344
Huntsman Spider, 233
Jumping Spider, 108
Lone Star Tick, 359
Nursery Web Spider, 171
Orb Weaver, 237
Redback Spider, 496
spider, 81
Tarantula, 382
tick, 503
Wolf Spider, 26
Arthropod
Arthropod, 197
Black Snake
 Millipede, 456
centipede, 177
millipede, 182
Tiger Centipede, 558
Bees / Wasps
bee, 16
Honeybee, 19
hornet, 174
Jewel Wasp, 503
Killer Bee, 98
Mason Wasp, 132
Mud Dauber, 87
Sweat Bee, 525

Bees / Wasps *(continued)*
Tarantula Hawk, 290
wasp, 407
Wood Wasp, 508
Wool Carder Bee, 101
Beetles
Asian Lady Beetle, 446
beetle, 323
Click Beetle, 84
Colorado Potato
 Beetle, 568
Dung Beetle, 431
Hercules Beetle, 160
Hibiscus Beetle, 492
Longhorn Beetle, 428
Sand Scarab, 242
Scarab Beetle, 38
Stag Beetle, 439
Tiger Beetle, 553
Tortoise Beetle, 526
Bugs
Assassin Bug, 539
Doodlebug, 379
June Bug, 414
Ladybug, 100
Lightning Bug, 337
Palmetto Bug, 385
Stink Bug, 488
Butterflies
Apollo Butterfly, 212
butterfly, 403
Cairns Birdwing
 Butterfly, 251
Lesser Wanderer, 199
Long Tail Skipper, 145
Monarch Butterfly, 410
Sulphur Butterfly, 489
Ulysses Butterfly, 513
Flies
Black Fly, 214
Damselfly, 161
Dragonfly, 18
Fairyfly, 50
Firefly, 159
fly, 262
Fruit Fly, 172
Horse Fly, 243
House Fly, 330
Maggot, 52
Mayfly, 370
Sawflies, 441
Moths
Guava Moth, 381
Hawk Moth, 463

Moths *(continued)*
Kawakawa Looper, 287
Madagascan Sunset
 Moth, 299
Magpie Moth, 107
Moon Moth, 134
moth, 329
Owl Moth, 355
Tiger Swallow Tail
 Moth, 560
Other Insects
aphids, 131
caterpillar, 436
Cicada, 208
cockroach, 479
cricket, 210
Earwig, 308
flea, 118
grasshopper, 419
Green Planthopper, 342
Katydid, 242
Leaf Hopper, 168
Leech, 526
Lice, 252
Locust, 193
mite, 310
Mole Cricket, 233
mosquito, 500
Pond Skater, 487
Praying Mantis, 163
Rice Weevil, 205
scorpion, 194
Silverfish, 229
Stick Insect, 310
Termite, 458
Tomato Fruitworm, 550
Tree Hopper, 455
Water Flea, 99
Weevil, 36

Mammals

**Amphibious African
Ungulate Mammal**
Hippopotamus, 412
Anteaters
anteater, 107
Pangolin, 219
Antilocapridae Family
Pronghorn, 331
Bears
American Black
 Bear, 536
bear, 292

Raise Your Frequency Through Number Messages 579

Bears *(continued)*
Brown Bear, 306
Giant Panda, 437
Grizzly Bear, 188
Kodiak Bear, 551
Moon Bear, 224
Panda, 514
Polar Bear, 29
Red Panda, 99
Sloth Bear, 416
Sun Bear, 96
Boars, Pigs, Hogs
boar, 58
Kune Kune, 163
pig, 148
Pot Belly Pig, 115
Warthog, 334
Wild Boar, 375
Bovines
American Bison, 324
antelope, 246
Black Angus, 261
Blackbuck, 125
Blue Bull, 285
Bohar Reedbuck, 144
Bongo, 309
Buelingo, 433
Buffalo, 399
Chamois, 302
cow, 360
Dik Dik, 226
Eland, 563
Gaur, 199
gazelle, 215
Gnu, 250
Hereford Cow, 139
Highland Cattle, 555
Holstein Cow, 252
Impala, 245
Jersey Cow, 423
Kob, 519
Kudu, 324
Lechwe, 274
Musk Ox, 438
Nyala, 348
Red Angus, 518
Saiga Antelope, 257
Scimitar-horned
   Oryx, 120
Springbok, 94
Takin, 447
Texas Longhorn, 521
Urial, 35
Water Buffalo, 524

Bovines *(continued)*
Wildebeest, 166
Yak, 75
Zebu, 25
Burrowing Mammals
Aardvark, 17
Mole, 411
Mole Shrew, 297
Star-nosed Mole, 498
Camels, Camelids
Alpaca, 258
camel, 405
Dromedary, 555
Llama, 70
Vicuña, 453
Canines
African Wild Dog, 293
Arctic Fox, 67
Arctic Wolf, 296
Bush Dog, 519
coyote, 16
Dingo, 221
dog, 36
Fennec Fox, 312
fox, 445
Gray Fox, 203
Island Fox, 397
Jackal, 187
Kit Fox, 64
Maned Wolf, 22
Red Fox, 332
Red Wolf, 435
Tanuki, 473
wolf, 525
Cervids
Axis Deer, 60
Caribou, 117
deer, 146
Elk, 347
Fallow Deer, 225
Key Deer, 200
Moose, 255
Mule Deer, 256
Muntjac, 319
Pampas Deer, 304
Red Deer, 358
Reindeer, 464
Sambar, 56
Water Deer, 541
Whitetail Deer, 47
Elephants
African Elephant, 490
Asian Elephant, 346
elephant, 289

Elephants *(continued)*
Indian Elephant, 142
Equines
African Wild Ass, 173
Akhal-Teke, 190
American
   Saddlebred, 141
Andalusian, 241
Appaloosa, 258
Arabian, 290
Barock Pinto, 387
Belgian, 291
Caspian, 454
Clydesdale, 215
donkey, 32
Dutch Warmblood, 400
Falabella, 86
Fjord Horse, 373
Friesian, 86
Gypsy Vanner, 236
Haflinger, 138
Hanoverian, 399
horse, 181
Icelandic Horse, 192
Lipizzan, 285
Miniature Horse, 206
Morgan, 120
Mule, 410
Mustang, 183
Onager, 184
Paint Horse, 247
Percheron, 284
Przewalski's Wild
   Horse, 383
Quagga, 33
Quarter Horse, 220
Shetland Pony, 272
Shire, 295
Standardbred, 444
Tennessee Walking
   Horse, 497
Thoroughbred, 548
Zebra, 150
Zonkey, 37
Felines
Amur Leopard, 92
Bengal Tiger, 27
Black Panther, 515
Bobcat, 383
Caracal, 255
cat, 385
Cheetah, 98
Clouded Leopard, 73
Cougar, 152

Felines *(continued)*
  Fishing Cat, 569
  Genet, 319
  Geoffroy's Cat, 362
  Golden Cat, 129
  Jaguar, 294
  Jaguarundi, 357
  KodKod, 402
  Leopard, 270
  Leopard Cat, 261
  Lion, 135
  Lynx, 34
  Marbled Cat, 318
  Margay, 185
  Mountain Lion, 381
  Ocelot, 382
  Puma, 59
  Ringtail Cat, 117
  Sand Cat, 118
  Serval, 77
  Siberian Tiger, 456
  Snow Leopard, 45
  Tasmanian Tiger, 541
  tiger, 416
  White Tiger, 119
Flying Mammals
  Bat, 426
  Flying Fox, 234
  Ghost Bat, 406
  Vampire Bat, 47
Giraffes
  giraffe, 191
  Okapi, 157
Hyaenidae Family
  Hyena, 431
Hyrax Family
  Hyrax, 336
  Yellow-spotted
    Hyrax, 561
Lemurs
  Colugo, 342
Marsupials
  Antechinus, 65
  Bandicoot, 528
  Bilby, 495
  Cuscus, 443
  Eastern Quoll, 352
  Greater Glider, 220
  Honey Possum, 111
  Kangaroo, 367
  Koala, 66
  Kowari, 228
  Kultarr, 218

Marsupials *(continued)*
  Mountain
    Pademelon, 314
  Mulgara, 283
  Musky Rat
    Kangaroo, 364
  Opossum, 363
  Possum, 78
  Potoroo, 132
  Quokka, 570
  Spotted Quoll, 409
  Squirrel Glider, 105
  Striped Possum, 481
  Sugar Glider, 72
  Tasmanian Devil, 182
  Tree Kangaroo, 567
  Virginia Opossum, 496
  Wallaby, 46
  Wombat, 408
  Yapok, 376
Mephitidae Family
  Skunk, 267
Mongoose
  Meerkat, 212
  Mongoose, 435
Monotremes (Egg-laying) Mammals
  Echidna, 486
  Platypus, 128
Mustelidae Family
  Badger, 340
  Black Footed Ferret, 147
  Ermine, 273
  ferret, 239
  Fisher, 531
  Honey Badger, 172
  Marten, 56
  Mink, 244
  otter, 423
  River Otter, 54
  Sable, 567
  Stoat, 29
  weasel, 438
  Wolverine, 491
  Zorilla, 103
Nasua Family
  Coati, 43
Ochotonidae Family
  Pika, 66
Other Antelope
  Natal Duiker, 158
Pinnipeds
  seal, 266
  walrus, 298

Placental Mammals
  Armadillo, 87
Primates
  Aye Aye, 420
  baboon, 164
  Bleeding Heart
    Monkey, 450
  Blond Capuchin, 189
  Bonobo, 390
  Bushbaby, 534
  Capuchin, 317
  chimpanzee, 218
  Drill, 523
  Gelada Baboon, 286
  Gibbon, 484
  gorilla, 377
  Howler Monkey, 121
  Lemur, 89
  Loris, 335
  Macaque, 85
  Mandrill, 469
  Marmoset, 137
  monkey, 179
  Orangutan, 376
  Peruvian Night
    Monkey, 328
  Proboscis Monkey, 239
  Ringtail Lemur, 71
  Slow Loris, 108
  Spider Monkey, 116
  Squirrel Monkey, 63
  Tamarin, 506
  Tarsier, 452
Procyonidae Family
  Kinkajou, 100
  Raccoon, 155
Rhinoceros
  Black Rhinoceros, 315
  Rhinoceros, 327
  White Rhino, 552
Rabbits, Hares
  Cottontail, 307
  hare, 480
  Jackrabbit, 59
  Marsh Rabbit, 94
  rabbit, 157
  Snowshoe Hare, 28
Rodents
  Agouti, 317
  Beaver, 51
  Black Rat, 259
  Capybara, 197
  Chinchilla, 64
  Chipmunk, 193

Raise Your Frequency Through Number Messages 581

Rodents *(continued)*
Deer Mouse, 114
Dwarf Hamster, 352
Flying Squirrel, 153
Fox Squirrel, 112
Gerbil, 308
Gopher, 101
Ground Squirrel, 475
Groundhog, 531
Guinea Pig, 61
Hamster, 374
House Mouse, 471
Jerboa, 316
Kangaroo Rat, 367
Lemming, 184
Marmot, 124
Mole Rat, 425
Mountain Beaver, 217
mouse, 457
Muskrat, 470
Naked Mole Rat, 186
Nutria Rat, 269
Paca, 394
Pack Rat, 284
Patagonian Mara, 264
Porcupine, 256
Prairie Dog, 174
rat, 504
Rat Squirrel, 546
Red Squirrel, 238
Small-toothed Harvest Mouse, 198
squirrel, 90
Swamp Rat, 537
Tuco Tuco, 522
Vole, 24
Woodchuck, 50
Zokor, 428
Seals
Antarctic Fur Seal, 167
Elephant Seal, 529
Leopard Seal, 63
Sheep, Goats
Angora Goat, 550
Bighorn Sheep, 465
Fainting Goat, 147
goat, 380
Ibex, 334
Kamori, 235
Merino Sheep, 316
Mountain Goat, 485
Mountain Sheep, 222
Pygmy Goat, 20
sheep, 391

Sheep, Goats *(continued)*
Tur, 556
Shrews, Moles and Hedgehogs
Elephant Shrew, 420
hedgehog, 332
Moonrat, 110
Shrew, 415
Sloths
Maned Sloth, 411
sloth, 476
Tapiridae Family
Tapir, 28
Tenrecidae Family
Tenrec, 516
Viverridae family (Cat-like Mammals)
Binturong, 534
Fossa, 123
Spotted Linsang, 389

Micro-animals
Tardigrade, 280

Mollusks
Banana Slug, 482
Mussel, 309
slug, 183
Spirula spirula, 179
Tusk Shells, 460

Other Water Animals
Amazon Dolphin, 79
Manatee, 83

Reptiles

Turtles/Tortoises
Alligator Snapping Turtle, 91
Box Turtle, 513
Desert Tortoise, 462
Galapagos Tortoise, 210
Green Turtle, 396
Map Turtle, 429
Mud Turtle, 162
Painted Turtle, 106
Russian Tortoise, 566
Snapping Turtle, 387
Softshell Turtle, 55
Sulcata Tortoise, 511
tortoise, 140

Turtles/Tortoises *(continued)*
turtle, 253
Snakes
Anaconda, 80
Ball Python, 355
Black Mamba, 241
Black Racer, 71
Black Snake, 502
Blind Snake, 265
Boa Constrictor, 169
Boomslang, 413
Brown Snake, 468
Bullsnake, 312
Burmese Python, 464
Bushmaster, 558
Cat Snake, 461
Cobra, 348
Coral Snake, 494
Corn Snake, 417
Cottonmouth, 327
Diamondback Rattlesnake, 300
Egyptian Cobra, 532
Gaboon Viper, 366
Garter Snake, 165
Golden Tree Snake, 221
Gopher Snake, 101
Grass Snake, 325
Green Anaconda, 110
Green Snake, 443
Indigo Snake, 231
King Cobra, 109
Kingsnake, 159
Mamba, 90
Milk Snake, 213
Moccasin, 369
Pit Viper, 39
Python, 467
Rainbow Snake, 395
Rat Snake, 535
Reticulated Python, 544
Sand Boa, 26
snake, 369
Taipan, 502
Tiger Snake, 93
Timber Rattlesnake, 562
Viper, 492
Wolf Snake, 494
Lizards
Agamid Lizards, 371
Anole, 318
Blue Tongue Skink, 433
Caiman, 288

Lizards *(continued)*
Chameleon, 206
Chinese Water
   Dragon, 517
Chuckwalla, 246
Collared Lizard, 516
Crested Gecko, 414
Crocodile Skink, 474
Desert Horned
   Lizard, 437
Fire Salamander, 477
Flying Dragon, 293
Flying Lizard, 180
Frilled Lizard, 253
Gecko, 244
Giant Salamander, 465
Gila Monster, 551
Green Iguana, 276
Horny Toad Lizard, 216
Iguana, 389
Inland Bearded
   Dragon, 486
Jackson's
   Chameleon, 162
Komodo Dragon, 41
Leopard Gecko, 282
lizard, 42
Monitor Lizard, 463
Panther Chameleon, 363
Plumed Basilisk, 452
Rainbow Lizard, 249
Red Salamander, 151
Salamander, 432
Savannah Monitor, 460
Skink, 30
Tegu Lizard, 154
Thorny Devil, 30
Tokay Gecko, 408
Uromastyx, 155
Veiled Chameleon, 512
Water Dragon, 31
Water Monitor, 405

Snails
Garden Snail, 371

Frog/Toads
Bufo Toad, 254
Bullfrog, 314
Frog, 542
Glass Frog, 339
Green Frog, 440
Pacman Frog, 268
Poison Dart Frog, 549
Surinam Horned
   Frog, 524

Frog/Toads *(continued)*
Tadpole, 295
Toad, 375
Tree Frog, 445
Tungara Frog, 566

Other Reptiles
Alligator, 209
Crocodile, 392
Gharial Crocodile, 384

Sea Life
Abalone, 568
Angel Shark, 390
Basking Shark, 313
Beluga Whale, 34
Black Dolphin, 93
Blacktip Shark, 527
Blue Dragon, 62
Blue Shark, 565
Blue Whale, 257
Blue-ringed
   Octopus, 475
Bottlenose Dolphin, 520
Box Jellyfish, 569
Brain Coral, 345
Bull Shark, 189
Cat Shark, 501
Clam, 17
Common Whelk, 449
Conch, 451
Conger, 562
Coral, 112
Cowries, 274
Crown of Thorns, 426
Demosponge, 388
Dolphin, 264
Dugong, 561
Eel, 403
Feather Star, 260
Fin Whale, 301
Frilled Shark, 280
Glass Sponge, 553
Goblin Shark, 202
Great White Shark, 287
Greenland Shark, 245
Hammerhead Shark, 351
Hooded Nudibranch, 137
Humpback Whale, 154
Jellyfish, 373
Leatherback Sea
   Turtle, 235
Lemon Shark, 259
Leopard Shark, 338
Loggerhead Turtle, 125

Sea Life *(continued)*
Mako Shark, 326
Manta Ray, 547
Marbled Electric
   Ray, 248
Moray Eel, 62
Mushroom Coral, 413
Narwhal, 173
Nurse Shark, 41
Octopus, 138
Orca, 238
Oyster, 91
Pencil Urchin, 84
Porpoise, 51
Portuguese
   Man o' war, 538
Reef Shark, 425
Saltwater Crocodile, 123
Sand Dollar, 171
Scallops, 240
Sea Anemones, 89
Sea Angel, 544
Sea Cucumber, 126
Sea Fans, 368
Sea Lily, 421
Sea Lion, 478
Sea Otter, 500
Sea Snake, 542
Sea Turtle, 23
Sea Urchin, 559
Sea Wasp, 57
Seahorse, 76
shark, 201
Sperm Whale, 116
sponge, 543
Squid, 418
Starfish, 133
Stingray, 409
Thresher Shark, 552
Tiger Shark, 45
Tube Sponge, 548
Vampire Squid, 523
Vaquita, 97
whale, 194
Whale Shark, 25

Worms
Earthworm, 127
Glow Worm, 313
Ice Worm, 134
Inchworm, 20
Silkworm, 122

Raise Your Frequency Through Number Messages

NATURE MESSENGERS

Cactus
Bunny Ear, 243
Cardón, 162
Eve's Pin, 528
Golden Barrel, 93
Ladyfinger, 64
Prickly Pear, 99

Clouds
Altocumulus, 561
Altostratus, 356
Cirrocumulus, 339
Cirrostratus, 445
Cirrus, 451
Cloud Iridescence, 534
Cloudburst, 550
Cumulonimbus, 424
Cumulus, 15
Irisation, 491
Kelvin-Helmholtz
  Wave, 456
Lenticular, 559
Nacreous, 391
Nimbostratus, 556
Noctilucent, 327
Roll Cloud/Morning
  Glory, 83
Stratocumulus, 173
Stratus, 224

Fruits
apple, 24
apricot, 84
Asian pear, 507
avocado, 281
banana, 542
bergamot, 352
bitter melon, 564
blackberry, 419
blueberry, 533
boysenberry, 410
cactus pear, 497
cantaloupe, 436
carambola, 525
casaba melon, 232
chayote, 387
cherimoya, 375
cherry, 347
cherry tomato, 58
clementine, 502

Fruits *(continued)*
coconut, 112
cranberry, 310
Custard-Apple, 563
Date fruit, 151
Dragonfruit, 476
dried plums, 490
elderberry, 143
feijoa, 452
fig, 382
gooseberry, 379
Granny Smith
  Apple, 516
grapefruit, 562
green grapes, 464
guava, 500
honeydew melon, 342
horned melon, 489
Hydnora Africana, 546
jackfruit, 202
java-plum, 34
jujube fruit, 454
key lime, 151
kiwifruit, 333
kumquat, 19
lemon, 114
lime, 246
lychee, 487
Mamey sapote, 294
Mandarin orange, 320
mango, 81
mangosteen, 433
mulberry, 378
nectarine, 512
olive, 354
orange, 157
papaya, 469
passion fruit, 412
peach, 135
pear, 544
persimmon, 292
pineapple, 55
pitaya, 308
plantain, 481
plum, 482
pomegranate, 160
pomelo, 142
prune, 334
pummelo, 295
pumpkin, 289
quince, 161

Fruits *(continued)*
raisin, 244
raspberry, 210
Red Delicious apple, 346
red grapes, 440
Rose-Apple, 332
soursop, 160
starfruit, 142
strawberry, 272
tangelo, 285
tangerine, 377
tomatillo, 249
tomato, 257
Ugli fruit, 123
watermelon, 61

Gemstones
Amazonite, 214
Amethyst, 192
Ametrine, 85
Ammolite, 51
Andalusite, 224
Aquamarine, 117
Aventurine, 231
Azurite, 390
Azurmalachite, 428
Benitoite, 549
Beryl, 274
Blue Diamond, 26
Blue Topaz, 357
Boulder Opal, 386
Brown Diamond, 481
Cat's-Eye Opal, 358
Charoite, 553
Chrysoberyl, 244
Chrysoprase, 269
Colored Diamond, 59
Common Opal, 152
Cordierite, 216
Corundum, 268
Diamond, 97
Dryhead Agate, 73
Emerald, 186
Ethiopian Opal, 409
Euclase, 389
Fancy Sapphire, 34
Fire Agate, 180
Fire Opal, 109
Fluorite, 241
Fuchsite, 317
Garnet, 522

584 Raise Your Frequency Through Number Messages

Gemstones *(continued)*
Goshenite, 436
Granite Obsidian, 471
Green Beryl, 338
Green Diamond, 373
Helenite, 103
Heliodor, 190
Hematite, 213
Iolite, 351
Iris Agate, 459
Jade, 154
Jet, 319
Jewels, 27
Labradorite, 79
Lapis Lazuli, 508
Larimar, 42
Lepidolite, 77
Malachite, 341
Marble Mariposite, 560
Marcasite, 521
Matrix Opal, 458
Maw Sit Sit, 478
Moldavite, 426
Montana Moss
  Agate, 340
Moonstone, 543
Morado Opal, 484
Morganite, 146
Nephrite, 545
Opal, 565
Orthoclase, 552
Peridot, 554
Polka Dot Agate, 179
Prasiolite, 492
Precious Opal, 470
Pyrite, 438
Realgar, 175
Red Beryl, 98
Red Diamond, 416
Rhodochrosite, 172
Rhodonite, 265
Rose Quartz, 298
Ruby, 405
Sapphire, 360
Scapolite, 485
Serpentine Stone, 29
Sodalite, 205
Sonora Sunrise, 113
Sphalerite, 542
Spinel, 385
Spodumene, 503
Staurolite, 327
Sugilite, 165
Sunstone, 527

Gemstones *(continued)*
Tanzanite, 510
Tiffany Stone, 239
Tiger's-Eye, 49
Topaz, 261
Tourmaline, 295
Turquoise Stone, 38
Turritella Agate, 108
Yellow Diamond, 52

Grass
American Beach
  Grass, 127
Bahia grass, 299
Bermuda grass, 532
Broomstraw, 16
Coastal Panic grass, 364
Common eelgrass, 139
crabgrass, 301
fescue grass, 323
Kentucky bluegrass, 362
lemongrass, 498
Neptune grass, 540
pampas grass, 404
rye grass, 391
sawgrass, 448
seagrass, 65
switch grass, 260

Herbs
basil, 233
bay leaf, 568
boneset, 201
chervil, 56
chickweed, 83
chives, 145
cicely, 277
cilantro, 293
coriander, 223
dill, 43
echinacea, 29
goldenrod, 318
lemon balm, 86
Mimosa Pudica, 168
mint, 272
oregano, 195
parsley, 282
peppermint, 541
rosemary, 413
rue, 325
sage, 127
spearmint, 500
starflower, 66
tarragon, 377

Herbs *(continued)*
thyme, 130
witch hazel, 276

Legumes
black beans, 255
broad bean, 544
cannellini beans, 195
fava beans, 121
great northern beans, 211
green beans, 282
hyacinth bean, 139
kidney bean, 473
lentils, 145
lima bean, 401
lupine, 476
mung bean, 236
navy bean, 487
Nuttall's Lotus, 132
red beans, 130
snap peas, 382
snow pea, 464
soybean, 162

Metal
beryllium, 204
bismuth, 529
copper, 196
gold, 193
lead, 469
limonite, 138
magnetite, 176
nickel, 181
silver, 21
titanium, 76

Minerals
anhydrite, 466
apatite, 355
augite, 35
barite, 85
biotite, 101
bloodstone, 152
bornite, 187
calcite, 362
cassiterite, 329
chalcopyrite, 538
chlorite, 147
chromite, 189
chromium, 231
cinnabar, 303
Clinozoisite, 519
desert rose, 287

Raise Your Frequency Through Number Messages 585

Minerals *(continued)*
- epidote, 267
- feldspar, 480
- fool's gold, 40
- galena, 407
- Gaspeite, 117
- gem silica, 87
- graphite, 218
- gypsum, 552
- halite, 412
- hornblende, 478
- ilmenite, 115
- jadeite, 113
- kyanite, 136
- limestone halite rock salt, 96
- magnesite, 375
- molybdenite, 444
- monazite, 468
- muscovite, 281
- olivine, 502
- orpiment, 337
- Painite, 442
- phlogopite, 178
- plagioclase, 453
- pyroxene, 352
- quartz, 57
- rutile, 314
- salt, 216
- smoky quartz, 39
- talc, 508
- titanite, 331
- uraninite, 68
- vanadinite, 73
- variscite, 46
- zinc, 54
- zircon, 229
- zoisite, 41

Mushrooms and Fungus
- Armillaria Ostoyae mushroom, 200
- fungus, 136
- Hydnellum Peckii, 507
- mold, 402
- morel mushroom, 316
- mushroom, 310
- stinkhorn mushroom, 494

Nuts, Drupes, Nut-like Legumes and Seeds
- acorn, 386
- almond, 526
- black walnut, 323
- Brazil nut, 444
- butternut white walnut, 141
- cashew, 273
- chestnut, 69
- chinquapin nut, 128
- English walnut, 245
- filbert, 446
- ginkgo nut, 148
- hazelnut, 251
- hickory nut, 268
- macadamia nut, 525
- paradise nut, 419
- peanut, 90
- pecan, 567
- pine nut, 79
- pistachio, 271
- poppy seed, 555
- pumpkin seed, 546
- sesame seed, 225
- Sheanut, 385

Other Things in Nature
- ash, 430
- beehives, 415
- bird nests, 567
- comet, 135
- current (water flow), 536
- dead leaves, 347
- dust, 302
- Earth's crust, 82
- ember, 456
- fossils, 120
- gas, 390
- gas fire, 181
- gravity, 20
- honeycomb, 33
- horizon, 461
- jungle, 479
- leaf, 264
- liquid asphalt, 205
- maple syrup, 493
- meteorite remnants, 399
- meteors, 70
- methane gas, 212
- mud puddles, 474

Other Things in Nature *(continued)*
- nitrogen, 422
- opalized wood, 187
- palm wood, 383
- peanut wood, 556
- pearls, 530
- petrified wood, 248
- petroleum, 227
- pinecones, 357
- quicksand, 143
- clay, 466
- red clay, 450
- rotting logs, 441
- seashells, 16
- seawater, 21
- sediment, 69
- silt, 229
- soil, 105
- solstice, 31
- spider webs, 63
- standing water, 275
- steam, 402
- stream, 299
- sulfur, 329
- sun, 485
- sunrise, 365
- sunset, 434
- termite mounds, 40
- volcanic ash, 71
- water, 45
- wilderness, 283

Plants
- algae, 335
- aloe plant, 564
- angelica, 414
- anise, 496
- anthurium plant, 492
- arum lilies, 344
- aster, 149
- azalea, 380
- baby toes, 307
- bamboo, 190
- baseball plant, 203
- beach bur, 328
- beach saltbush, 477
- bear's breeches, 378
- bearberry, 220
- Bee Orchid, 324
- bellflower, 425
- bindweed, 191
- Birdsfoot Trefoil, 227
- black bat flower, 451

Plants *(continued)*
black currant, 204
black medic, 119
black nightshade, 280
Black-eyed Susan, 565
bladderwort, 179
blazing star, 321
bleeding heart, 358
bloodroot, 538
blossom, 111
bluebells, 429
Bok Choy, 486
borage, 140
Boston fern, 215
bougainvillea, 307
broadleaf
 arrowhead, 403
bulrush, 392
burnet, 209
burro's tail, 346
buttercup, 120
butterfly milkweed, 156
buttonbush, 483
camellia, 269
campion flower, 230
Canada thistle, 245
cardinal flower, 191
carnation, 194
catnip, 354
cattail, 371
cattleya, 379
cedar sedge, 439
Centaurea, 528
chocolate cosmos, 158
chokecherry, 170
Christmas fern, 183
cistus, 458
clasping-leaf
 pondweed, 455
clover, 144
coast wallflower, 339
cocoon plant, 370
coffee plant, 105
colt's foot, 67
coneflower, 177
Coontail, 185
coral bells, 209
cornflower, 259
costmary, 285
Creeping Charlie, 336
curly-leaf
 pondweed, 463
cycad plant, 278
daffodil, 153

Plants *(continued)*
dahlia, 235
daisy, 311
dancing lady orchid, 448
dayflower, 322
devil's claw, 398
devil's thorn, 308
dracaena plant, 462
duckweed, 184
durian, 233
early dog violet, 215
elephant's foot plant, 495
evening primrose, 345
exotic angel plant, 280
fatsia, 78
fenugreek, 415
Ficus Lyrata plant, 283
fiddle leaf fig plant, 342
flaxseed, 17
fleabane, 482
flying duck orchid, 137
foam flower, 107
forget-me-not, 80
four o'clock flower, 174
four-leaf clover, 202
foxglove, 250
frangipani, 301
gardenia, 401
gazania, 104
ghost orchid, 80
ghost plant, 184
ginger lily, 537
glade coneflower, 182
glade thistle, 296
glory of the snow, 213
golden alexander, 150
golden currant, 67
Golden Pothos, 273
gorse, 416
grape hyacinth, 534
gray-head
 coneflower, 173
happy alien flower, 309
heather, 148
heliconia flower, 91
hibiscus, 261
holly, 313
honeysuckle, 373
horehound, 438
horse tails, 566
Hosta, 183
hyacinth, 121
hydrangea, 569
Hydrillia, 252

Plants *(continued)*
hyssop, 309
iris, 398
Irish eyebright, 530
ivy, 235
Jacob's ladder, 169
jade vine, 126
jasmine flower, 58
Kadupul flower, 563
king's holly plant, 551
lacy blue self-heal
 plant, 64
lady fern, 44
lady slipper, 141
lamb's quarter, 171
laughing bumblebee
 orchid, 344
lavender, 447
leatherwood, 188
lemon verbena, 388
licorice, 164
lilac, 536
lily of the valley, 223
Lithop, 238
living rocks, 171
lizard's tail, 278
log fern, 297
longan, 359
loquat, 383
lotus, 400
lovage, 418
marigold, 475
Marsh Blazingstar, 417
Middlemist Red, 315
milfoil, 122
mist flower, 336
mistletoe, 489
money tree plant, 172
monstera plant, 298
moonflower, 447
morning glory, 267
moss, 15
musk thistle, 332
myosotis, 351
naiad, 421
naked man orchid, 446
nettle, 221
night blooming
 cereus, 97
night blooming
 jessamine, 439
Nottingham Catchfly, 61
nutsedge, 207
orchid, 166

Raise Your Frequency Through Number Messages 587

Plants *(continued)*
oxalis, 353
Pachira plant, 180
pansy, 424
parachute flower, 547
parrot's beak flower, 232
passion fruit flower, 535
patchouli, 558
peace lily, 176
peacock plant, 114
pelican flower, 423
pencil plant, 435
peonies, 494
periwinkle, 337
petal, 270
petunia, 206
phlox, 175
phragmites, 159
pickerel plant, 118
pitcher plant, 422
poinsettia, 293
poison ivy, 276
poison oak, 203
poppy, 89
primrose, 360
purple loosestrife, 484
purslane, 465
Quackgrass, 39
Queen Victoria
 Agave, 122
ragweed, 211
red algae, 154
red hot lips flower, 408
red rose, 531
red sand verbena, 543
reed, 343
rhododendron, 146
rice, 348
Rodgersia, 95
rose, 210
rose mallow, 247
rubber plant, 511
running cedar, 241
Russian sage, 200
safflower, 317
sago pondweed, 155
sassafras, 396
sea holly, 345
sea lettuce, 404
sea oats, 380
sea rocket, 303
sea thrift, 197
seabeach sandwort, 124
seaweed, 237

Plants *(continued)*
sensitive plant, 47
Shameplant, 367
Siberian Iris, 44
smartweed, 107
snake plant, 361
Spathiphyllum, 399
spicebush, 555
stevia, 442
stinking corpse lily, 549
sugarcane, 161
sundew, 265
sunflower, 277
swaddled babies
 orchid, 72
sweet alyssum, 527
Swiss cheese plant, 250
tea plant, 291
telegraph plant, 324
tempest, 32
titan arum, 256
trillium plant, 467
tulip, 514
velvetleaf, 28
Venus fly trap, 54
vernal witch-hazel, 53
Veronica flower, 106
Victoria Amazonica, 305
virgin's bower, 129
Virginia bluebells, 510
Virginia creeper, 222
wasabi, 125
water canna, 509
water chestnut, 72
water lily, 32
water poppy, 264
winterberry holly, 45
wisteria, 147
wolfsbane, 53
yellow sweet clover, 242
Youtan Poluo, 106
zebra haworthia, 90
zinnia, 23

Rainbows
double, 443
fire, 193
full circle, 185
quaternary, 103
rainbow, 405
supernumerary, 455
tertiary, 66
twinned, 260
white, 168

Rocks
amphibolite anthracite
 coal, 116
andesite basalt, 284
anthracite gneiss, 545
anyolite, 400
arsenopyrite, 225
basalt dacite, 25
bauxite, 533
bedrock, 291
breccia caliche, 465
caliche chalk, 306
chalk chert, 557
chert bituminous coal, 43
coal conglomerate, 199
columnar basalt, 77
conglomerate
 diatomite, 174
dacite diabase, 78
diabase quartz
 diorite, 411
diatomite dolomite, 63
diorite gabbro, 330
dolomite flint, 355
flint hematite iron
 ore, 524
gabbro granite, 95
geodes, 60
gneiss hornfels, 262
gravel, 158
iron ore limestone, 566
mariposite
 novaculite, 443
metamorphic, 350
novaculite phyllite, 87
obsidian pegmatite, 312
pebble, 495
pegmatite peridotite, 392
peridotite pumice, 384
phyllite quartzite, 129
pumice rhyolite, 60
quartzite muscovite
 schist, 76
rhyolite, 302
rock salt sandstone, 300
sand, 372
sandstone, 198
scoria welded tuff, 517
shale, 290
siltstone, 432
skarn, 499
slate, 81
soapstone, 486
tephra, 239

Rocks *(continued)*
  tuff, 506
  unakite, 157
  volcanic rock, 50
  Wonderstone, 242

Spices
  allspice, 457
  black cumin, 22
  black mustard, 217
  black pepper, 407
  brown mustard, 381
  caraway, 562
  cardamom, 275
  cassia, 322
  cayenne pepper, 425
  chili pepper, 102
  cinnamon, 319
  clove, 554
  cumin, 374
  curry, 547
  ginger, 462
  grains of paradise, 457
  mace, 506
  marjoram, 463
  nutmeg, 188
  paprika, 540
  pepper, 520
  saffron, 101
  star anise, 110
  turmeric, 501
  vanilla, 38

Topography, Terrain, and Landforms
  atoll, 170
  ayre, 246
  backwater, 471
  badlands, 30
  basin, 389
  bay, 182
  beach, 75
  butte, 134
  canal, 201
  canyon, 477
  cape, 503
  cascade, 254
  cave, 406
  cavern, 338
  cay / key, 393
  cenote, 523
  cliff, 515

Topography, Terrain, and Landforms *(continued)*
  coast, 262
  cove, 288
  crater, 320
  creek, 330
  dale, 414
  dam, 437
  Danxia landforms, 472
  delta, 366
  desert, 387
  dry lake, 537
  equator, 304
  escarpment, 460
  estuary, 431
  fairy chimneys, 110
  field, 363
  fjord, 420
  fluvial island, 403
  geyser, 36
  giant cliff, 305
  glacier, 22
  glen, 254
  gorge, 388
  grassland, 165
  grove, 473
  hill, 294
  hogback, 263
  hot springs, 133
  ice cave, 376
  island, 274
  knoll, 551
  lagoon, 169
  lake, 134
  land bridge, 234
  marsh, 149
  meadow, 258
  mound, 356
  mountain, 394
  mountain lake, 426
  mountain stream, 526
  mountain top, 116
  mud volcano, 144
  mudslide, 84
  natural fault line, 104
  ocean, 326
  plains, 196
  plunge pool, 553
  pond, 133
  prairie, 504
  puddle, 315
  rainforest, 461
  reef, 539

Topography, Terrain, and Landforms *(continued)*
  ridge, 370
  Riverbank, 394
  riverbed, 428
  rock formation, 17
  rock pit, 255
  sand boil, 271
  sand dunes, 427
  sandhill, 92
  sandstone arches, 159
  sea, 531
  sea cave, 257
  sinkhole, 470
  slot canyon, 522
  swamp, 518
  terra, 41
  thermal pools, 89
  tide pool, 156
  tundra, 112
  tunnel, 449
  valley, 49
  volcano, 286
  waterfall, 292
  wetlands, 289

Trees
  acacia, 20
  apple, 349
  aspen, 266
  atemoya, 102
  bald cypress, 25
  banana, 542
  banyan, 125
  beech, 395
  birch, 186
  black ash, 57
  blackthorn, 247
  blue jacaranda, 111
  bonsai, 36
  bristlecone pine, 520
  cacao, 548
  cannonball, 406
  cat palm, 331
  cedar, 493
  chinquapin oak, 86
  coast redwood, 311
  Coco de Mer, 393
  cypress, 65
  dogwood, 333
  dragon's blood, 474
  elder wood, 198
  fig, 382

Raise Your Frequency Through Number Messages

Trees *(continued)*
  fir, 452
  flowering talipot
    palm, 348
  forest, 62
  giant baobabs, 279
  giant sequoias, 397
  green ash, 212
  henna, 236
  Japanese maple, 82
  Joshua, 423
  juniper, 519
  key lime, 341
  lemon, 51
  lime, 47
  mahogany, 228
  majesty palm, 140
  mangrove, 453
  maple, 529
  Montezuma cypress, 367
  oak, 207
  palm, 137
  pawpaw, 228
  peach, 334
  pecan, 365
  pin oak, 94
  pine, 74
  pinyon, 30
  ponderosa pine, 108
  rainbow eucalyptus, 314
  red maple, 472
  red oak, 505
  river birch, 230
  royal poinciana, 483
  rubber, 532
  sapodilla, 217
  shagbark hickory, 253
  sugar-apple, 514
  sweet chestnut, 517
  sweetgum, 513
  sycamore, 349
  tamarind, 366
  wahoo elm, 219
  weeping willow, 131
  white ash, 512
  willow oak, 238
  wintergreen, 94
  yew, 42

Vegetables, Roots, and Grains
  acorn squash, 119
  alfalfa sprouts, 226
  artichoke, 368
  asparagus, 569
  bamboo shoots, 418
  bean sprouts, 559
  beet, 206
  Belgian endive, 237
  black-eyed pea, 488
  boniato, 128
  Broccoflower, 432
  broccoli, 459
  Brussel sprouts, 480
  butternut squash, 288
  cabbage, 518
  carrot, 219
  cassava, 300
  cauliflower, 395
  celery, 499
  chickpea, 71
  chicory, 91
  collard greens, 48
  corn, 251
  cucumber, 353
  daikon, 313
  Davidor, 192
  eggplant, 56
  endive, 197
  escarole, 496
  fennel, 516
  garlic, 491
  green bell pepper, 306
  green onion, 24
  hominy, 328
  horseradish, 445
  hot pepper, 167
  iceberg lettuce, 361
  Jerusalem artichoke, 222
  jicama, 409
  kale, 433
  kelp, 515
  kohlrabi, 208
  leek, 138
  lettuce, 28
  malanga, 266
  napa cabbage, 468
  okra, 252
  onion, 535
  parsnip, 374
  pea, 199
  potato, 521
  radicchio, 163

Vegetables, Roots, and Grains *(continued)*
  radish, 177
  red bell pepper, 115
  red cabbage, 304
  rhubarb, 290
  romaine lettuce, 164
  rutabaga, 240
  scallion, 460
  shallot, 343
  spinach, 243
  sprouts, 541
  squash, 376
  string bean, 325
  sweet pea, 429
  sweet pepper, 435
  sweet potato, 501
  turnip, 37
  watercress, 240
  waxed beans, 55
  wheat, 286
  yams, 98
  yellow squash, 126
  yuca/cassava, 131
  zucchini squash, 48

Weather
  arctic air, 335
  arid (dry) climate, 150
  atmosphere, 68
  autumn, 194
  avalanche, 96
  biosphere, 163
  black ice, 155
  blizzard, 75
  blood moon, 368
  breeze, 490
  calm air, 284
  carbon dioxide, 350
  chinook wind, 124
  clear ice, 467
  clear sky, 488
  cold front, 70
  condensation, 166
  crystallization, 312
  cyclone, 100
  dawn, 253
  daytime, 316
  derecho, 381
  dew, 19
  drift ice, 498
  drizzle, 505
  drought, 523
  dusk, 287

Weather *(continued)*
 dust devil, 479
 dust storm, 214
 El Niño, 74
 equinox, 570
 evaporation, 363
 eye of the storm, 62
 fire, 568
 flash flood, 449
 flood, 557
 fog, 33
 frost, 411
 frost flowers, 550
 frozen lake, 420
 gale wind, 279
 hail, 558
 haze, 297
 heatwave, 118
 humid climate, 93
 humidity, 99
 ice, 340
 ice circles, 167
 ice crystals, 31
 ice jam, 153
 ice pellets, 189
 ice storm, 270
 iceberg, 321
 icicle, 430
 jet stream, 384
 La Niña, 100
 lava, 396
 lava hair, 218
 lightning, 109
 lightning storm, 504
 lunar eclipse, 427
 maelstrom, 437
 mist, 23
 moisture, 364
 monsoon, 234
 moon, 570
 moonlight, 369
 muggy weather, 359
 nighttime, 524
 nor'easter, 92
 overcast sky, 497
 oxygen, 18
 ozone layer, 178
 precipitation, 440
 prevailing wind, 408
 pyroclastic flow, 410
 rain, 249
 rain shower, 413
 rainclouds, 548
 rainstorm, 441

Weather *(continued)*
 saturation point, 417
 sea breeze, 539
 sky, 220
 sleet, 37
 slush, 318
 snow, 434
 snowflakes, 35
 solar eclipse, 59
 spring, 513
 sprite, 397
 stars, 560
 static electricity, 259
 storm surge, 50
 summer, 421
 sun shower, 221
 supercell, 450
 temperature, 326
 thaw, 46
 thermal energy, 208
 thunder, 26
 thunderstorm, 123
 tide, 132
 tornado, 263
 tropical storm, 88
 trough, 371
 tsunami, 475
 typhoon, 454
 ultraviolet light, 88
 updraft, 27
 volcanic lightning, 258
 warm front, 372
 Wasatch Wind, 226
 water vapor, 256
 waterspout, 509
 whirlwind, 52
 wildfire, 511
 wind, 248
 wind chill factor, 369
 wind speed, 18
 winter, 296

Raise Your Frequency Through Number Messages 591

UNIVERSE / ENERGY MESSENGERS

Actions

acceptance, 19
accuracy, 23
active thought, 122
adaptability, 466
adventure, 387
advice, 421
agreement, 547
align with your goals, 519
allow yourself to receive, 302
alone time, 241
alternative, 287
answers, 436
art, 169
ask a question, 141
attention to details, 51
bake cookies, 241
bathe, 526
be an inspiration, 114
be decisive, 541
be exceptional, 543
be fully present in life, 569
be modest, 401
be punctual, 566
be resilient, 561
be romantic, 203
beauty, 558
become more organized, 525
beginnings, 298
belief, 169
bike ride, 183
bounce a ball, 321
brainstorming, 415
breathing, 485
broaden your horizons, 50
burn your favorite candle, 66
call to action, 459
carnival, 341
challenge yourself, 218
chance encounter, 392
change a habit, 347
character, 507

Actions *(continued)*

charisma, 535
charitable giving, 121
cleverness, 110
climb over a fence, 95
coincidence, 371
color, 483
communication, 154
companionship, 231
compose a song, 378
conceptualization, 528
confession, 476
confetti, 493
conformity, 85
congratulate someone, 434
connect with your soul song, 270
consequence, 167
consider little things, 342
consider the big picture, 442
consider your past, 181
consistency, 377
contemplation, 192
contribution, 287
conversation, 381
cooking, 97
creation, 144
creative expression, 299
cuddle with a pet, 126
cultivate, 143
dance, 468
dance in the rain, 565
daydream, 124
decision making, 418
declutter your space, 77
decorations, 346
define yourself, 274
detour, 339
diligence, 18
diplomacy, 211
disciplined, 185
discover your life purpose, 311
discovery, 256
discretion, 148
don't hesitate, 497
dream, 285

Actions *(continued)*

ecstatic, 71
effervescence, 176
embrace a moment, 29
encourage others, 568
energetic self-starter, 529
engagement, 164
ethics, 380
evaluate your frequency, 267
examine your inner self, 313
examine your multifaceted self, 322
examine your opinions, 160
exceed, 130
exercise, 57
express your empathy, 555
feedback, 437
find treasure at a yard sale, 517
fireworks, 313
flexibility, 409
float on a raft, 451
focus, 133
follow through, 526
follow your gut instincts, 490
forgiveness, 101
fork in the road, 69
friendliness, 387
gathering, 114
gaze at the night sky, 456
gift, 440
give back, 359
go camping, 373
go canoeing, 197
go for a drive, 80
go for a run, 556
go rafting, 71
goodwill, 496
hold someone's hand, 533
hug, 372
ignore, 163
illumination, 191

592 Raise Your Frequency Through Number Messages

Actions *(continued)*
 imagery, 253
 imagination, 281
 improvisation, 460
 included, 120
 industrious, 295
 insightfulness, 336
 inspired action, 529
 integrate opposites, 301
 intelligence, 214
 intention, 137
 interest, 248
 interpretation, 277
 introspection, 460
 investigate, 99
 isolate briefly for clarity, 391
 just sit, 366
 kindness, 182
 knowledge, 337
 laugh at yourself, 567
 learn a new skill, 519
 learn something new, 105
 lend a sympathetic ear, 509
 let go, 484
 lighten up, 369
 listen, 355
 longevity, 134
 look for a divine sign, 233
 look for symbols, 461
 look for the lesson, 317
 make a choice, 61
 make a craft, 557
 make a request, 76
 make something out of beads, 518
 make things happen, 516
 massage your scalp, 122
 memories, 300
 mercy, 349
 mingle, 188
 modesty, 465
 motivated reasoning, 488
 motivation, 282
 move your body, 532
 muse, 292
 music, 412
 never forget, 561
 nirvana, 434
 nonverbal communication, 415

Actions *(continued)*
 notice buildings, 366
 notice your world, 252
 nourish, 397
 nurture a good habit, 383
 nurture a plant, 380
 observe nature, 29
 observe patterns, 48
 open the door for a stranger, 88
 opportunity, 429
 originality, 253
 painting, 262
 pamper yourself, 184
 pay attention to psychic impressions, 129
 pay attention to your surroundings, 78
 perseverance, 254
 persistence, 20
 perspective, 295
 pick a place on a map and go there, 170
 plan your time, 524
 plant a garden, 138
 play, 63
 play a game, 83
 play in a sprinkler, 237
 play with a yoyo, 501
 pleasure, 98
 practice gratitude, 139
 praise, 301
 preparations, 467
 proactive, 386
 problem solving, 416
 productivity, 426
 progressive relaxation, 108
 promises, 456
 pronoia, 463
 propose a new concept, 266
 prowess, 251
 pull up weeds, 357
 quiet your mind, 348
 reach out to someone, 372
 read a book, 493
 read poetry, 559
 read random book text for inspiration, 147
 reading, 52
 reaffirm, 188

Actions *(continued)*
 rearrange your furniture, 97
 reconnect with someone, 62
 rejoice, 189
 relate, 304
 relationship building, 424
 relax in a hammock, 182
 relax in a sauna, 495
 relaxation, 325
 release control, 311
 release doubt, 198
 release drama, 395
 release something that no longer serves you, 351
 reliable, 213
 remember someone, 497
 remembrance, 151
 repetition, 494
 resourceful, 306
 rest, 80
 reward others, 496
 ride a bike, 234
 ride a horse, 400
 run, 179
 searching, 548
 secrets, 542
 see a plan to completion, 190
 see opportunities everywhere, 525
 seek, 560
 self-discovery, 141
 self-reflection, 376
 set a goal, 155
 share knowledge, 546
 share your possessions, 98
 sincerity, 197
 sing, 25
 sing a song in your mind, 68
 sit and think on a park bench, 429
 sit by a fire, 45
 sit in darkness, 501
 sketching, 47
 skip stones on water, 388
 sleep, 331
 slide, 125
 slow concentrated breathing, 102

Raise Your Frequency Through Number Messages 593

Actions *(continued)*
- slow down, 59
- smiles, 17
- socialize, 411
- solutions, 550
- solve a puzzle, 551
- sort through your closet, 180
- spend quality time, 438
- spend time alone, 106
- spend time with friends, 428
- stop and consider, 307
- stretch, 196
- study something new, 550
- suspension of disbelief, 441
- sweeping, 103
- swimming, 491
- swinging on a swing, 47
- tackle a goal, 382
- take a chance, 537
- take a nap, 232
- take a photo, 220
- take a positive action, 507
- take a step out of your comfort zone, 278
- take control of your life, 500
- take in the view around you, 165
- teach, 142
- tenacity, 222
- test your theory, 438
- time, 16
- togetherness, 152
- tolerance, 288
- tradition, 230
- transparency, 344
- travel, 329
- truth, 17
- trying, 421
- understanding, 219
- unveil your spiritual truth, 303
- use reason, 91
- use time wisely, 516
- validation, 252
- value, 236
- viewpoint, 502
- visit a farmer's market, 238

Actions *(continued)*
- visit a loved one, 553
- volunteer, 226
- wading in water, 385
- wait, 566
- wake up early, 373
- watch fish in an aquarium, 341
- watch the clouds, 70
- willingness, 365
- willpower, 437
- wisdom, 385
- write a letter, 216
- write an abundance check, 360
- writing, 48
- yodeling, 49
- yoga, 225

Colors
- amber, 266
- antique white, 457
- apricot, 330
- auburn, 558
- azure, 306
- baby blue, 482
- black, 192
- blue, 401
- blue green, 298
- blue violet, 406
- blush, 31
- brown, 191
- byzantine, 163
- cadet blue, 408
- carrot orange, 485
- cerulean, 212
- cherry blossom, 462
- chestnut, 390
- citrine, 165
- cobalt blue, 173
- copper penny, 413
- cornsilk, 329
- cranberry, 240
- dark sienna, 53
- deep cerise, 34
- deep fuchsia, 183
- denim, 203
- ecru, 469
- emerald, 332
- fawn, 410
- fire brick, 215
- fire opal, 345
- gold, 64
- gray, 302

Colors *(continued)*
- green, 338
- honeydew, 471
- hunter green, 417
- inchworm green, 78
- indigo, 428
- iris, 509
- ivory, 352
- Kelly green, 100
- key lime, 476
- lemon chiffon, 221
- light periwinkle, 375
- magenta, 231
- maize, 118
- melon, 263
- metallic bronze, 250
- midnight, 514
- mint, 236
- misty rose, 381
- mulberry, 126
- mustard, 157
- Nickel, 384
- olive, 436
- orange, 363
- pale blue, 258
- peach, 511
- pine green, 262
- pink, 419
- purple, 533
- red, 244
- red ochre, 432
- rosewood, 294
- saddle brown, 388
- saffron, 444
- scarlet, 332
- sienna, 294
- sky blue, 315
- smoke, 398
- straw, 393
- sunflower yellow, 541
- tan, 53
- tangerine yellow, 453
- terra cotta, 528
- tree bark, 204
- ultramarine, 534
- white, 382
- winter sky, 271
- yellow, 551

Emotions and Feelings
- accomplishment, 94
- admiration, 178
- adoration, 319

Emotions and Feelings
(continued)
- affection, 481
- affectionate, 143
- affirmation, 498
- alive, 570
- alluring, 189
- amazement, 300
- ambition, 246
- amicable, 474
- amusement, 85
- anticipation, 557
- appetizing, 326
- appreciated, 96
- appreciation, 187
- approachable, 486
- ardent, 430
- aspire, 81
- astonishment, 316
- astuteness, 15
- attentive, 399
- attractive, 356
- aware, 259
- awe, 36
- bemusement, 107
- blessings, 81
- bliss, 161
- bonding, 420
- bravery, 494
- breathtaken, 379
- calmness, 290
- camaraderie, 310
- candor, 16
- capable, 224
- carefree, 151
- caring, 209
- certainty, 207
- cheerfulness, 530
- cherish, 544
- cold, 471
- comfortable, 414
- comforting someone, 171
- commitment, 84
- compassion, 351
- complimentary, 278
- confidence, 520
- confident, 65
- connected, 198
- consolation, 46
- contentment, 15
- courageous, 57
- curious, 357
- daring, 290

Emotions and Feelings
(continued)
- delight, 83
- delight in the happiness of others, 479
- desire, 522
- determination, 316
- devotion, 269
- duty, 368
- eagerness, 348
- easy, 447
- elation, 93
- embarrassment, 147
- emotional bonds, 36
- enchanted, 531
- engaged, 276
- enthusiasm, 72
- entrancement, 106
- epiphany, 155
- euphoric, 448
- excitement, 279
- exhilaration, 393
- expectation, 257
- explore ideas, 91
- expression, 86
- exuberance, 195
- faith, 480
- fascinated, 145
- festive, 56
- focused, 28
- frivolous, 444
- fun, 400
- gaiety, 211
- gallant, 272
- generosity, 362
- gentleness, 390
- genuine, 468
- giddy, 416
- gladness, 378
- glee, 555
- glorious, 284
- graceful, 150
- grounded, 256
- happiness, 248
- heart-warming, 405
- helpfulness, 469
- heroism, 487
- hilarity, 82
- honor, 172
- hope, 153
- humble, 412
- humor, 508
- important, 473
- infatuation, 441

Emotions and Feelings
(continued)
- inquisitive, 404
- intimate, 268
- jolly, 402
- jovial, 564
- joviality, 117
- joy, 132
- joyful surprise, 54
- jubilant, 229
- jubilation, 157
- love, 135
- love yourself, 569
- loyal, 77
- luck, 150
- luminous, 296
- merriment, 184
- noble, 407
- optimism, 234
- overjoyed, 470
- pardon, 186
- passion, 237
- patience, 405
- peace of mind, 358
- peaceful, 491
- perception, 41
- playful, 101
- pleased, 318
- present, 216
- pride, 293
- protective, 37
- puzzled, 339
- radiance, 277
- rapturous, 480
- reflection, 121
- refreshed, 22
- regeneration, 458
- rejoice, 222
- rejuvenated, 199
- relief, 320
- resolve, 377
- respect, 261
- respected, 40
- reverence, 394
- satisfaction, 478
- satisfied, 88
- secure, 99
- sentimentality, 424
- settled, 249
- shyness, 417
- silliness, 159
- spacious, 285
- spellbound, 158
- spontaneous, 542

Emotions and Feelings
(continued)
spunky, 361
strength, 52
strong feeling of belonging, 90
surprise, 245
sweetness, 320
tenderness, 337
thrilled, 35
time standing still, 41
tranquility, 505
triumphant, 364
trust, 340
uniqueness, 364
unity, 275
unselfish, 537
uplifting, 152
vibrant, 205
vivacious, 367
welcoming, 124
witty, 419
wonderment, 51
worthy, 210
zeal, 549
zest, 49

Scents

after it rains, 379
amber, 196
apple cinnamon, 142
apple pie, 148
apricot, 281
baking, 219
balsam fir, 484
banana, 359
bay rum, 194
bergamot, 156
black spruce, 270
blueberries, 540
bubblegum, 264
burning wood, 324
cake, 467
campfire, 355
caramel apples, 75
carnations, 275
cedar, 140
chamomile, 111
cherry, 559
chimney smoke, 115
chocolate, 207
cinnamon, 261
citronella, 291

Scents *(continued)*
citrus, 125
clary sage, 504
clothes right out of the dryer, 128
clove, 200
clover, 309
coffee, 344
cold mountain air, 522
cologne, 223
cookies fresh from the oven, 413
cool fall air, 201
cotton candy, 272
cream soda, 54
crisp linen, 260
crisp spring morning, 505
cucumber, 109
cypress wood, 442
damp earth, 445
dew, 247
dry woods, 478
embers, 342
eucalyptus, 20
fire in a fireplace, 50
floral, 43
forest, 554
frangipani, 139
frankincense, 260
fresh cut pine, 392
freshly baked bread, 202
freshly cut grass, 59
freshly popped popcorn, 303
freshly washed sheets, 103
frosting, 46
fudge, 56
funnel cakes, 104
gardenia, 69
gasoline, 170
geranium, 217
ginger, 239
gingerbread, 84
grape, 175
grapefruit, 315
grilling outside, 425
hay, 159
honeysuckle, 208
horse's coat, 133
hot cocoa, 293
hot summer night, 343
jasmine, 55

Scents *(continued)*
juniper, 153
juniper berry, 506
labdanum, 233
lavender, 498
leather, 68
leaves in the forest, 545
lemon, 154
lemongrass, 350
lilacs, 308
lime, 334
magnolia blossoms, 112
mango, 44
menthol, 250
mint, 430
moonflower, 439
musk, 162
myrrh, 511
new baby smell, 431
new car smell, 396
nutmeg, 477
ocean breeze, 545
old books, 138
oranges, 506
orchids, 58
palo santo, 258
pastries, 79
patchouli, 325
peach nectar, 564
pepper, 177
pineapple, 175
pipe, 426
pizza, 190
pumpkin spice, 131
puppies, 515
rich soil, 123
roses, 473
rosewood, 206
sage, 305
sandalwood, 454
shower fresh, 326
spruce, 321
sugar cookies, 123
summer air, 136
swimming pool, 343
tea tree, 280
the beach, 446
toasted coconut, 323
toasted marshmallow, 502
tobacco, 514
vanilla, 465
warm apple cider, 286
white sage, 312

596 Raise Your Frequency Through Number Messages

Scents *(continued)*
   wisteria, 291
   worn leather, 228
   ylang ylang, 523
   your favorite
     perfume/cologne, 220

Sensations
   airy, 205
   alertness, 22
   breathless, 226
   buoyant, 254
   cleanliness, 433
   cold wind, 174
   cool, 517
   craving, 552
   electric, 243
   eloquence, 21
   energized, 374
   feel the wind on your
     face, 67
   flavorful, 113
   fluid, 282
   fluttery, 353
   fulfillment, 74
   goodness, 327
   innocent, 540
   lightheartedness, 19
   lively, 431
   mellow, 181
   shimmering, 335
   smooth, 229
   snappy, 562
   soft, 242
   sparkly, 314
   splendid, 396
   stillness, 317
   thrill, 32
   time passing, 38
   tingling, 45
   touch healing, 43
   warmth, 333
   zippy, 483

Sounds
   air conditioner turning
     on/off, 422
   airplane taking
     off/landing, 283
   alarm going off, 107
   applause, 411
   babble of a brook, 79
   baby chicks, 486
   baby laughing, 279

Sounds *(continued)*
   bagpipes, 521
   barking, 162
   basketball bouncing, 267
   beep, 158
   bells, 61
   birds singing, 263
   birds tweeting, 193
   bleating, 352
   blender, 230
   boiling water, 457
   boom, 186
   bubble wrap
     popping, 204
   bubbling, 297
   bumblebee buzzing, 349
   buzzing, 356
   buzzing of bees, 23
   camera shutter, 398
   car horn, 503
   car starting, 119
   cat purring, 195
   cat's meow, 117
   chanting, 459
   chirping, 156
   chorus of the
     katydids, 439
   cicadas at night, 489
   clapping, 354
   clatter of coins, 245
   clicking, 100
   clock ticking, 209
   coins jingling, 451
   coughing, 242
   crackle, 131
   crickets chirping, 328
   crowd chatter, 75
   crunch of walking on
     snow, 149
   cuckoo clock, 89
   cymbals, 406
   dog panting, 423
   door opening and
     closing, 86
   doorbell, 127
   drip, 472
   drum roll, 448
   drumbeat, 42
   electric guitar, 202
   electric saw, 30
   elevator, 113
   engine cranking, 563
   film projector reel, 440
   flaming torch, 539

Sounds *(continued)*
   foghorn, 458
   footsteps, 518
   forest ambience, 384
   frogs croaking, 455
   gasp of surprise, 247
   giggle, 513
   gong, 404
   gurgle of a coffee
     machine, 466
   hammering, 70
   harmonica, 128
   harp, 187
   hawk calls, 386
   heartbeat, 273
   helicopter flying, 443
   hiccup, 532
   horse running, 82
   horse walking, 166
   humming, 470
   ice dropped into a
     glass, 324
   jackhammer, 340
   jet fly by, 449
   jungle ambience, 420
   ker-ching, 173
   kettle whistling, 92
   knocking, 299
   laughter, 489
   lawn mower, 549
   leaves crunching under
     your feet, 255
   lighting a match, 284
   lion's roar, 338
   liquid being poured, 323
   listen to the sea in a
     conch shell, 310
   mooing, 235
   muscle car, 535
   om, 244
   opening a can of
     carbonated
     beverage, 212
   owl hooting, 243
   people laughing, 269
   person whistling, 423
   phone ringing, 361
   piano playing, 297
   ping pong ball
     bouncing, 308
   pop of a cork, 24
   popping popcorn, 225
   pots and pans
     clanging, 454

Sounds *(continued)*
pouring a beverage, 327
purring, 560
quiet, 265
rain on a tin roof, 353
ring, 96
rocking chair, 515
rolling ocean waves, 65
rooster crowing, 402
rumble, 453
running water, 95
rustling, 228
rustling of leaves in the wind, 447
saw, 166
school bell, 433
seagulls calling, 214
sewing machine, 452
shouts of joy, 422
sighing, 28
silence, 33
sizzle, 94
sleigh bells, 395
slurp, 446
sneezing, 475
snoring, 492
sonar, 394
splashing, 521
spoon clinking in cup, 223
squeak of the floor when stepped on, 34
squeaky toy, 538
squish, 238
stillness after a snowstorm, 273
tap dancing, 481
tapping, 92
tears of joy, 206
telephone ringing, 504
thunder, 249
Tibetan singing bowl, 389
timer beeping, 280
tractor, 563
train moving, 452
train whistle, 475
trumpets, 335
turkey gobble, 500
turning a page, 408
typing, 464
underwater, 399
vacuuming, 55
whinny, 527

Sounds *(continued)*
whirr of a fan, 354
whisper, 227
whooshing, 530
wind blowing outside, 524
wind chimes, 350
wind gusts, 418
wind through the trees, 201
windshield wipers, 487
wolf howl, 180
wood burning in a fireplace, 199
yawning, 546
zipper, 544

Phenomenon and Events
Absorption, 72
Antarctica's Blood Falls, 510
anthelion halo, 554
aurora borealis, 27
ball lightning, 145
barometric pressure, 63
black hole, 314
blood moon, 116
blue moon, 539
Catatumbo lightning, 168
circumzenithal arc, 346
corona effect, 136
crepuscular rays, 345
doldrums, 435
earth rhythms, 319
echo, 108
electricity, 26
electromagnetic energy, 410
eternal flame, 90
fata morgana, 368
freezing, 44
giant permafrost explosions, 304
green flash, 403
hair ice, 474
heat lightning, 168
hybrid eclipse, 35
ice blink, 370
light waves, 414
magnetic field, 538
microburst, 289
midnight sun, 251

Phenomenon and Events *(continued)*
mirage, 309
moon dog, 305
moonbow, 391
nebula, 292
Novaya Zemlya Effect, 215
ocean current, 536
radio waves, 407
Russian light pillars, 167
sailing stone, 171
second summer, 218
shooting star, 111
sky punch, 174
sound waves, 425
sparks, 397
St. Elmo's Fire, 271
striped iceberg, 369
Subsun, 450
sun dog, 562
thundersnow, 110
transient lunar phenomenon, 112
turquoise ice at Lake Baikal, 257
Tyndall effect, 149
U Burst, 32
water sky, 89

Psychic, Paranormal, Unexplained
after death communication, 543
astral body, 362
astral plane, 464
astral projection, 513
aura, 116
aura balancing, 93
auric sight, 115
channeling, 450
Clairaudience, 62
Claircognizance, 87
Clairempathy, 109
Clairgustance, 164
Clairscent, 221
Clairsentience, 265
Clairtangency (Psychometry), 307
clairvoyance, 328
cloud messages, 119
crop circles, 130

Psychic, Paranormal, Unexplained *(continued)*
déjà vu, 427
dream interpretation, 512
dream travels, 556
empathic ability, 370
fairy ring, 403
gut instinct, 371
hunch, 534
intuition, 296
lucid dreaming, 87
orbs, 127
phantom phone call/text, 64
phantoms, 330
poltergeist, 178
precognition, 367
prophecy, 499
prophetic dreams, 520
retrocognition, 255
see beyond the veil, 462
sense connections around you, 322
sensitive, 552
shadow people, 477
spontaneous drawing, 140
superstition, 235
telekinesis, 73
telepathy, 146

Spirituality
abundance, 24
akashic records, 137
ascended masters, 135
attraction, 30
attunement, 26
authenticity, 132
awaken, 200
awakened interest, 461
awareness of self, 38
awareness of the obvious, 495
balance, 568
be aware of the present moment, 129
biorhythm, 232
centering, 185
chakras, 274
Chills of Universal Truth, 217
cocreation, 432
color healing, 312
creative visualization, 74

Spirituality *(continued)*
crown chakra, 33
crystals & gemstones, 105
destiny, 383
divination, 179
divine connections, 161
divine guidance, 25
dowsing, 240
empathy, 445
empowerment, 482
energy balancing, 565
enlightened, 288
familiars, 523
free will, 176
frequency, 427
gratitude, 246
greater good, 160
grounding, 479
growth, 358
guardian, 194
guidance, 120
harmony, 21
healing, 259
heart chakra, 31
higher self, 553
infinity, 449
inner guide, 510
inner peace, 488
journeying, 67
karma, 239
law of attraction, 508
leap of faith, 144
lightness of being, 177
living in the moment, 40
power of thought, 374
mandalas, 73
manifesting, 42
mantra, 118
meaningful occurrences, 39
meditation, 60
mediumship, 104
mercury retrograde, 334
mindfulness, 409
miracles, 443
nature spirits, 268
near death experience, 286
open mindedness, 360
oracle, 213
out-of-body experience, 60
past life, 146

Spirituality *(continued)*
positive self-talk, 66
positive thinking, 58
prayer, 347
prosperity, 547
purity, 264
purposeful realization, 76
pursuit of dreams, 435
raising consciousness, 570
realization, 37
reason for being, 499
receive, 102
receptivity, 492
recurring words/phrase, 210
root chakra, 376
sacral chakra, 333
secret codes, 548
self-care, 18
self-image, 567
selfless, 365
self-reliance, 531
self-respect, 363
serenity, 27
simplicity, 193
solar plexus chakra, 134
solstice, 536
soul energy, 503
spirit, 490
spirit guides, 208
spirit messengers, 318
spiritual self, 463
synchronicity, 389
the unexpected, 276
third eye chakra, 227
thought forms, 224
throat chakra, 172
unblock energy, 527
veil to the other side, 289
vibration, 455
vibrational healing, 283
visions, 39
vortex energy, 331
well-being, 336
wellness, 472
wholeness, 375

Raise Your Frequency Through Number Messages 599

OTHER BOOKS BY MELISSA ALVAREZ

Published by Llewellyn Worldwide

Published by Adrema Press

Journals

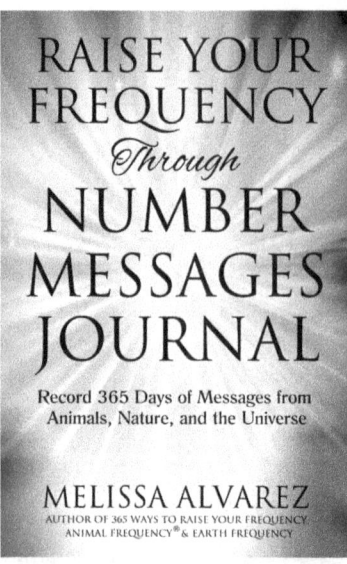

CPSIA information can be obtained
at www.ICGtesting.com
Printed in the USA
JSHW012041100523
41553JS00005B/236